THE *SAVVY* GUIDE TO MOTORCYCLES

Other books in the *SAVVY* Guide series

The Savvy Guide to Home Theater, ISBN 0-7906-1303-4

The Savvy Guide to Digital Photography, ISBN 0-7906-1309-3

The Savvy Guide to Fantasy Sports, ISBN 0-7906-1313-1

The Savvy Guide to Home Security, ISBN 0-7906-1315-8

The Savvy Guide to Digital Music, ISBN 0-7906-1317-4

THE *SAVVY* GUIDE
TO MOTORCYCLES

SHIRLEY DUGLIN KENNEDY

INDY-TECH®
PUBLISHING

Indianapolis

International Standard Book Number: 0-7906-1316-6

Chief Executive Officer:	Alan Symons
President:	Scott Weaver
Chief Operating Officer:	Richard White
Acquisitions Editor:	Brad Schepp
Editorial Assistant:	Dana Eaton
Copy Editor:	Cheryl Hoffman
Technical Editors:	Glenn L. Tussing Jr., Richard White
Typesetter:	Cheryl Hoffman
Cover Design:	Robin Roberts
Cover Photos:	Courtesy of Fairchild Sports/FirstGear
Interior Illustrations:	Provided by the author
Interior Photos:	Provided by the author
Drawings:	Provided by the author

"Savvy Guide Icons" section adapted from *The Savvy Guide to Home Security* by John Paul Mueller.

Manufactured in the USA, at Ripon Community Printers, Ripon WI.

CONTENTS

SAVVY GUIDE ICONS

As part of Sams' Savvy Guide series, this book may use a number of icons to identify special kinds of information. These icons alert you to something unique, something that you should pay particular attention to as you read the book. Here are the four icons that may be used in this book and a description of what they mean.

Savvy Tip: A Savvy Tip gives you special information—usually something that you won't find anywhere else. Often the Tip is based on the author's experiential knowledge, or as a result of an interview with an expert.

For More Information: Sometimes you need just a little more information about a topic discussed in the book. Yes, the book described the topic well but possibly not in enough detail to meet your specific needs. This icon alerts you to additional information that you can find online. Normally, this icon points you to a detailed resource provided by a third-party resource.

For Skeptics: Not everyone will accept the information in this book at face value; many people want proof. Although this book strives to provide as many details as possible, sometimes it will direct you to a resource that provides detailed proof about a concept. You can skip this information if you agree with what the text is saying; only the skeptic needs to read further.

Information identified by the magnifying glass icon is of three sorts:

- *Added Detail.* This is information that is nice to know but not essential for your understanding of the topic. In fact, the information might not even relate directly to the current discussion; it might have only a casual relationship to the topic as a whole. The ancillary details are sometimes important for a complete understanding of a topic.

- *Background Info.* Some people like to know the basis for a piece of information or the reason that the information is so important. Text identified by this icon provides that information, which you can use as a basis for additional research.

- *Elaboration.* Sometimes it's better not to include every detail in a discussion. This information elaborates on the current discussion, extending it in a way that completes the discussion for those who want to know more than the minimum required. You can skip this information if you're happy with the level of discussion provided in the standard text.

ACKNOWLEDGMENTS

So many people to thank for getting me to this point. Where do I even begin? At the most logical place, of course.

Matt Wagner—An agent with enough imagination to think that a nice, middle-aged, lady librarian could write a book about motorcycling.

Brad Schepp—An editor with the patience and understanding to realize it is an ordeal to do a whole freakin' book when you're also tied to a day job.

Captain Glenn L. Tussing Jr.—Officer, gentleman, Motorcycle Safety Foundation instructor and friend, a very busy man who nevertheless agreed to be the technical editor for this book. Good luck on your retirement; we're glad you decided to stick around with us. Ride safe.

Rick Emerson—Who did not succeed in getting me killed on that beast of an old Suzuki—you can stop feeling guilty now, Rick—but did provide assistance with some of the more gearheaded aspects of this book … and did a whole lot of virtual hand-holding. Ride safe, guy.

Ray Eydmann—Because of and in spite of … and you know exactly what I mean. Ride safe, always. But I don't have to tell you that.

Tom Tait—For giving me a lift to all those ballgames because I never take the bike when I'm drinking beer (which really helps when you're watching the Devil Rays). A true friend.

Sean and Patrick Kennedy—My two risk-averse sons, who never deliberately chose to have a "motorcycle mama" but ended up with one anyhow. My love for you both is the most important reason I ride safe. You are the best part of me.

My fellow riders in the About.com Motorcycle Forums—An amazingly diverse and knowledgeable bunch of folks who also functioned as a collective cheering section and emotional support group. Ride safe, guys. I miss Vinnie; his moral support at a critical time definitely helped get me to this point. Ride free, brother.

The staff at the MacDill Air Force Base Library—Y'all tolerate my eccentricities on a daily basis and were generally polite enough not to mention how damn tired I looked the entire time I was working on this book. What more could I ask? Enjoy your retirement, Bill. I wish you well, but I am also green with envy.

INTRODUCTION

The first time around, I was in my early 20s. The guy I was dating had a full-size Yamaha of some kind and a brother with a garage where all sorts of vehicles were brought for repair. Someone had dropped off a small Yamaha Enduro—175 cc—and never came back to pick it up. The two of them thought I might like to ride it. I got on it and rode it—not very proficiently, mind you, but well enough to get around a little bit on quiet semirural streets and controlled-access roads in parks. I wore no protective gear.

We do things like this when we are young. Most of us survive. I did. I also moved on—away from the guy, away from my hometown, away from the life I was living. It was time. It never occurred to me to take the little motorcycle. That was part of "then" and this was now.

An interesting couple of decades followed. When the smoke had cleared, I had lived and worked in four states, spent way too much time in graduate school, and was the single mother of two amazing sons. An old friend came back into my life on a BMW street bike. He had no car, so I rode behind him on his bike. And I liked it. And I started thinking more and more about that little Yamaha Enduro—and about my late father, who owned and raced old Indians through the streets of Philadelphia years before I was born.

I told my friend I wanted to learn to ride. He backed off. "I know you can do this," he said, "but I don't want anything to do with it. Take the MSF course." I realize now that he did not want to think that this was something I was doing because of him. He needn't have worried. This was very much something I wanted to do for me. And pointing me in the direction of the Motorcycle Safety Foundation was the best advice he could have given me.

My first go-around with the MSF Basic Rider Course was a disaster. Since I already had a motorcycle endorsement on my license from having ridden that little Enduro many years ago, the instructors put me—the only woman—in a group of 10 relatively experienced people. Most of these guys owned bikes. I did not. Most of them rode almost every day. I hadn't ridden, except as a passenger, for more than two decades. They were taking this class to get an insurance reduction, a motorcycle endorsement, or because you have to take and pass a motorcycle safety class if you want to ride on a military installation. We had guys from the Navy and the Coast Guard in that group.

I was beyond nervous. Awkward, uncoordinated. . . . It didn't take long before I fell well behind the rest of the group, frustrated and unable to do the various exercises successfully. Both of our group's instructors focused their attention on me. One was barking instructions into my right ear. The other was barking instructions into my left ear. All of a sudden, it all started sounding like a bunch of buzzing bees . . . and I got light-headed . . . and passed out . . . and fell over with the little loaner bike. Apparently, I'd held my breath—something they'd warned us about during the classroom part of the course. I'd blown it off, of course, because it had never happened to me before in my life, and I tend to be somewhat of a daredevil by nature

The instructors told me to sit down, eat and drink something, chill out . . . and think about whether learning to ride a motorcycle was something I really wanted to do. I was too demoralized to rejoin the class that day. I got in my car and drove home… and took a hot bath . . . and thought about what had happened . . . and made lunch . . . and thought some more about what had happened. It was pouring rain outside. I stopped thinking. I got into the car, drove to the closest motorcycle dealership and bought a used Suzuki Savage.

I was afraid to ride it home in the rain on the busy streets. A guy from the dealership delivered it to me in the back of a pickup truck. I'd extracted a promise from the salesman that, if after a week, I decided this was really not for me, I could bring the little green bike back for a complete refund.

I did not love that bike that first week, but I am nothing if not stubborn. I kept the thing. I made myself ride it every single day, even if it was just for a trip around the block. I practiced with it in parking lots. I dropped it and hurt my leg badly enough to require stitches. When I came limping into work, my staff was appalled. "If you have one more incident with that thing," I was told, "we're gonna put it up for sale on eBay."

Five weeks later I went back to the MSF class and passed it. The chief instructor walked over to me, raised the face shield on my helmet and removed my sunglasses. "I thought that was you," he said. "We didn't think you would be back. What the hell happened? You were a completely different person out there today."

Not long after that, I took my first white-knuckle ride to work on the bike. I work on an Air Force base. I had to register the bike at the visitor's center and get a Department of Defense sticker for it. I showed the young airman behind the counter my license (with required motorcycle endorsement), my registration, my insurance card, and my MSF card. She spread these things out in front of her and began entering my information into the computer system. When she handed my cards back to me, along with the new sticker for my bike, this lovely young girl—about the age of my oldest son—said, "I think you are so cool. How hard is it to learn to ride a motorcycle?"

And I thought, for you at your age, probably not that hard. You're still young enough, probably, to feel you are immortal. And you had enough moxie to join the military. At my age . . . well, I know bad things can happen. I was scared. I was intimidated. But something in me really, really wanted to do this.

So I did.

◆ ◆ ◆

I'm no longer intimidated, but I still feel that flicker of fear every time I get ready to start up the bike and take off. I have learned that this is a good thing, because the adrenaline will keep you alert. I ride almost every day, and I keep trying to be a better, more skillful motorcyclist.

At any rate, this is the book I wish I'd had when I was making the decision to learn to ride. It is not a book for dummies or idiots. It is not a book that will teach you how to ride a motorcycle.

You cannot learn that from a book.

It is not a book that will delve deeply into the physics of how motorcycles work, and it will not teach you how to maintain and repair motorcycles. This is certainly not my area of expertise.

It is not a book that will tell you what kind of motorcycle to buy or what kind of gear you absolutely must have. How you spend your money is up to you—and depends completely on the type of riding you plan to do, where you live, and many other variables. And, ultimately, what you really want. If nothing but a Harley-Davidson will do and your bank account permits it, so be it. If you crave a Ducati sport bike and can afford and learn to handle one, go for it. If you have your heart set on a restored 1974 Norton Commando and you can find one, you should have one. And if what you really need is a good, reliable, start-it-up-and-go Japanese cruiser or standard bike, there are many from which to choose.

It's all up to you. And my job here is to arm you with the information you need to make intelligent decisions about motorcycling—including, first of all, whether this is something you really want to do. What will be covered between these covers:

- A brief history and explanation of motorcycling's allure
- How motorcycles work (low-tech version)

- Different types of motorcycles and how to decide which one is right for you
- Buying a motorcycle, new or used
- Choosing motorcycle gear and accessories
- Getting trained, licensed, insured
- Staying safe on the roads
- Taking care of your bike (for nonmechanics)
- Group riding and touring
- Good-to-know things like motorcycling etiquette and how to ship a bike

Oh, and you'll also get to meet several different riders—men and women maybe a lot like yourself—who will tell you, in their own words, why they ride. Some of them have expertise to share with you beyond what I can provide. You'll see that when you take up motorcycling, you are joining a brotherhood (and sisterhood) of riders who are basically accepting, nonjudgmental, and very helpful.

I can't even count the number of people who have been kind, helpful, and informative since I began my motorcycling journey in January 2004. I've thanked some of them in the acknowledgments in this book, but there are so many others who have crossed my path. Sometimes I like to think that my dad, whose love of motorcycles most assuredly resides in my DNA, has been Out There Somewhere, making sure that all of these incredible motorcyclists keep appearing in my life.

I'm glad you've given me the opportunity to appear in yours.

Onward. Let's take a look at what makes motorcycling so very cool.

◆ ◆ ◆

Since I'm a librarian as well as a writer, you'll find lots of pointers to additional information—books, magazines, Web sites, and other resources. Keep in mind that Web site links can be here today, gone tomorrow, so if you hit a dead one, try using a search engine to find out if it's moved. By the time you have this book in your hands, I will have put together a Web site that includes all of the links here. You'll be able to get to it from my personal Web site: www.uncagedlibrarian.com.

Also, you'll find some terms boldfaced in the text. These are words that are included in the glossary.

1 WHAT IS IT ABOUT MOTORCYCLES?

◆ The mystique

◆ When did all of this start?

◆ Bad boys, bad boys

◆ Your dentist on that Gold Wing . . .

◆ You take your life in your hands

◆ Your wife, your sister . . . your mom

Despite the many years this country has had to accustom itself to sharing the highway with motorcycles, the distinctive sound of American iron and the sight of the tattooed hordes thundering down the interstate can still inspire dread just by appearing in the rear view mirror.

—*Ross Fugslang*

THE MYSTIQUE

It was one of my first forays out into traffic on the little Suzuki Savage. One cylinder . . . but 650 cc . . . OK. Thumper bike. I'd last ridden more than 20 years ago—and not all that much—on a 175 cc Yamaha Enduro. At any rate, I was still rather timid about venturing out onto busy streets, but the only way you learn to ride in traffic is to ride in traffic.

I had to make a left turn in a few blocks, so I was sticking to the left-hand lane. The light turned

The epigraph is from Ross Fuglsang, "Media Genres and the Construction of a Deviant Culture" PhD diss., University of Iowa, 1997 (http://webs.morningside.edu/masscomm/DrRoss/Research.html).

red at the next intersection, and I pulled up next to a minivan stopped in the right lane. There I was on this little green bike, wearing a red-and-black hand-me-down Cordura jacket (way too big . . . yeah, not a good idea), and a white helmet that, while still serviceable, had seen better days with its previous owner, who had also given me a pair of old black leather gloves. (At least I was wearing my own jeans and boots.)

The lady driving the minivan had two little kids in there with her. As I pulled up beside her, she looked down at me. Then she quickly looked away, and I heard . . . *click, click, click* . . . the unmistakable sound of electric vehicle doors being locked. The driver glanced down at me again, and I just sat there with my mouth half opened, thinking, "Geez, lady. Do I really look *that* scary?" (See figure 1-1.)

What is it about motorcycles? They evoke an emotional—in some cases, a visceral—response in so many people. It's either a yearning for freedom and the open road or sometimes an almost primal fear. Even as motorcycling has become such a mainstream activity that your family dentist is probably cruising around on a Honda Gold Wing, people will still gawk at bikes and their riders. You know . . . that bar, with a passel of Harleys parked out front; it simultaneously attracts and repels. "Loud pipes save lives" . . . and annoy the hell out of everybody else. Which is kind of the point, no?

And those young kids weaving in and out of traffic at high speed on their high-tech sport bikes (e.g., **crotch rockets**) . . . Yeah, we hate 'em, but at the same time we are kind of in awe of them. Was I ever *that* young and *that* fearless? (I probably *was* that stupid, even though I never owned one of *those* things.)

Meanwhile, millions of people tune in regularly to the Discovery Channel's *American Chopper* series. And you know it's not just to watch the antics of the dysfunctional-but-amusing Tuetul clan. Think of all those Orange County Chopper t-shirts adorning the bodies of folks who have never been within spitting distance of a motorcycle, let alone have ridden one. Those wishing to immerse their

Fig. 1-1: Your author . . . big, scary biker type.

olfactory sense in the whole experience can now buy Orange County Chopper Full Throttle cologne. ("Your Road. Your Rules.")

WHEN DID ALL OF THIS START?

Actually, not that long after the invention of the bicycle in the late nineteenth century. Someone apparently decided it did not go fast enough and felt a need to attach a motor to it. Gottlieb Daimler . . . yeah, vaguely familiar name, that one . . . is acknowledged to be the inventor of the motorcycle, in 1885. His machine, made mostly of wood, had a single-cylinder gas engine. Although motorcycles weren't very useful small vehicles till the early 1900s, people had already started racing them by then. The first documented motorcycle race was in France, in 1895.

Some of us, it seems, are hardwired with the Need for Speed.

In 1901, Indian Motorcycles—the first American motorcycle company—began production. Indian ceased production in 1953, although the marque was briefly resurrected in 1998 in Gilroy, California, until that factory closed its doors in 2003. In 1903, William Harley and Arthur and Walter Davidson got together and started the firm that stands today as America's oldest motorcycle company. In 1909, Harley-Davidson's v-twin bike became the first commercially manufactured motorcycle that was actually able to climb hills.

Motorcycle manufacturing began across Europe during this era—Italy was already making Ducatis and Moto Guzzis—and motorcycles were beginning to emerge as useful transportation. The U.S. Army started using motorcycles in 1913. General John J. Pershing was astride a Harley in 1916 while in pursuit of Pancho Villa, the rebel general of the Mexican Revolution. By 1917, roughly one-third of Harley-Davidson's production was being snapped up by the military. The army used approximately 20,000 motorcycles in World War I; by some accounts, the first American to enter Germany after the cease-fire was a motorcycle dispatch rider. And speaking of Germany, BMW, originally an aircraft engine manufacturer (Bayerische Motoren Werke), cranked out its first motorcycle in 1923.

H-D again started gearing up for action as World War II was breaking out, producing a bike that could stand up to the harsh African desert terrain. Alas, as the troops moved through Africa, the motorcycle began to lose ground to the jeep. Still, Harley-Davidson manufactured roughly 90,000 bikes for the war effort during World War II. And the military has continued using motorcycles—in Korea, in Vietnam, right up to now, in the Middle East. In *Soldiers* magazine, Specialist First Class Lisa Gregory writes, "The vehicle's ability to keep going, even after the road ends, was an important factor in Afghanistan, as it is today in Iraq, where the terrain doesn't always allow access for heavier, four-wheeled vehicles" ("War Bikes," August 2003, www.findarticles.com/p/articles/mi_m0OXU/is_8_58/ai_106981877).

Motorcycles became an established fixture in American popular culture after World War II, when many GIs returning home found in these two-wheeled vehicles a substitute for the adrenaline rush of serving in a tank unit or flying in a plane. These thrill-seekers were perceived in some quarters as a menace to society—the genesis of the so-called biker stereotype.

Bad Boys, Bad Boys . . .

Nobody—except another cyclist—likes a man on a motorcycle.

—Hal Burton

Fourth of July weekend 1947. Hollister, California. Roughly 4,000 people—mainly motorcyclists and their hangers-on—converged on and more or less overwhelmed the small town. Despite rather sensational media coverage in such popular magazines of the era as *Life* and the *Saturday Evening Post,* there really was not much damage and few arrests, with those mainly for drunkenness and public urination (probably because there were not enough bathrooms). A reprint of the original *San Francisco Chronicle* article about the event is still floating around on the Internet: www.cestcop.com/chron1.htm.

In January 1951, *Harper's* magazine carried a short story based on this event, "The Cyclists' Raid," by Frank Rooney. This became the genesis of Stanley Kramer's 1954 film, *The Wild One*, featuring an iconic Marlon Brando in a black leather jacket, riding his own Triumph motorcycle. This is still the image that appears in our collective mind's eye when we hear the word "biker." Unless it's a group of Hell's Angels, "the oldest, and biggest original 1% motorcycle club in the world." The club was founded in 1948 in San Bernardino, according to, yes, their own Web site: www.hells-angels.com (see figure 1-2).

Throughout the 1950s and on into the 1960s, the Hell's Angels developed something of a counterculture reputation that was, historian John Wood wrote in the November 2003 *Journal of Popular Culture*, more illusion than reality. "With the possible exception of all but the earliest Angels and their immediate predecessors," Wood said, "the Hell's Angels were very definitely not a part of the counterculture. In fact, the Hell's Angels actually mimicked the mainstream American society that the counterculture fought so hard to eliminate" ("Hell's Angels and the Illusion of the Counterculture").

The epigraph is from Hal Burton, "Most Unpopular Men on the Road," *Saturday Evening Post*, September 25, 1954.

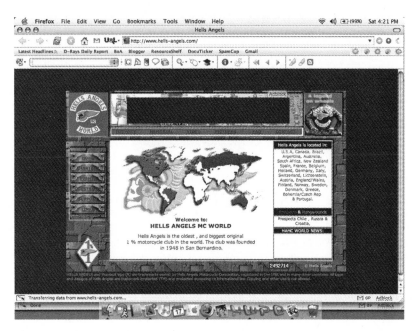

Fig. 1-2: Who isn't on the Web these days? www.hells-angels.com.

At any rate, the Hell's Angels counterculture bubble burst for good on December 6, 1969, at the notorious Altamont Speedway Rolling Stones concert in California, where a group of Angels, hired as security for the event, stabbed an 18-year-old man to death. Even though the Angel charged with the stabbing was acquitted of murder in 1971—the victim had pulled a gun and the Angel was found to be acting in self-defense—the party was over.

Meanwhile, the FBI amassed some 233 pages' worth of information from the 1960s and 1970s about this motorcycle gang's "involvement in violent activities in various parts of the country," which you can peruse on their Freedom of Information Act Web site, http://foia.fbi.gov/foiaindex/hellsang .htm. (See figure 1-3.) The late Hunter S. Thompson offered an interesting take in his classic, "The Motorcycle Gang: Losers and Outsiders," which ran in the *Nation* on May 17, 1965: "The Hell's Angels try not to do anything halfway, and anyone who deals in extremes is bound to cause trouble, whether he means to or not. This, along with a belief in total retaliation for any offense or insult, is what makes the Hell's Angels unmanageable for the police and morbidly fascinating to the general public" (www.thenation.com/doc.mhtml?i=19650517&s=thompson).

That morbid fascination persists. And more than a few in the motorcycling community cultivate it—overtly or covertly. You may be a government worker in a cubicle all week long, but when you're out riding around on the weekends and you pull up at a red light on that DynaGlide, sometimes you just can't help but make eye contact through those dark-tinted shades with that errand-running cager in

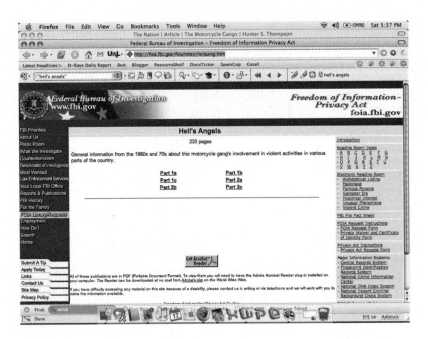

Fig. 1-3: The FBI offers more than you probably want to read about the Hell's Angels.

his Toyota Camry . . . and you stare till he looks away . . . and you are glad that you are not he. At least not at that particular moment in time.

These days, outside of the fringe criminal element, motorcycle groups are in the news more for charity poker runs, holiday toy runs, and other good works–type fundraising events or memorial rides. One organization of note, Rolling Thunder (www.rollingthunder1.com), seeks to focus attention on those who died in the Vietnam War and on American POW/MIAs from all armed conflicts. Each Memorial Day weekend, they sponsor a commemorative ride that attracts hundreds of thousands of motorcyclists to Washington, D.C. (See figure 1-4.)

YOUR DENTIST ON THAT GOLD WING, YOUR LAWYER ON THAT ROAD KING

Harleys were, of course, always the ride of choice for the so-called **1%-ers.** Big, loud, American iron—yeah, that's the ticket. But H-D began losing ground; in the 1970s and 1980s light, inexpensive Japanese bikes came to dominate the American market. Kawasaki. Suzuki. Yamaha. "You meet the nicest people on a Honda," right? Motorcycling was starting to become more diverse.

Struggling Harley-Davidson, bought out by AMF in 1969, continued to struggle until 1981 when a

Fig. 1-4: "Joint Chiefs Chairman Air Force Gen. Richard B. Myers and his wife, Mary Jo, get ready to rumble across the Memorial Bridge during Rolling Thunder May 30. The chairman and his wife joined about 400,000 riders in the annual Memorial Day weekend tribute." (Photo: Petty Officer 1st Class Bob Lamb, USN; Armed Forces Press Service; June 1, 2004.)

group of employees, including Willie G. Davidson, one of the founders' grandsons, bought the company back for $80 million. And it's well known what happened after that. A classic American success story, Harley-Davidson was profitable again by 1987, and it's pretty much been nothing but boom times ever since, as motorcycling in general has surged in popularity. It's nice to have a Harley, but it's been even nicer to own Harley-Davidson stock.

The company commands a mystique all its own, and its customer loyalty is legendary. To those who don't ride, Harley-Davidson is pretty much synonymous with motorcycle. The machines have a distinctive sound; the engine is tuned so that the pistons fire unevenly. It's *supposed* to sound like that; Harley owners would have it no other way. And many would ride nothing else: "I'd rather push a Harley than ride a (insert the name of your favorite Japanese bike here)." The bikes command a premium price and hold their value well. (Only BMW motorcycles come close, and they attract an entirely different type of owner.)

And where else can you find such a breathtaking assortment of licensed and logo'ed merchandise as in a Harley-Davidson dealership? Barbie dolls, clocks, shot glasses, yada yada yada . . . and lots of clothes for everyone, from babies to babes. You may not be able to afford a bike, but you can certainly buy yourself a T-shirt, if black and orange is your thing.

Motorcycling continues to grow even more diverse, both in terms of who is riding and what is being ridden. Harley-Davidson is scratching its corporate head, trying to figure out how to appeal to a younger demographic than its traditional deep-pocketed Baby Boomer clientele, who are poised to age out of the motorcycling population sooner rather than later. (See figure 1.5.) Harley partnered with the Buell Motorcycle Company, which makes sportier, less expensive bikes, in 1993, and they bought the company in 1998. Other motorcycle manufacturers are in the same boat. Younger riders tend to prefer, on one hand, high-tech, light Japanese sport bikes, and, on the other hand, chic, urbanized motor scooters—both options considerably less expensive than a **fully dressed** Harley-Davidson Road King.

According to the H-D Web site, in 2004 the median age of its customers was somewhere in the late 40s, with a median household income of just over $80,000 annually (http://investor.harley-davidson.com/demographics.cfm?locale=en_US&bmLocale=en_US). At this point in time, baby boomers remain the solid core of the motorcycling industry, and all the manufacturers are still trying hard to cater to them with tricked-out cruisers and luxury touring bikes. Many in this demographic are trying motorcycling for the first time, but a sizable number of others are so-called reentry riders, who tooled around on bikes in their youth but drifted away during the career-and-family years. (Some 27 percent of Harley-Davidson's customers are either new riders or have not owned a bike within the past five years, according to the company.) This is having its consequences.

Fig. 1-5: The roads are full of middle-aged motorcyclists, and they do have money to burn. Photo courtesy of Fairchild Sports/FirstGear.

YOU TAKE YOUR LIFE IN YOUR HANDS

It's really kind of astonishing. You would think it would be all of the young kids on those fast bikes, but it's not.

—State highway safety coordinator

Safety experts nationwide are flat-out alarmed by the sharply rising number of fatalities among this tidal wave of not-so-young riders. The National Highway Traffic Safety Administration tells us that the average age of motorcyclists killed in accidents went from 32 in 1994 to 38 in 2003. A NHTSA statistical analysis done in August 2004 looked at ten-year fatality trends, which showed:

- An overall decline in the under-age-30 group.
- A roughly 25 percent increase in the 30–39 age group.
- An over 200 percent increase in the 40-plus age group (which includes an increase of 300 percent in the 50-plus age group. Wowie kazowie!)

A 10-year trend analysis (*Motorcycle Rider Fatalities: Where Are the Increases?* www.nrd.nhtsa.dot .gov/pdf/nrd-30/NCSA/PPT/PresMCIncreases.pdf) by motorcycle engine size revealed the following:

- A decline in the under-500 cc engine size range.
- No change in the 501–1,000 cc engine size range.
- A more than 100 percent increase in the 1,001–1,500 cc engine size range.

Actually, this makes a lot of sense. Here you are, a baby boomer with all that disposable income now that the kids are grown and gone. You're gonna go out and buy the biggest honkin' cruiser you can afford. But whether or not you want to admit it, you're not so young anymore. You haven't ridden a motorcycle in years. And as we'll see when we discuss buying a bike later in this book, motorcycles are a lot different than they were when you were a kid. Maybe you need to ease into it with a smaller bike that is easier to maneuver. It's something to consider. According to the NHSTA, two-thirds of the riders who bought the farm on 1,001–1,500 cc bikes were over 40 years of age. (See figure 1-6.)

Something else to consider: Do you really need that beer? The Centers for Disease Control and Prevention analyzed motorcycle fatality statistics from 1983, 1993, and 2003. According to results published in the ominously titled *Morbidity and Mortality Weekly Report*, among alcohol-impaired motorcycle drivers, the mortality rate was highest among persons aged 20 to 24 in 1983 and among persons aged 40 to 44 in 2003. In 1983, 8.2 percent of alcohol-impaired, fatally injured motorcycle drivers were 40 and over; by 2003, 48.2 percent of such drivers were in this age group (*Trends in*

The epigraph is from a state highway safety coordinator quoted by David Sharp, "Motorcycle Safety Activists Worried about Baby Boomer Deaths," Associated Press, January 21, 2005).

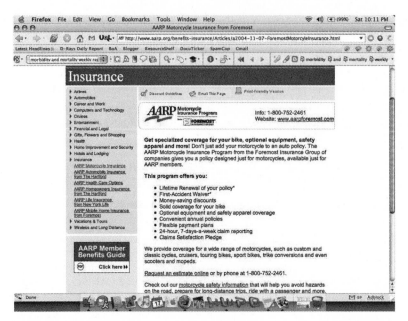

Fig. 1-6: You can buy motorcycle insurance through the AARP now. What does this tell you?

Motorcycle Fatalities Associated with Alcohol-Impaired Driving–United States, 1983–2003, www.cdc.gov/mmwr/preview/mmwrhtml/mm5347a2.htm).

The CDC surmised that mortality rates among motorcyclists 40 and over are increasing not only because more people in this age group are riding, "but also because older motorcyclists might be more likely to consume alcohol before driving than younger motorcycle drivers." For one thing, middle-aged motorcyclists grew up in the days before MADD and SADD, when it had not yet become socially unacceptable to drink and drive. Additionally, older motorcyclists are more likely to be doing most of their riding recreationally on weekends in "circumstances that might involve alcohol consumption," noted the CDC. You know, all those rides from bar to bar. Unfortunately, alcohol has always held a prominent place in motorcycle culture. Maybe this is something that needs to change.

Additionally, the CDC pointed out that "motorcyclists who drink are also less likely to wear helmets, a factor that increases the risk for death in a motorcycle crash."

YOUR WIFE, YOUR SISTER . . . YOUR MOM

You block my breeze!

—Every woman who finally got tired of riding around behind some guy, hopped off, and bought a bike of her own

For better or for worse, women have traditionally gotten into motorcycling via a man—a dad, a brother, a significant other. And there was a time when we were all pretty much content to ride **pillion**, to go wherever we were taken.

This is changing fast.

As for me, I happily rode around behind a guy for a while. Then he made the mistake of taking me over the spectacular Sunshine Skyway, at the mouth of Tampa Bay. I'd been over this bridge countless times in a car, but never on a bike. My jaw dropped open inside my full-face helmet. The view was absolutely magnificent and I felt like I was part of it instead of just observing it. And suddenly, it occurred to me, "I'll bet it's even better up there, where he is sitting."

Less than six months later, I rode over the Sunshine Skyway on my own bike for the first—but not the last—time. (See figure 1-7.)

I have to be honest with y'all, it was not easy to get there. I beat back fear, I ignored all the people who thought I was nuts, I got over the guilt of embarrassing my sons, I took a Motorcycle Safety Foundation class, and I practiced countless hours in the back parking lot of the local dog track, constantly on the lookout for the guy in the white security golf cart who ran me off every time he saw me. I went down with the bike once, the shift lever punched a hole in my shin, and I got to listen to a doc-in-the-box lecture me about how dangerous motorcycles are while he stitched me up. (Always, but *always* wear good boots.)

I don't ride on the back of anybody's bike anymore. And that is the way I like it.

That is the way a growing number of women like it these days. And don't think the motorcycle manufacturers haven't noticed. According to various industry sources, women now purchase roughly 10 percent of new motorcycles. And we are a desirable demographic, a relatively untapped market to motorcycle companies biting their nails over all those aging-less-than-gracefully baby boomer males.

Fig. 1-7: The first time I rode over the Sunshine Skyway bridge on my own bike, it took me a week to wipe the grin off my face.

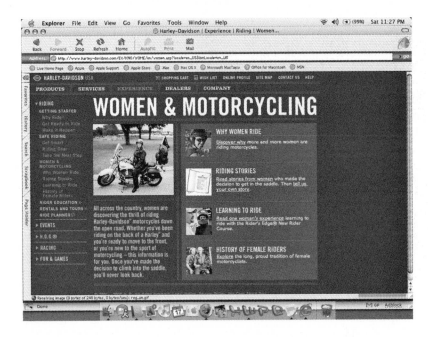

Fig. 1-8: Ladies! Harley-Davidson is interested in your business. Can you tell? Visit www.harley-davidson.com/wcm/Content/Pages/ Women/women_motorcycling.jsp?locale=en_US.

"That female riders are an emerging force in motorcycling is no secret," declared an article in *Brandweek* all the way back in June 2000. "How to market to them is another question. Said one industry insider, 'No one wants to be seen as building a 'girl's bike.'" Yet even then, according to the article, every major manufacturer was already offering models with low seat heights and featuring pictures of women riders in their ads ("Leaders of the Pack," Robert Francis, February 26, 2000).

The bike manufacturers—as well as the companies out there selling gear and other accessories—are now much more active in their efforts to reach women riders. Harley-Davidson's Women in Motorcycling Web site is one striking example of this (see figure 1-8).

Interestingly, though women are purchasing just 10 percent of new motorcycles, the Motorcycle Safety Foundation says one out of every three new riders enrolling in its classes is a woman. I think we can all take that as a pretty good sign, no?

You'll find information on Web sites and other resources for women riders, including organizations, in the bibliography. And when we discuss buying motorcycles a little further on in this book, we'll offer information for smaller, shorter riders. (Your author, who is on her third motorcycle, is five feet two inches tall on a good day and has a 28-inch inseam.)

Cecilie Hoffman
Project Manager/Business Process
Engineer
Mountain View, Calif.
1994 Triumph Sprint ST
Cecilie's Moto Journal:
www.balsamfir.com/motorcycle.htm

When I was a kid and watched motorcycles go by, I saw an individual astride a mechanically elegant two-wheeled vehicle. Simple, minimal, nimble—but dangerous. At least that is what I was sure my parents thought. And the way my college boyfriend rode his Honda Nighthawk ensured that I stayed away from motorcycles for the next 20 years.

I decided to learn to ride when I reached a point in my life where I stopped putting off doing things that I have always wanted to do. The decision was both enabled and fueled by hormonal changes; the perimenopausal phase of my life started when I turned 44. For many women, this is a time when we finally allow ourselves to act independently of the voices from our pasts that counsel caution or provide well-intentioned guidance about how a woman should comport herself properly in society.

After taking the MSF class, I progressed quickly from a used Suzuki GZ 250 to BMW's entry-level F650 CS, a single-cylinder 650cc bike with its gas tank below the seat (low center of gravity). I owe the rapid development of my riding ability to Karolyn Bachelor, who took it upon herself to go riding with me and coach me for about a year. Karolyn is a fellow student of Aikido who had been riding for around 15 years when I met her.

The three people I rode with cared about riding well and shared an interest in the track. They described the track environment as a place with no potholes, no traffic lights, no stop signs or intersections, no dogs, no children, and no cops. Not really understanding why I was doing it, I signed up for a "novice day" at a local track with only about eight months' riding experience. Novice didn't mean "novice rider"; it meant "novice to track riding," but I went anyway. I get stubborn about some things. I was the slowest person on the track that day and for many track days to come. I'm still slow on the track, but I don't care. I'm out there learning more control—and getting faster.

My current two-wheeled love is a Triumph Sprint ST, a triple-cylinder, 955 cc, 108 bph beauty with plenty of torque. I bought the Sprint because my other half, Peter, rides a Honda VFR. The Sprint and the VFR are well matched for size and power, and we will have no trouble riding cross-country together on these beasts.

In the future looms a dual-sport bike so that some day I'll be able to ride the Silk Road, starting at the Western terminus, Istanbul, crossing central Asia, entering northwestern China through the Korgas pass, and crossing China to the Eastern terminus, Xian.

2 GETTING ROLLING

- ◆ How does a motorcycle work?
- ◆ What happens If I press this gizmo?
- ◆ What do I do with my feet?
- ◆ How does it go?

- ◆ How does it stay up? How does it steer?
- ◆ It's fallen and I can't pick it up
- ◆ The fear factor
- ◆ Can you do this? Do you really want to do this?

To many, shifting seems an arcane, almost black art. Like tracking tigers in the jungle, weaving rope or starting fires with flint and steel, shifting is an almost-lost skill, taught within families, passed down to generations. But if dad or mom were raised on automatics, who will teach the kids?

—*George P. Blumberg*

HOW DOES A MOTORCYCLE WORK?

With a few eccentric exceptions, all motorcycles come with a standard transmission. What this means is that you will have to shift gears manually. If you don't know how to drive a car with a stick shift, understanding how a motorcycle's clutch works in conjunction with the shift lever is one more hurdle you're going to have to get over.

The epigraph is from George P. Blumberg, "Transmission Choice Undergoes a Radical Shift," *Chicago Tribune*, February 11, 2005. (www.chicagotribune.com/technology/chi-0502110440feb11,1,1603641.story?coll=chi-technology-hed&ctrack=3&cset=true).

Or maybe not. Bear with me here if you think this is all pretty basic stuff. Operating a motorcycle is really not very similar to driving a car. Many things about riding a motorcycle are not intuitive to the average person with no experience or very limited experience—or experience that was so far in the past that it is no longer relevant and/or particularly helpful. I'm going to try and explain things here that I'm glad someone explained to me or, in some cases, I wish someone *had* explained to me.

Even if you do know how to drive a car with a stick shift, it's different enough on a motorcycle that most beginners will be starting from scratch. In the average car or light truck, you have a clutch pedal on the floor and a shift lever within reach of your right hand, either on the steering column or somewhere between the front seats. On a motorcycle, you work the clutch by squeezing a lever on your left handgrip, and you operate the shift lever with your left foot.

Although some motorcycles have a linked braking system or an antilock brake system (**ABS**), most bikes have separate controls for the front and rear brakes, much like a bicycle. The rear brake is operated via a pedal on the lower right side. The front brake works via a lever you squeeze on the right handgrip.

The front brake supplies roughly 70 percent of a motorcycle's stopping power.

That is in boldface for a reason. Remember it. You'll be seeing it again.

In a car, you go faster via "pedal to the metal"—pressing down on the accelerator pedal on the vehicle floor. On a motorcycle, you control your speed via "twist of the wrist"—rolling on and off the throttle that is integrated into the right handgrip.

And . . . oh yeah. In case you've forgotten, you're rolling along on two wheels rather than four. Balance comes into play—big time. Which means that knowing how to ride a bicycle is more valuable, in some respects, than knowing how to drive a car, at least when you are first learning to operate a motorcycle.

WHAT HAPPENS IF I PRESS THIS GIZMO?

Although there is no real standardization in this industry, most motorcycles have, more or less, all the same controls in fairly similar locations. My Yamaha V-Star 1100 Custom (see figure 2-1) is pretty typical. The lever behind the left handgrip is the clutch. Squeeze it in to release it when you shift gears. The three switches to the right of the handgrip are operated with your left thumb. The up-and-down toggle switch on the top is high beam/low beam headlights. The switch in the middle operates your turn signals. Slide it to the left for a left turn and to the right for a right turn. Push it in to turn the signal off. Note that some motorcycles have self-canceling turn signals (like cars), but

Fig. 2-1: If you ride a lot, especially in traffic, you will build up a significant amount of strength in your left hand, which operates the clutch lever. If you're feeling somewhat deficient here, you may want to get yourself one of those soft rubber "stress balls" that you can repeatedly squeeze and release, squeeze and release.

many do not. After you make your turn, you will have to turn it off manually or you will be putt-putting down the road with your blinker flashing, confusing other motorists and creating a potentially hazardous situation as your intentions are misread. You will soon get into the habit of punching that button repeatedly with your left thumb when you are out riding.

The left-and-right toggle switch below the turn signal with the picture of the little trumpet on it is—you guessed it—the horn. There will be times when you will feel the urge to ride along with your thumb hovering just over the horn switch; shopping center parking lots always bring out this urge in me.

On my motorcycle, you can see a sliding lever underneath the horn switch. This is the **choke** control. On other motorcycles, this is a knob that is pulled out and pushed in, often located on the side of the bike. (See figure 2-2.) Its purpose is to "choke off" air to the carburetor so an enriched fuel mixture is available to help get the bike started. I slide this lever all the way to the left before I start up my bike if it has been sitting idle for any length of time, or if it is cold. With a knob-type choke, you pull it all the way out before you start. As the bike warms up, you can set the choke back to its normal position. Some bikes are more cold-blooded than others and will need more vigorous choking. There's a bit of voodoo involved in trying to figure out the appropriate amount of choke. Generally speaking, if you smell gas in the air, you've given it too much choke. If the engine doesn't seem to want to turn over at all, you're not giving it enough choke.

Note that many motorcycles now have electronic fuel injection, which precludes the need for a choke control.

You operate the front brake lever, found behind the right handgrip, by squeezing it with your right hand (see figure 2.3). Yes, it is like a bicycle's brake . . . and remember: **The front brake supplies roughly 70 percent of a motorcycle's stopping power.**

Fig. 2-2: If you don't have a fuel-injected motorcycle, your bike will have some sort of choke control. Choke knobs are common.

The bright red up-and-down toggle switch is the motorcycle's engine cutoff switch. Basically, it allows you to shut the engine off quickly without removing your hand from the handgrip. It must be in the On position (down) or the motorcycle will not start. The starter switch is below the engine cutoff switch. When you've turned your ignition to the On position with your key, put the engine cutoff switch in the On position and, if necessary, set your choke. Give the starter switch a quick flick and, with any luck, your engine will roar to life. (When you hear it start, release the starter button immediately or you risk damaging the machine.) If it doesn't start, well, see the troubleshooting box (sidebar "Help! It Won't Start!") before you panic. The problem is usually something simple. (It could always be worse; older motorcycles typically had to be kick-started via a kick lever. This could be physically intense at best, downright dangerous at worst.)

Almost every motorcycle has a fuel supply valve (also called a **petcock**), which controls the flow of gasoline to the engine. (See figure 2-4.) This is commonly found on the left side of the bike under-

Fig. 2-3: Your right hand operates the motorcycle's throttle—integrated into the right handgrip—which is how you control your speed. Pull your hand toward you for more speed; push your hand away to let up on the throttle and slow down. Because your right hand is busy all the time when you are riding, you generally won't find a lot of controls on the right handgrip. Here you see only the engine cutoff and the starter switch.

HELP! IT WON'T START!

Different motorcycles have different starting procedures. The dealer or the person you bought it from should show you what to do. (And be sure to read the owner's manual.) But most machines are similar enough that if something is going wrong, you may be able to figure out what it is.

- Is the fuel valve in the On position?

- Is the key in the ignition turned to On?

- Is the engine cutoff switch in the On position?

- Is the bike in gear? It is dangerous to start up when the motorcycle is in gear; the machine will lunge forward and you will lose control. You should always make sure you are in neutral when starting up; an indicator light (typically green) should come on when you turn the ignition key on to let you know you are in neutral—but squeeze the clutch in anyhow, just to be sure. Many bikes will not start unless they are in neutral and/or the clutch is squeezed in. Most bikes have a switch that automatically cuts off the engine if the sidestand is down while the bike is in gear.

- Do you smell gas? Maybe you've given it too much choke and the engine is flooded. Wait a few minutes and try again.

- It does have gasoline in it, right? You didn't forget to reset the fuel petcock to On after going on reserve and then stopping for a fill-up?

- When you hit the starter switch, do you just get a couple of pathetic clicks and groans? Your battery is probably dead. If you're game, Walter Kern, the motorcycles guru at About.com, tells you how to jump-start a motorcycle: http://motorcycles.about .com/cs/maintenance/ht/howtojumpstart.htm. Warning: If you're using your car battery, do not turn the car on or you may burn out your motorcycle's electrical circuitry.

More complicated problems—possibly involving spark plugs, electrical circuitry, and miscellaneous engine gremlins—are best tackled by a professional unless you are comfortable with such things. Roadside assistance plans are available with many motorcycle insurance policies, and the cost is usually quite reasonable.

neath the fuel tank and is operated by hand. (Some fuel valves are completely automatic and are not accessible to the rider.)

Most of these have at least three positions: On, Off, and Reserve. When you're using the motorcycle, you will want this in the On position. If you're riding regularly, you can usually just leave it On; if the motorcycle will be sitting for a while, turn it to Off. Check your owner's manual or query your service department about this.

The Reserve setting is . . . interesting. Many motorcycles do not have a fuel gauge. As you get used to your bike, you will quickly learn how far it will travel on a tank of gas, depending on the size of its tank and its fuel consumption rate. By watching your odometer—or your trip odometer, if you have one—you will know when it's time to start looking for a gas station. But sometimes, you may not be paying attention, or you may be in some out-of-the-way location, or you may just decide to try to make it home. And suddenly, you . . . feel . . . your . . . engine . . . start . . . to . . . sputter . . . and . . . die. This is not a good feeling, even when you realize what it is, especially when you've been flying along a busy interstate at a high rate of speed.

What you are supposed to do, quickly and automatically, is to reach down and flip your petcock to the Reserve position. This allows the motorcycle to draw on a small reservoir of fuel at the bottom of the tank that will, with any luck, get you to a gas station in time for a fill-up before you go completely bone dry. In your bike's owner's manual, you'll find information about how large its gas tank is and what portion of that is reserve. If you know roughly how many miles to the gallon your motorcycle is getting, you can figure out how far you can go on Reserve before the machine dies completely and strands you.

It's important to know exactly where your fuel valve is and how it operates so that you can reach down and flip the switch to Reserve without having to look down—and take your eyes off the road, a very bad thing under most circumstances. (I know of one rider who started running out of fuel,

Fig. 2-4: On this fuel valve, On is in the 6 o'clock position, Off is in the 9 o'clock position, and Reserve is in the 12 o'clock position. Some fuel valves also have a Prime position, often at 3 o'clock, which is used to "prime" or enrich the engine with fuel after the bike has been sitting idle for a long time.

reached for and could not locate the petcock with his left hand, and so he looked down for it . . . and ran off the road and hit a tree. He survived—blessedly, he was not going all that fast—but he had several broken bones, and his bike was a total loss.) Practice reaching for and operating the fuel valve when you're in a noncritical situation. If you suddenly find that you need it and can't locate it promptly with your hand, pull over onto the shoulder, look down, flip the switch to Reserve, and make sure your bike is running smoothly again before you attempt to pull back onto the highway.

Oh, and when you get to the gas station and finish filling up, be sure to flip the fuel valve from Reserve to On again. If you don't, you risk running out of gas completely next time, with no Reserve to bail you out.

What Do I Do with My Feet?

While the motorcycle's front brake is operated with your left hand—and **the front brake supplies roughly 70 percent of a motorcycle's stopping power**—the rear brake is operated with your right foot. Just press down on the brake lever (see figure 2-5).

Maximum stopping power is achieved by using the front and rear brakes together, without locking up either of the wheels. The good folks at the Motorcycle Safety Foundation strongly encourage the use of both brakes under all circumstances, so you will instinctively know how to do this in an emergency, when you have to make a panic stop. Some motorcyclists are a bit timid about the front brake, fearing that the motorcycle will do a **stoppie**—rise up on the front wheel as the rear wheel leaves the ground—and they will be thrown headfirst over the handbars. On some touchy sport bikes . . . yeah, maybe. But on the average modern street motorcycle . . . nah, unlikely.

While your left hand operates the clutch, your left foot shifts the gears (see figure 2-6). With a few exceptions, the gearing arrangement on motorcycles is "one down, four up." That is, from neutral, you step down on the lever when the clutch is squeezed in to shift into first gear. Let the clutch out and roll on the throttle until you're moving smoothly. To speed up, release the throttle, squeeze in the clutch again, put your foot under the shift lever and kick it up as far as it will go, then let it drop back. Release the clutch. You are in second gear. Roll on the throttle. Repeat for third, fourth, and fifth gear.

You can see that even if you are familiar with driving a manual-transmission car, the mechanics of shifting a motorcycle are quite different—and you've got a lot of other things going on here that require your attention as well. What is similar, though, is that you shift upwards and downwards according to the sound and feel of the engine. The principle is the same; you are matching gears and engine speed.

Fig. 2-5: The rear brake pedal is located in front of the right foot peg.

Fig. 2-6: The shift lever is located in front of the left foot peg.

When you slow the motorcycle, you downshift by squeezing in the clutch and stepping on the lever once for each gear, until you are back in first, with the clutch squeezed in, and then you put your foot under the shift lever and raise it slightly till you pop the bike into neutral. It can sometimes be hard to get the hang of this right away; it's easy to go right on by neutral into second and have the bike lurch forward when you let the clutch out. Every bike is a little bit different. Hint: The neutral light on or near your speedometer is green. Watch for it to come on when you think the bike is in neutral. (But as the Motorcycle Safety Foundation will tell you, don't trust that light completely. Ease off the clutch slowly and make sure you really *are* in neutral.)

How Does It Go?

So here you are with this motorcycle. If you haven't yet had the opportunity to take a motorcycle safety class—and you *will* take one, right?—give this a try in your driveway (provided that it's paved and not on a slope).

Fire up the bike.

OK. You've got the engine running and you are perched atop the motorcycle with your feet on the ground on either side. Now what?

Take several deep breaths. Smoothness and patience are everything here. And be forewarned: You may well stall the engine while trying this exercise. But it certainly won't be the last time you stall your bike, and . . . well, that is why they have starter switches. Note that this exercise typically works better on a bike that has been warmed up; a rider/friend could be a big help here.

In this order (on a typical modern motorcycle):

- Squeeze in the clutch while also holding in the front brake.
- Step down on the shift lever until—clunk—you are in first gear. (Look down and see if the green neutral light has gone out, which will confirm that you are in gear.)
- Gradually release the clutch lever until you feel it "catch." You'll hear the engine slow down and feel the bike start to move forward.
- Squeeze the clutch back in again. What you've just done is locate the sweet spot where the bike's engine and transmission come together to create forward motion.
- Now do it again. But this time, when you hear the engine slow down, get off the brake and ease onto the throttle so that the bike travels forward slowly. Pick your feet up off the ground if you dare.
- After you've gone a dozen feet or so, get back on the brake and squeeze in the clutch as you bring the bike to a complete stop and plant your feet solidly back on the ground.
- Get your left foot under the shift lever and gently raise it until the bike pops back into neutral. (Did the green light come back on?) Hit the engine kill switch and turn off the bike.
- Put the sidestand down. Turn the ignition key to the off position and remove it. Take several deep breaths.

How Does It Stay Up? How Does It Steer?

A motorcycle is a big, heavy, two-wheeled machine. As such, it is inherently unstable. When it's standing still or moving slowly, it is extremely unstable. Beginning riders are often timid about speed, but we all quickly learn that it is far easier to manage a motorcycle when it's up and running at a consistent speed than when we're attempting to maneuver it around in a tight parking lot or near crowded gas pumps. When you ride yourself, you gain a new appreciation for the skills of the motorcycle officer (see figure 2-7) who executes a flawless U-turn in a confined space on his or her enormous Harley-Davidson or BMW police bike. (As long as he or she isn't turning around to chase you, that is.)

I am not a physicist, and I am sure you did not pick up this book for a long physics lesson on how motorcycles work. But you do need some basic knowledge to understand what is happening when you ride.

Speed stabilizes the motorcycle. This is pretty basic. As the bike moves forward, inertia will tend to

Fig. 2-7: This Key West motor officer was probably not going to execute a U-turn anytime soon. Definitely not a bad law enforcement gig. Photo courtesy of the Monroe County (Fla.) Public Library.

keep it moving in a straight line. The faster it goes, the less susceptible it will be to outside forces trying to change its direction.

Motorcycles turn by leaning. At all but the slowest speeds, you don't actually turn the motorcycle by steering. You **countersteer**, by leaning into the turn and pressing forward on the handgrip in the direction of the turn. Heed the Motorcycle Safety Foundation's mantra: "Press left, lean left, go left. Press right, lean right, go right" (www.msf-usa.org/downloads/Motorcycle_Operator_Manual.pdf)

You really don't want to think too hard about this. Most people do it instinctively because it feels right. When you first begin riding, it can certainly be a bit unsettling to feel the motorcycle lean over, but you'll quickly get used to it. There may come a day when you will experiment with your bike and see how far over you can make it lean in a turn. Probably, farther than you think—although that enormous Honda Gold Wing is not going to lean as readily as some nimble crotch rocket.

One day, you may scrape your heel or your footpeg on the ground when you are leaned over in a turn. That's a sign that you are reaching the bike's limit as to how far it will lean over before it falls down. But you're not quite there yet, so don't panic. Your gut reaction may be to hit the brake, but that is exactly the wrong thing to do as it may result in a **low-side**—a crash resulting from the bike's loss of traction, wherein the low side of the bike hits the ground. Which is what you were afraid was going to happen to begin with, no?

The right thing to do is to give it more throttle. Remember: Speed stabilizes the motorcycle. The bike will begin to stand up again as you emerge from the turn. And you've learned another little tidbit of conventional motorcycling wisdom: When in doubt, gas it.

IT'S FALLEN AND I CAN'T PICK IT UP

Sooner or later you will drop your bike. If you're just starting out, it will be sooner rather than later. Some fortunate souls manage to escape the stress and indignity of a dropped bike. But it happens to most of us at least once. Maybe you will forget to put the sidestand down before you get off. Maybe you will turn the wheel a little too sharply when you're moving the bike around in your garage. Maybe you will lose your footing on a slick spot when trying to maneuver the bike into a parking spot somewhere.

With any luck, you will not be on the motorcycle when it falls over. With even more luck, you will not have an audience there watching you when it happens.

One motorcycling maxim holds that you should not be riding around on any bike that is too big for you to pick up by yourself if it goes over. That would seem to cut a lot of us smaller folks off from anything much larger than a moped, but in truth, you *can* learn to pick up a bigger bike on your own.

True story: I was riding around the Philadelphia area on a motorcycle that was far too large for me—a 1980 Suzuki GS1000G, with a full **Vetter fairing** and **hard bags**. It's a long, convoluted tale how I came into possession of this monster (see figure 2-8), but it was very heavy, and I could not get both feet to touch the ground when I was on it. I was scared to death of the thing but too stubborn not to try and ride it. I did, however, have enough common sense not to take it into Center City, where I was meeting a friend for dinner.

I parked the bike near a commuter railway station on a cobblestone side street in a hilly neighborhood—a major challenge in and of itself—and I took the train downtown. When I returned on the last outbound train of the evening, it was close to 1 a.m. I walked a couple of blocks to retrieve the bike and my heart sunk. There it was, lying on its side in the street, like a fallen mastodon. Someone had obviously messed with it and it had gone down.

I stood there—my armored jacket on, my helmet and gloves in my hand—and stared at the poor bike for a while. Then I began looking around for somebody, anybody, who could help me pick it up.

Fig. 2-8: Your author's 1980 Suzuki GS1000G. Definitely a case of Too Much Motorcycle.

It being 0-dark-30, the streets were not exactly teeming with viable possibilities. Suddenly, I spotted a police car slowly cruising through the nearest intersection, which immediately raised my spirits.

"Officer! Officer!" I ran toward the cruiser. The policeman rolled down the window and leaned out. "Can you help me?" I asked. "My bike fell over."

The guy looked pretty bored, didn't say anything, pulled over to the curb and got out of the car. "Where is it?" he asked. Then he saw the helmet in my hand and did a double take. "Uh, you're talking about a motorcycle, not a bicycle," he said. I nodded. He rolled his eyes. I led him to the fallen bike.

He looked down at the bike. He looked over at me. "Lady," he said, "that thing is a *beast*! No way in hell am I going to be able to pick that up." He started making noises about having back problems. I interrupted him, informing him that, between the two of us, we *should* be able to pick up the bike . . . and besides, I reminded him, "You lift with your legs, not your back."

We did manage to get the bike upright—the officer grumbling and muttering under his breath the entire time—and I did manage to ride it back to the hotel where I was staying. (I managed, in fact, to ride it all the way to southern Virginia before I chickened out and had it shipped the rest of the way back to Florida, which made my relatives and friends very happy.)

I am convinced that no matter who you are, the best way to pick up a dropped bike is to get help. Alas, help is not always readily available. My little Suzuki Savage weighed about 385 pounds. When it fell over (and took me with it), I was able to pick it up by myself, in spite of the fact that the shift lever had gone through my shin and I was bleeding all over the intersection where I'd been done in by a stop sign and loose gravel—not quite one week after I'd brought the bike home.

My 600-pound V-Star went over (in the grass, thank heavens), when I attempted to park it in an unstable spot. Picking this one up was a little more challenging. But I did it (after first checking to be absolutely certain that the tall, 30-something contractor who lives next door to me was not around). You, too, can pick up a large fallen motorcycle. Carol Youorski—a five-foot three-inch, 118-pound Atlanta woman—has developed a technique that has made her somewhat of a motorcycling legend. She travels around the country giving demonstrations, and you can watch a video or a slide show on her Web site, www.pinkribbonrides.com/dropped.html. (See figure 2-9.)

- First, hit the kill switch to shut off the engine.
- Then put the bike in gear (or, if you can't get to the shift lever, tie the front brake lever down tight to lock the wheel).
- If the bike is lying on its left side, turn the handlebar all the way to the left. If it's lying on its right side, turn the handlebar all the way to the right.
- Clear away gravel or anything else lying around that could interfere with your traction.
- Turn around, facing away from the bike, crouch down and grab the lower handgrip with one hand. Find something solid to grab onto with the other hand—part of the frame, for example—as close to your body as possible.

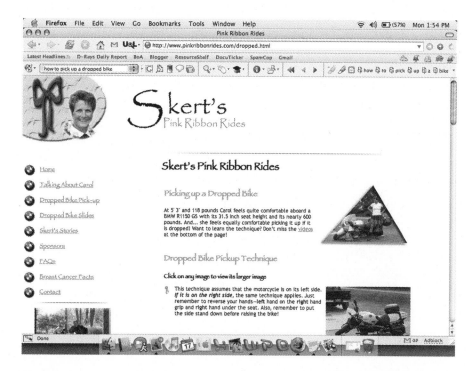

Fig. 2-9: Yes, you can pick up a large fallen motorcycle by yourself. This lady, who is five feet three inches tall and weighs 118 pounds, will show you how (www.pinkribbonrides.com/dropped.html).

- Back your butt up solidly against the bike's seat and start walking backward with small steps as you push the bike upright. Keep your feet close together. Move your butt higher or lower as needed to maximize your leverage.
- When the bike is almost upright, put the sidestand down with your heel. (If it was lying on its right side, you should put the sidestand down before you start lifting.)
- Walk the bike slowly past upright and then let it settle back onto its stand.

THE FEAR FACTOR

There's a lot to think about here, right? A motorcycle safety course will shorten the learning curve somewhat, but it will not completely eliminate it. Only practice will do that. Don't ever kid yourself into thinking this is easy. As with many other activities, some folks will pick up on it quite readily while others struggle. Some of us are naturally more coordinated than others, and some of us are more comfortable with machines.

And there is the fear factor. In the beginning, it can be almost overwhelming. Motorcycling is risky, no doubt about it. You could get hurt. You could get killed. Not that you can't get hurt or killed doing other things. But an inexperienced motorcyclist is in a much dicier place than an inexperienced tennis player.

The risk inherent in motorcycling can certainly be managed, even if it can't be completely eliminated. The fear can be managed as well. Make sure you have a bike you are capable of handling. Hang in there, get instruction, practice. Avoid busy streets and stay off the interstate. If your neighborhood is full of children and free-running dogs, find a quieter place to ride—business or light industrial parks on the weekends are often good. Large, deserted parking lots like the local mall, early on Sunday morning before the stores open, are excellent. Take it slow and easy and don't push yourself—or allow yourself to be pushed by anyone else.

Sometimes your significant other, friend, or relative can be more of a hindrance than a help. Here is this person close to you—maybe he or she has been riding for years and is eager to share this beloved activity with you. He or she wants you out there riding around sooner rather than later. This can make for a very stressful situation.

For all the obvious reasons, most people are better off learning to ride a motorcycle from a trained, professional instructor. But friends and relatives who ride can be very helpful when you want to practice.

Even after taking and passing the Motorcycle Safety Foundation's Basic Rider Course, I spent many

Fig. 2-10: Big, empty parking lots are excellent places to practice riding and gain confidence. You may, however, encounter security guards who will run you off.

hours riding around in the back parking lot of the local dog track before I had enough self-confidence to mix it up out there on the streets with all the other vehicles. It is possible to get to the dog track from my house largely on back roads, but the trip does involve about six blocks of riding on a six-lane, congested urban street that is nerve-racking even in a car. In the beginning, I could not bring myself to ride on that street. A (riding) friend, bless his heart, volunteered to ferry me over to the dog track on the back of my own bike, and there he would sit, making business calls on his cell phone and doing paperwork, while I rode around and around, practiced weaving in and out of the light poles, and made panic stops from different speeds. (See figure 2-10.)

Meanwhile, if you're feeling hopeless and discouraged, emotional support (and sometimes a buddy to practice with) can be found online. Several Web sites include forums that cater to beginning riders. One of the most active and very best, in terms of the quality of the people who hang out there, is About.com's Motorcycling for Beginners forum (see figure 2-11).

Dropped your bike? Had a bad day at the MSF course? Wondering why you are still so afraid of riding? Not sure what kind of bike is best for you because you are significantly taller/shorter/heavier/lighter than the average person? Did some cager practically run you off the road? Confused about what kind of gear to buy and where to buy it? You'll find empathy and advice here.

Or maybe you just passed the MSF course, rode to work on your motorcycle for the first time, bought a shiny new bike . . . and you want to crow about it. You'll find a cheering section here. Your nonriding friends, relatives, and coworkers may get sick of hearing you talk about motorcycles, but your online compatriots will not.

About.com has several other motorcycling forums as well—for women, for Harley-Davidson riders, for those interested in sport bikes and racing, for maintenance and repair discussions, etc., plus a

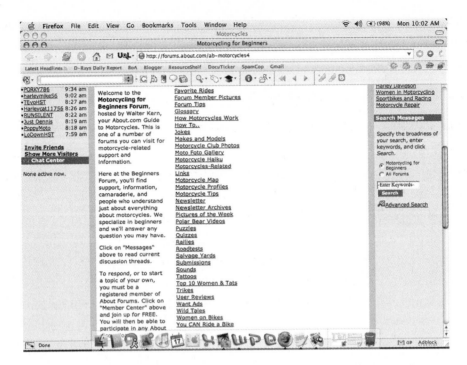

Fig. 2-11: You can find good information and lots of moral support at About.com's Motorcycling for Beginners forum, where the only stupid question is the one you don't ask. Browse to http://forums.about.com/ab-motorcycles/start and choose Motorcycling for Beginners. You can read forum postings as a guest, but if you want to participate, you will need to register (free).

general motorcycling discussion group. Bookmark http://forums.about.com/ab-motorcycles/start/ and visit often. You never know when you might be able to help someone else.

CAN YOU DO THIS? DO YOU REALLY WANT TO DO THIS?

Some people should not ride a motorcycle.

A little bit of fear is good—essential, even, because it will keep you alert and help keep you alive. (It's another little piece of motorcycling's conventional wisdom that if you ever lose that little bit of fear you typically feel as you are gearing up and getting ready to go, then you should not be riding.) But when the fear is incapacitating—when day after day, you cannot look at that bike in the garage without getting sick to your stomach—maybe motorcycling is not for you, regardless of how your significant other feels about it. If you want it badly enough, you *will* overcome the fear. But if it's more a case of what someone else wants you to do—even with the best intentions—maybe it's time for a Come-to-Jesus discussion.

Some people should not ride a motorcycle.

You've had five speeding tickets in the last two years. You've totaled several vehicles and had more close calls than any sane person should rightly survive. You can't even park without causing damage to at least two other cars around you. You think it is normal to eat, drink, talk on the cell phone, and groom yourself—simultaneously—while driving. You routinely overimbibe and drive home with your hand over one eye to reduce the double vision, hoping you're not weaving so erratically that you attract the attention of law enforcement. Speaking of which, you are on a first-name basis with half the local cops in your area, and with highway patrol officers in your state and five contiguous states. Your monthly car insurance nut is higher than your mortgage or rent payment. You are a lousy driver. You are a dangerous driver. You will probably not last two weeks on a motorcycle.

Some people should not ride a motorcycle.

If your middle finger gets more use than all of your other fingers and your thumb combined, if you take it personally when someone passes you, if your eyeballs bulge out of your head because the driver in front of you stopped when the light turned yellow instead of flooring it and barreling through the intersection, if you think it's cool to play chicken with fuel tankers and loaded, oversized gravel trucks, if you would never, ever stop to let someone merge or slide in front of you on a congested highway, if you routinely cut off school buses and ambulances . . . uh, do yourself a favor and stay away from motorcycles. Road rage and motorcycles is a deadly combination. And if you attempt to occupy the same spot in the time-space continuum as a larger vehicle, you will lose. Count on it.

Some people should not ride a motorcycle.

Your eyes have never been that good and they seem to be getting worse. You have a health condition that requires you to take a medication with side effects like dizziness, fatigue, etc. You are hopelessly uncoordinated and have been that way your entire life. You are so out of shape that you get winded walking to the mailbox at the end of your driveway and the only exercise you get involves a knife and fork. You are a substance abuser without the inclination or ability to get it under control. Riding a motorcycle is both physically and mentally demanding. If you're not up to it, you could die. And take others with you. Time for a reality check. If you really want to ride, there may be something you can do to fix the problem. Perhaps you should talk to a health professional. Do a little research and see how others cope. Or maybe you need to adjust your expectations.

The truth is, most people who really want to ride will be able to ride. Realistically, you may not be able to manage a touchy, high-tech sport machine or wrestle with an 1800 cc supercruiser.. Maybe you know you are better off not riding at night and/or have no inclination whatsoever to ride in urban/suburban traffic or on the freeways. Possibly, a trike conversion or a sidecar can make motor-cycling a little less physically challenging for you. Online communities can be invaluable for work-ing through these sorts of issues because the odds are great that someone else has Been There, Done That and is willing and eager to share his or her experience.

3 GETTING TRAINED, GETTING LEGAL

- ◆ Yes, you need a special license

- ◆ Getting trained

- ◆ Insurance: Heaven forbid you should ever have to use it, but . . .

> The safe operation of a motorcycle requires different knowledge and skills than driving a car. Testing and licensing of motorcycle operators help ensure that riders can demonstrate basic knowledge of motorcycle operation and safely perform basic handling skills. While all 50 states require a separate driver's license endorsement to operate a motorcycle, it is estimated that about 20% of the national motorcyclist population is either unlicensed or improperly licensed. Low compliance with state licensing laws is indicated by federal statistics showing that more than 40% of motorcyclists involved in fatal crashes are not properly licensed.
>
> —*American Medical Association*

YES, YOU NEED A SPECIAL LICENSE

There is a reason states have separate licensing requirements for motorcyclists. Every statistical report, analysis, and study shows that unlicensed motorcyclists are overrepresented in fatal accidents; have a look at figure 3-1. We can all sit back and debate the cause-and-effect arguments here,

---

The epigraph is from American Medical Association, *Options for Improving Motorcycle Safety*, December 1998, www .ama-assn.org/ama/pub/category/13623.html.

To find out exactly what is required in your state to get a motorcycle license, check your state DMV Web site. The Federal Highway Administration maintains a comprehensive list of links at www.fhwa.dot.gov/webstate.htm. The Canadian Motorcycle and Moped Industry Council offers licensing information for all provinces at www.mmic.ca/license.asp.

but it's a fact that simply obtaining a proper license immediately decreases the statistical odds that you will die on your motorcycle.

Depending on where you live, you may be able to locate a state-funded or state-subsidized motorcycle training program using some version of the Motorcycle Safety Foundation's Basic Rider Course. MSF-certified rider/coaches often conduct these sessions. Some states have outsourced motorcycle training to the MSF—a somewhat controversial issue, as you'll see below.

In most states, if you successfully complete one of these courses, you can take your MSF card to the local department of motor vehicles office and walk out with a new driver's license that includes a motorcycle endorsement. Alternately, you can go to the DMV, take a written and/or vision test, obtain a learner's permit, practice on your own or have a friend/family member teach you (not recommended), and then go back to the DMV and take a motorcycle skill test. If you pass, you get your motorcycle endorsement. In some states, successful completion of a rider training course is required for anyone under the age of 21.

Note that a motorcycle learner's permit usually allows you to ride your bike on any public highway, but it may impose some restrictions, such as no passengers, no riding after dark, helmet must be used, bike cannot be larger than a certain size, etc. Usually, too, a learner's permit from one state is valid in that state only.

GETTING TRAINED

People really need to think about taking one of these classes. They come in here, they buy a bike, then they ask me to go out into the parking lot with them and show them how to ride it. And I'm like . . . hey, guy, I'm a salesman. I don't even own a motorcycle.

—Sales dude at powersports dealership near my house

Will a formal motorcycle training course turn you into a competent rider? Think you'll automatically be able to manage a 700-pound cruiser in rush hour traffic? Or be ready to maneuver one of the

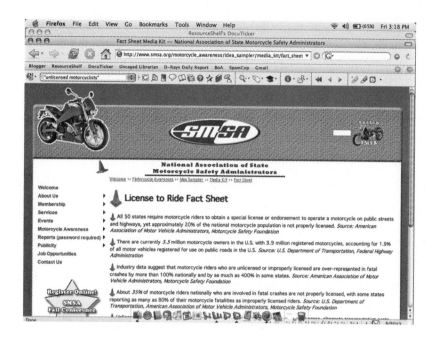

Fig. 3-1: The National Association of State Motorcycle Administrators has accumulated a variety of statistics that demonstrate why obtaining a motorcycle license is a really good idea: www.smsa.org/motorcycle_awareness/idea_sampler/media_kit/fact_sheet.

higher-end Suzuki sport bikes through Deal's Gap? (That's U.S. 129 in North Carolina, which boasts 318 curves within just 11 miles. See figure 3-2.)

Think again. When you complete the Motorcycle Safety Foundation Basic Rider Course, you will basically be qualified to operate a 125 cc or 250 cc motorcycle in a parking lot. Unless you've had a fair amount of riding experience before you take the class—and some students do; they may be taking the class as a refresher or to qualify for insurance discounts—you are hardly ready to venture out onto the public roads. You're still looking at a lot of practice time before you're ready to take on the challenges of heavily trafficked highways or "the **twisties**."

So why even bother spending time and money on a class? Why not just let your spouse or your brother-in-law give you a few lessons and then venture out into your neighborhood on your own and ride around until you have enough confidence to join the flow of traffic? You can learn by doing, can't you?

Well, yes. To a certain extent. But most experienced riders recommend a motorcycle training course. If you wander into any of the beginning motorcyclists' forums on the Internet, it's almost always the first piece of advice anyone is given. "Find an MSF class."

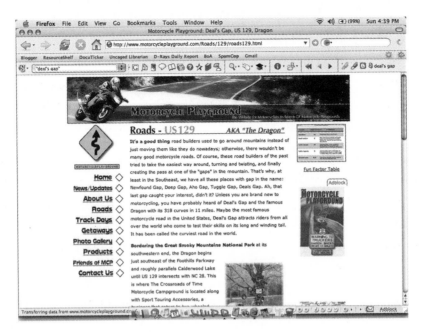

Fig. 3-2: Motorcyclists come from all over the world to "slay the Dragon," the nickname for Deal's Gap, U.S. 129 in North Carolina, which has 318 curves in 11 miles. Plenty of businesses in the area are happy to cater to the two-wheeled tourist trade. Have a look at this page from the Motorcycle Playground: www.motorcycleplaygr ound.com/Roads/129/roads129.html.

Why?

Well, for one thing, it's a good way to find out if motorcycling is for you without making a sizeable investment in bike and gear. (Or worse, borrowing a friend's bike for a trial run and not surviving long enough to return it.) When you register for the MSF BRC, small motorcycles and proper helmets are provided. Even if you already own a bike, you will not normally be allowed to use it in the basic. (Although after you're riding a while and decide you want to take the MSF's Experienced Rider Course, you will need your own bike.)

The standard MSF basic course is 20 hours long. It's not unusual for someone to decide, at some point within those 20 hours, that motorcycling is not for him or her. No harm, no foul. You've lost some time and maybe a few bucks, but the odds are that it's only your ego that has gotten a bit bruised. And the instructors, for the most part, know what they are doing and can weed out the occasional student who really doesn't want to be there but was been pushed by a spouse or significant other. (Instructors often frown on SOs who want to "hang around and watch." This can make even an enthusiastic student nervous.)

What else do you get from a basic motorcycle training course? Well, it's a chance to start your learning experience off in a controlled environment—no children or dogs darting out in front of you, no traffic signals, no cell-phone-engrossed SUV drivers poised to run you down, etc. And most of the folks in the group with you will largely be in the same boat and can provide moral support above and beyond what you'll get from the instructors. And one or more of them may end up as future riding partners.

Interestingly, as Art Friedman points out in his safety column in the February 2005 issue of *Motorcycle Cruiser* magazine (http://motorcyclecruiser.com/streetsurvival/training/), research has shown that rider training courses really do not provide any long-term benefit. "The only measured difference between training course graduates and those who start riding without any formal training shows up during the first six months, when those who take the course suffer somewhat fewer lapses—events such as crashes and tickets—than unschooled riders."

More than one researcher has demonstrated that those first few months or first few hundred miles are, statistically, the riskiest period for the rookie motorcyclist. If a class can help get you through that learning curve in one piece . . . well, that's a good thing, no? Friedman acknowledges this halo effect in his column and recommends that new riders "absolutely not" pass on the opportunity to take a training class.

Motorcycle Safety Foundation

On its home page, the Motorcycle Safety Foundation boasts that some 250,000 novice and experienced motorcyclists enrolled in its courses in 2004, and nearly 3.2 million riders have graduated from MSF courses. (The screen shot in figure 3-3 was taken in May 2005.) What, exactly, is the MSF and how did it get to be the 800-pound gorilla of motorcycle training in the United States?

The MSF is industry funded. According to its Web site, "The Motorcycle Safety Foundation is a national, not-for-profit organization sponsored by the U.S. manufacturers and distributors of BMW, Ducati, Harley-Davidson, Honda, Kawasaki, KTM, Piaggio/Vespa, Suzuki, Victory and Yamaha motorcycles." It's been around since 1973, and it works with various other entities—the National Highway Traffic Safety Administration, state governments, the military, etc.

The MSF has begun managing some states' rider training programs and appears to be moving more and more in this direction, and there has been debate over this. Some feel that since the MSF is industry-funded, there is a bottom-line interest in selling more motorcycles to more riders, which may sometimes conflict with the goals of rider training. And some states prefer to use their own locally developed courses. But the MSF has a lot of industry money behind it, so some feel the playing field is not exactly even, and that other entities are being shut out. How much of this is politics

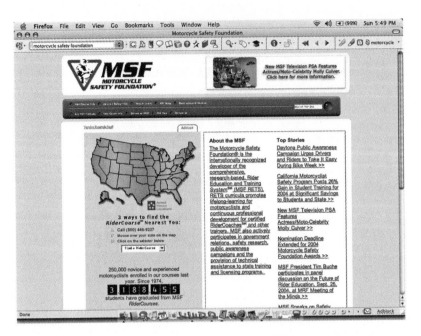

Fig. 3-3: The Motorcycle Safety Foundation's Web site offers plenty of good information. Start your browsing in the Library / Safety Tips section; www.msf-usa.org.

among the different organizations involved I cannot say. I do know that, from the standpoint of the average motorcyclist, "MSF" is becoming synonymous with rider training.

As mentioned before, the MSF Basic Rider Course is 20 hours long. Four hours is spent in the classroom and 16 hours on the "range," during which you'll be riding most of the time. Cost varies according to location. In the classroom, you'll learn about different types of motorcycles, controls, operation, protective gear, safety strategies, etc. On the bike, you'll learn straight-line riding, turning, shifting, stopping, cornering, swerving, and emergency braking. At the end, you must pass a written test and a riding skills test in order to get a card certifying successful completion. Find an interactive tour of the course on the MSF Web site, shown in figure 3-4.

David Hough, a longtime columnist for Motorcycle Consumer News and author of the well-regarded Proficient Motorcycling and More Proficient Motorcycling books, wrote a number of articles about the motorcycle training controversy for MCN. These are available in PDF format on MCN's Web site. See www.mcnews.com/mcn/proficient_motor.asp.

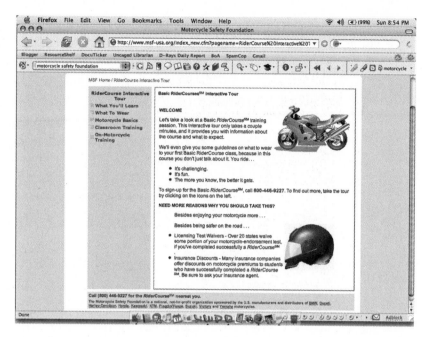

Fig. 3-4: The MSF offers an interactive tour of its Basic Rider Course on its Web site. Find it by clicking on the Rider Course Info link near the top left of the home page. There's also a review questionnaire and an interactive "Motorcycle Challenge." You can download a PDF copy of the course manual at www.msf-usa.org/CurriculumMaterials/BRC RiderHndbk_2005v6.pdf.

MSF's Experienced Rider Course, a one-day course, is designed for riders with at least six months or 3,000 miles of recent riding time. It covers such things as risk management, conspicuity, lane positioning, etc. You'll need your own bike and helmet, and you'll practice such skills as managing traction, controlling skids, panic stopping, stopping, cornering, and swerving. Many experienced riders take this course every couple of years to brush up their techniques and break bad habits they may have developed.

Harley-Davidson Rider's Edge

Harley-Davidson's Rider's Edge new rider course is analogous to the MSF's Basic Rider Course. Successful completion will net you an MSF card, which, as mentioned above, may enable you to get your motorcycle endorsement without further testing. You'll need to bring your own helmet, but you'll be provided with a lightweight, sporty Buell Blast for the duration of the course. According to the H-D Web site (figure 3-5), the cost of the course is determined by the dealer—anywhere from

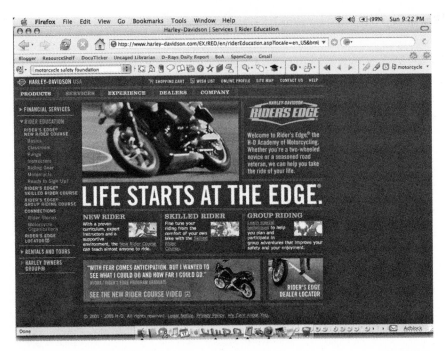

Fig. 3-5: Harley-Davidson's Rider's Edge training program uses the MSF curriculum; www.harley-davidson.com/EX/RED/en/riderEducation.asp.

$195 to $350—although one woman told me she was offered the course for free when she bought a new Sportster.

The Skilled Rider Course uses the MSF Experienced Rider Course curriculum and, as with the ERC, you'll need your own bike, although rentals may be available.

The Rider's Edge Group Riding Course, which covers such things as ride planning and preparation, formations, hand signals, and dealing with road hazards, is basically a self-study program that includes a handbook and a video. It can be ordered online.

Other Training Options

Ever wonder what it would be like to ride a motorcycle on a racetrack? After you've got some street experience behind you, you might want to sign up for a **track day,** where you pay a fee for the experience of riding your own bike around a track. You may have to make certain modifications to it such as taping up your headlights; each track has its own rules. Generally, riders are grouped according to experience and/or comfort level.

Browse webBikeWorld's Motorcycle Training, Motorcycle Track Days page, www.webbikeworld .com/motorcycle-training, for links to all sorts of interesting options.

INSURANCE: HEAVEN FORBID YOU SHOULD EVER HAVE TO USE IT, BUT . . .

It is easier to ride illegally in Florida than almost anywhere else in the country because it is one of six states that do not require motorcycle insurance. In the other states, proof of insurance is needed to register a bike, and insurance companies won't insure unlicensed riders, according to the Insurance Information Institute.

"Unlicensed Bikers Risk Lives," Orlando Sentinel, *March 27, 2005*

Whether you need insurance, and how much insurance you need, depends on where you live. What kind and how much insurance to buy is a confusing mess unless you are an insurance agent, but it's definitely worth trying to sort out. Even if you live in one of the few states that doesn't require motorcycle insurance, most experienced riders feel that you'd be a fool to ride without it.

The first thing you should know is that the same company that insures your house and/or your car may not be willing to insure your motorcycle. And even if it will give you coverage, its rates will often not be the best. Generally speaking, the companies that insure the most motorcycles tend to offer the best rates, and the same names come up again and again: Foremost, Geico, Markel/Bikeline, Progressive, Sentry. Check the bike rags; they're always full of ads from insurers. Ask your dealer (but verify what you are told). Ask other riders. Ask in online forums. But remember that not every company operates in every state. And if you're 19 years old with a lousy driving record and want to insure your new Suzuki Hayabusa, you will need to shop around for the best rate.

Motorcycle insurance rates are a lot like auto insurance rates. They're based on your age, your driving record, where you live, what kind of bike you have, engine size displacement, number of miles you estimate that you will ride, your riding experience, and whether or not you keep the bike in a garage. Some insurers will give you a discount if you've completed an MSF or comparable training course. Expect to pay more to insure a highly customized bike or one to which you've added a lot of costly accessories.

You can get an online quote from all of the companies mentioned above; plug the names into Google to locate their Web sites or try one of the sites that offers quotes from a variety of companies. You'll want a reputable site such as Insure.com, InsWeb.com, or Insurance.com. For a description of insurance coverages, see the sidebar "Insurance without Tears."

Savvy Tip

The American Motorcyclist Association maintains a database of state motorcycle laws, including insurance requirements. See www.amadirectlink.com/legisltn/laws.asp. This is something that will also likely be covered in your local MSF class.

INSURANCE WITHOUT TEARS

You need to know something about the different types of coverages available before you can even attempt to get a quote. I am not and never have been an insurance broker, but I'll do my best here.

Bodily Injury Liability: This covers your legal liability in an accident where you are at fault and someone else is injured. If your state mandates insurance, this is one of the coverages that will be required. Usually some minimum will be specified, such as $15,000/$30,000, meaning no more than $15,000 would be paid per person, and no more than $30,000 per accident. Usually recommended is a minimum of $100,0000/$300,000, which will not really be that expensive as a percentage of the total premium.

Property Damage Liability: Pays for the damage to someone else's property caused by your motorcycle in an accident where you are at fault. If your state has an insurance requirement, some minimum coverage here is usually specified, for example, $5,000. This means a maximum of $5,000 would be paid for property damage in one accident—which isn't very much, really. Twenty-five thousand dollars or more is usually recommended; again, this is not one of the more expensive coverages.

Collision Coverage: Covers your bike for damage sustained in an accident. You can choose deductibles ranging from $50 to $1,000; sport bikes (with all that expensive plastic to repair) are sometimes required to carry a deductible of $500 or more. The higher the deductible, the lower the premium.

Comprehensive Coverage: Covers your bike for damage caused by anything other than a collision—for example, fire, theft, or vandalism. Deductibles of $50 to $1,000 apply; again, the higher the deductible, the lower the premium. Note: Although neither collision nor comprehensive coverage is required by any state, if your motorcycle is financed, your lender will usually require these coverages.

Uninsured/Underinsured Motorist Coverage: If the other driver is at fault and does not have insurance, or doesn't have enough insurance, this coverage will pay for your medical bills, lost wages, pain and suffering, etc. Premiums for this coverage have skyrocketed. Some feel that if you have adequate health insurance and disability insurance, you don't need this coverage. If you choose to purchase it, you can only buy up to your own bodily injury liability limit. For example, if you've only got $15,000/$30,000 in bodily injury liability coverage, you can only buy $15,000/$30,000 in UM/UMI.

Medical Payments: Pays the cost of all medical treatment received as a result of a motorcycle accident, regardless of who is at fault. Usually limited in dollar amount and to a specific time period—for example, within three years following the accident. In some states, it kicks in only after other insurance coverage has been exhausted.

Towing or Road Service: This is fairly inexpensive, usually around $50 a year. Even if you have AAA or similar auto club membership covering your car, most of these plans do not include roadside service or towing for a motorcycle. Towing a bike requires special equipment lest the bike be seriously damaged. This coverage includes towing to the nearest qualified repair location and/or any necessary labor at the spot where your bike became disabled due to mechanical or electrical problems, dead battery, flat tire, missing key/broken lock, running out of gas/oil/water, getting stuck in mud/sand/snow/water, etc.

Other Coverages: You can usually buy coverage for add-on accessories, custom parts, trailers and sidecars, riding gear, etc.

Insurance is confusing. Premiums vary widely. I am in no way qualified to make any recommendations as to what coverage you need and how much. Talk to as many experienced local motorcyclists as you can, and get at least three quotes. If you take an MSF course, the instructors are usually a decent source of information. Geico offers a glossary of motorcycle insurance terms that might be helpful at www.geico.com/cycle/about/terms.htm.

An article appeared in the March 21, 2005, issue of *National Underwriter Property and Casualty* magazine with the intriguing title, "Tattooed Bikers Pay Less for Coverage" (www.nationalunder writer.com/pandc/nuonline/032105/p11tattooed_bikers.asp). The gist of the story was that Harley owners, 52 percent of whom are likely to have tattoos and/or body piercings compared to 40 percent of sport bike owners, pay less for insurance coverage than sport bike owners. Even though Harleys are usually more expensive out the door, considerably so in some cases, they "have a better loss history." When a sport bike gets damaged, there's a lot of expensive plastic to repair.

The difference in premiums can be quite significant; the article quotes a full coverage premium for

Savvy Tip

As with any other type of insurance, you will not want to buy motorcycle coverage from a company that is financially shaky. Check the status of an insurance company at the A.M. Best Web site, www.ambest.com. Plug in the name of the company and get a financial rating; secure companies are A++ to B+, vulnerable companies are in the B to C- range, and if a company has an A.M. Best rating of D–F, well . . .

a 25-year-old male at $1,487 if he's riding a 2004 1450 cc H-D Springer Softail, versus $2,799 for a 2004 750 cc Suzuki Katana. (The article was based on a nonscientific online survey by Progressive and contains some interesting findings—for example, 69 percent of riders daydream at work about motorcycling, 18 percent call in sick at least once a year to go riding, etc.) See the sidebar "Oh, No! It's Gone Missing!" for a discussion of preventing motorcycle theft.

OH, NO! IT'S GONE MISSING!

You shouldn't be surprised to learn that, as motorcycling has grown in popularity with the general public, motorcycles have grown in popularity with thieves. Higher-end Harleys are a particularly desirable target—they can be whisked away in a van and either resold as is or stripped down in a "chop shop" and sold for parts; they are particularly desirable as a luxury item outside the United States. Discouragingly, only 20–25 percent of stolen bikes are ever recovered.

Interesting factoid: The National Insurance Crime Bureau (NICB) says the stolen parts market is hotter in colder climates because the riding season is shorter. Makes sense. You don't want any downtime for that bike if you've only got a limited amount of time to ride it. These tips to thwart motorcycle theft were culled from the NICB and insurers:

- Keep your bike out of sight—in a locked garage, if possible. The NICB recommends chaining it to a stationary object even when it's in the garage. And if it's a high-end Harley in a low-end neighborhood, you may want to think about an alarm system.

- If garaging your bike is not an option, buy a motorcycle cover and use it. Don't choose one with a logo or brand name on it, as a potential thief may pass it by if it's unclear what kind of bike is under it. Keep the cover secured to the bike with a cable lock, and chain the bike to a stationary object. Park it in a well-lit place that is not within direct view of the street.

- Don't cheap out on a lock for your bike. Make an investment in a good one and then record key numbers and file them off if they are stamped on the lock. Here's something you may not have thought about: When the lock is secured to your bike, make sure it is not touching the ground. If the lock is lying on the ground, a thief could use a hard object to pound on it until it breaks.

- If you're so inclined, there are a number of mechanical or electrical antitheft devices that can be installed on a motorcycle; check the back of any bike rag. The well-known Lojack device is now available for motorcycles. See Lojack for Motorcycles—FAQ,

---

www.lojack.com/products-services/auto-security-system/lojack-for-motorcycles-faqs.cfm.

- If you're buying a used bike, the NICB cautions you to take a hard look at any machine that is titled or registered as an "assembled vehicle." In particular, make sure that any used Harley—though titled and registered as such—is not, in fact, "an assembled clone made from aftermarket components." Further, the NICB advises that you closely scrutinize any used cycle with "a title history that reveals numerous manufacturers' statements of origin for major component parts." (Motorcycles Offer a Tempting Target for Criminals, National Insurance Crime Bureau, www.nicb.org.

- Be especially wary of "all-custom" bikes that may have been assembled from stolen or altered aftermarket parts, especially chrome parts, or bikes allegedly assembled from parts acquired at a "swap meet."

- You may want to consider a professional appraisal or prepolicy insurance company inspection before buying a higher-end used motorcycle.

For more information and advice about motorcycle theft, see Art Friedman's article, "Anti-Theft Strategies for Motorcyclists," *Motorcycle Cruiser* magazine, August 1997, www .motorcyclecruiser.com/tech/antitheft.

4 YOUR OWN RIDE

- ◆ Awash in confusion
- ◆ Two-stroke, four-stroke . . .
- ◆ Chain drive, belt drive, shaft drive
- ◆ It goes, it stops
- ◆ So what's it gonna be?
- ◆ And if you're an absolute novice?

No matter what marque you ride, it's all the same wind.

—*Conventional motorcycle wisdom*

AWASH IN CONFUSION

Maybe you already had your dream bike picked out before you even started riding.

What image pops into your mind when you think about motorcycles? Maybe it's a big, low-slung cruiser with a custom paint job and chrome, chrome, chrome everywhere. After all, turning heads is the whole point, no?

Or you can only see yourself on one of those hot high-tech sport bikes, your helmet and your gear matching its bold paint job as you lean way, way over in the curves. Need for Speed. Yep, that is you.

Your soul is filled with wanderlust. You yearn to pack everything you could possibly require onto one of those big touring machines and head off who knows where for who knows how long. And you'd like to have every possible creature comfort, as you'll be spending hours and hours astride that big boy.

Maybe, though, you are just kind of confused. You're not sure what you want, and the more you look around, the more confused you get. If you have little or no experience with motorcycles, this is not uncommon. Even after you've taken the Motorcycle Safety Foundation class—where you typically ride around on loaner 125/250 cc bikes—you still don't know what you want to buy.

Well, read on. While I can't pretend to know exactly which machine will be the right one for you, I can share some information that will help you decide.

Two-Stroke, Four-Stroke . . . V-Twin, Inline Four . . .

My knowledge of internal combustion engines pretty much stops with the basics, but that's really all you need to know unless this kind of stuff really turns you on—in which case, check the bibliography for additional book suggestions.

Motorcycle engines come in two basic flavors—two-stroke engine or four-stroke engine. "Stroke" refers to the number of movements a piston makes within a cylinder during each power cycle. In a four-stroke engine cycle, the piston first moves down, sucking in the air/fuel mixture (intake), then moves up, causing the mixture to ignite and burn (compression), which pushes the piston down again (power). When the piston pushes back up again to expel the burned gases, this is the fourth stroke (exhaust). In a two-stroke engine, the piston moves down, sucking in air/fuel, and then moves up until the mixture ignites, forcing the piston back down again, for a more rapid power cycle. In simple terms, this means there is one power stroke for every engine revolution instead of every second revolution, as in a four-stroke engine.

Most street motorcycles you're going to see these days have four-stroke engines, as does pretty much every other motorized vehicle out there on the roads. While two-stroke engines are lighter and simpler and produce twice as much power, they also wear out faster, use much more oil, and create more pollution; characteristically, these engines produce a visibly smoky exhaust.

So, we're going to be talking about four-stroke engines here. And when we talk about different types of four-stroke engines—please forgive me—we use the words torque and horsepower. To really, really oversimplify this, horsepower is how fast your machine is capable of going, and torque is how fast it can get to that speed. From a practical motorcycling standpoint, at least generally speaking, torque is more useful than horsepower. Lots of horsepower can be cool, but mostly at speed limits that will attract the attention of law enforcement.

The more cylinders a bike has, everything else being equal, the smoother it will run. Single-cylinder bikes were once a lot more common than they are now, mainly because people figured that fewer moving parts made for a simpler, lower maintenance machine. Perhaps, but the vibrations from that

Timberwoof's Motorcycle FAQ, at www.timberwoof.com/motorcycle/faq/hp-torque.html, offers a lucid explanation of horsepower and torque that doesn't involve so much physics that your head will explode.

one oversized cylinder could definitely loosen the fillings in your teeth. Rubber engine mounts and engine counterweights have made the few single-cylinder bikes around today much less of a rugged ride, and these so-called "thumper" bikes—like the Suzuki Savage (which has morphed into the Boulevard S40) and the Buell Blast—can be excellent motorcycles for a beginner. (See my 2000 Suzuki Savage in figure 4-1.) They have enough torque to get you out of trouble but not enough high-end horsepower to get you into trouble. And they are light, maneuverable, and lots of fun to ride.

The V-Twin engine design has been around for a long time—Harley-Davidson was using it back in the early 1900s—and is arguably the most recognizable motorcycle engine type. It looks like what it is: two cylinders arranged in a V shape. This is what you'll find on classic cruising bikes, which tend to deliver a lot of torque as opposed to horsepower, even in the big-cc bikes. My V-Star 1100, in figure 4-2, is a good example.

All twins are not V-Twins. Especially if you are riding a BMW. The opposed twin—or boxer—was originally developed by BMW engineers for use by the German army in WW II. Harley Davidson used it briefly for military motorcycles, and Russian engineers subsequently copied the design. You can still buy a Ural motorcycle that employs it; these typically come with attached sidecars, like the one in figure 4-3.

Fig. 4-1: Your author's 2000 Suzuki Savage, a classic single-cylinder ("thumper") bike.

Fig. 4-2: Your author's 2005 Yamaha V-Star 1100 Custom, a traditional V-Twin cruiser.

Fig. 4-3: Specialist Sarah Houtler (left) and Sergeant Danielle Derosier, both of Headquarters Company, First Calvary Division, sit on the most popular of the three bikes on display during the Brotherhood of Bikers rally at Camp Blackjack (July 2004), a Russian copy of a BMW motorcycle. Photo: Courtesy of U.S. Army; by Corporal Benjamin Cossel.

The boxer's opposed pistons—one going left and one going right—generate less vibration than the standard V-Twin, and produce comparable torque. But they also offer a little more at the high end, and they run somewhat cooler. Typically, these are relatively long-lasting engines. It is not unusual to find BMW motorcycles with more than 100,000 original miles on the odometer.

Three cylinders . . . well, OK. This is a British thing—the inline triple—and in this day and age, that pretty much means Triumph. Those who like them tend to like them a lot—some compare the sound they make to a Porsche. Browse through the different models on their Web site, pictured in figure 4-4.

Four-cylinder bikes, besides running more smoothly, also tend to put out more power higher up the range than two-cylinder bikes. Some of the earlier four-cylinder bikes—inline and V-Four—were rather bulky, but over the years, designers have shifted components around to make for a somewhat more compact engine. These are common designs and, though a bit more complex than the twins, are pretty reliable.

Moving on up, yes, there are some six-cylinder bikes around. The standout example is Honda's radically styled Valkyrie, shown in figure 4-5. It's heavy, the parts tend to be more expensive, but the engine runs very smoothly.

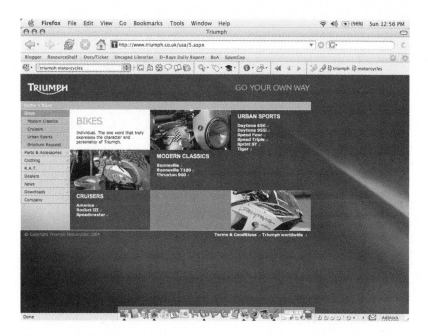

Fig. 4-4: Three-cylinder engines . . . very much a British thing. In today's motorcycle market, that means Triumph, which is turning out some pretty nice machines these days. To see them, visit www .triumph.co.uk/usa/t.aspx.

Fig. 4-5: Honda's Valkyrie Rune, with its six-cylinder, 1800 cc boxer engine, is a lot of motorcycle. A retired military acquaintance of mine hit a deer while riding one of these behemoths in Wisconsin. The deer got up and staggered away into the woods, making crackling noises, as if numerous bones had been broken. There wasn't a scratch on the Valkyrie; the man's son had added a chrome railing to the front fender for looks, and apparently it had served as a sort of cowcatcher. "But I'll tell you what," the guy said to me, "I had to pull off to the side, shut the bike down, get off and just sit there on the ground for half an hour or so until my heart rate dropped back

If you'd like to read more about motorcycle engines, check out the Beginner's Guide to Motorcycling on the Total Motorcycle Web site, www.totalmotorcycle.com/school-SectionSix.htm.

CHAIN DRIVE, BELT DRIVE, SHAFT DRIVE

Somehow, power has to get from the engine to the rear wheel, which moves the motorcycle forward. This so-called **final drive** comes in one of three flavors, each of which has its advantages and disadvantages. (See sidebar "So What Kind of Drive System Do I Want?")

For a long time, chain drives ruled the motorcycling world. If you're familiar with bicycles, you know what a chain drive looks like. This is a simple, reliable, easy-to-repair technology. It does, however, require more periodic maintenance than the other two alternatives; basically, the motorcycle's rear wheel has to be adjusted every so often to take up the slack as the chain elongates with use. It is also somewhat messy, as a chain must be lubricated regularly with nasty, greasy stuff. And replacing the chain, if it becomes necessary, can be a major production—although many chains today include a "maintenance link" that facilitates the process. It's just something else you have to keep an eye on, in case it decides to disassemble spontaneously.

A sales dude at my local dealership told me that a chain was the most efficient final drive system, since pretty much all the power from the engine gets transferred directly to the read wheel. This is why you'll find chain drives on sport bikes; see the rear wheel of a Honda CBR600F4i in figure 4-6.

The shaft final drive has become extremely popular because it is largely maintenance-free, but it

Fig. 4-6: You can see the chain on the rear wheel of this 2001 Honda CBR600F4i. Photo courtesy of Honda Motorcycles.

Fig. 4-7: Your author's V-Star 1100 Custom has a shaft drive. If you look toward the front of the rear wheel, you can see it.

Fig. 4-8: Suzuki's Boulevard S40 Cruiser, formerly known as the Suzuki Savage, has a belt drive. You can sort of see it if you look at the rear wheel here. Photo courtesy of Honda Motorcycles.

does have some disadvantages that you should take into consideration. For one thing, it is much more expensive to manufacture a shaft drive than a chain or belt drive. If, however, you're going to keep a bike for several years, the money you'll save on parts and labor—especially if you're not going to work on the bike yourself—will probably negate the extra expense. My Yamaha V-Star 1100 Custom, shown in figure 4-7, has a shaft drive.

A shaft drive adds noticeably more weight to the motorcycle than a chain or belt—and it is "unsprung" weight, not supported by the bike's suspension. Handling is somewhat affected; the motorcycle will not change directions as readily. And a shaft drive transmits to the motorcycle's chassis some of the energy normally absorbed by the chain, which causes the rear of the bike to move up when it should move down, and vice versa. In some cases, engineers have managed to mitigate this so-called **shaft jacking** by rearranging certain rear end suspension components.

The earliest motorcycles employed a leather belt to transmit power from the engine to the rear wheel, and today's belt final drive systems have evolved pretty much directly from that. You'll find belt final drive systems on all Harley-Davidson motorcycles and a scattering of other models. Suzuki's small Boulevard S40 cruiser, seen in figure 4-8, has a belt drive.

A belt drive eliminates the weight and motion weirdness often associated with the shaft drive and needs none of the messy maintenance a chain drive requires. However, if something goes bad with a belt drive, you've got a major problem on your hands. On a typical belt-driven bike, replacing one of these bad boys involves pulling a fair amount of the machine apart. Overall, today's toothed drive belts tend to be pretty reliable, but if you buy a belt-driven bike, be sure to check the owner's man-

---

So What Kind of Drive System Do I Want?

Each of the three types of final drive systems has advantages and disadvantages. Weigh the options and decide what will work best for you.

Chain Drive

Pro: Lightweight; efficient in terms of transmission of power to the rear wheel; easiest of the three to replace

Con: Noisy; Requires more maintenance, which is messy; can be dangerous if it suddenly snaps

Shaft Drive

Pro: Quiet; reliable; maintenance-free

Con: More expensive; heavier, performance issues due to shaft jacking

Belt Drive

Pro: Quiet; clean; economical

Con: Very difficult to replace; major service

---

ual to see when the manufacturer recommends that the belt be replaced and have the work done by service professionals. It could be very ugly if the belt suddenly fails when you are out in the middle of nowhere.

It Goes, It Stops

OK, without getting overly technical, here are a couple more things you ought to know about, right here, right now: "induction systems" and brakes.

Induction systems for motorcycles come in two basic flavors: carburetion and fuel injection. Carburetors are the tried-and-true-traditional, while fuel injection has finally started making some inroads. (Odd that it's taken this long, since the automobile industry embraced fuel injection a number of years ago; cost, apparently, has been an issue.) Both systems have the same purpose—inducing the proper air/fuel mixture the engine needs to run.

In very simple terms, a carburetor blends a mixture of air and fuel that is then sucked into the compression chamber—the area at the top of the cylinder where the air/fuel mixture burns—because of a difference between internal and external pressure. Each cylinder has its own carburetor. Fuel injection depends on an electronic pump that forces fuel into the cylinder's intake port.

BMW was the first manufacturer to make fuel injection available on its motorcycles, back in the mid-1990s. Other manufacturers have followed suit, with fuel injection available on many models either as standard equipment or as an option. But at this point, you are still likely to find more bikes with carburetors than fuel injection systems.

Motorcycle brakes also come in two basic flavors: disks and drums. In the standard setup, you use a hand lever on the right side of the bike to activate the front disk brakes (which provide roughly 70 percent of the bike's stopping power), and a foot pedal on the right side to activate the rear drum brakes. Some bikes have disk brakes front and rear—a good thing, generally, since disk brakes are self-cleaning and self-adjusting. They do, however, involve a hydraulic system—one more item that needs to be monitored.

Some manufacturers—Honda and Moto Guzzi are two—offer linked braking systems on some models that essentially decide for you how much front and rear brake should be applied regardless of whether you squeeze the front brake hand lever or step on the rear brake foot pedal. And antilock braking systems (ABS), computer controlled to keep you from locking up the brakes and preventing a skid, are becoming more widely available on motorcycles.

Opinions among experienced motorcyclists and gearheads are decidedly mixed here. Some riders are uncomfortable relinquishing braking control to a computer. Another issue is that all of these systems are at least slightly different, requiring different braking techniques from one machine to the next. Most experts seem to feel that beginners, especially, should stick with the standard front/disk rear/drum set-up. Simpler can definitely be better . . . and is usually cheaper.

So What's It Gonna Be?

According to the Motorcycle Industry Council—"a not-for-profit, national trade association created to promote and preserve motorcycling and the U.S. motorcycle industry"—cruisers are by far the most popular bikes in the motorcycle market, capturing some 55 percent of sales in 2004. Sport bikes were a distant second, at 24 percent, followed by touring bikes at 19 percent. Standard bikes comprised just 2.7 percent of the market, with dual sports (including adventurer-tourers) bringing up the rear, at 2.4 percent. (These latter two categories, however, were gaining ground fast at the time this book went to the printer.)

Why are cruisers so popular? Where do sport touring bikes fit in? Standard bikes? Huh? Are there nonstandard bikes? And what the heck is an "adventure tourer," anyhow?

What's it gonna be?

In case you were wondering about brand popularity, a 2004 motorcycle sales forecast in the January 2005 issue of *Dealernews* ("The voice of the powersports industry")—showed Honda with a 29.38 percent market share, followed by Harley-Davidson, at 25.86 percent, Yamaha at 16.54 percent, Suzuki at 12.11 percent, and Kawasaki at 9.58 percent. Everybody else—KTM, BMW, Triumph, the Italian manufacturers, etc.—shared the remaining slice of the motorcycle market pie.

Once you decide what type of bike you want, you'll have to decide which manufacturer. Or maybe it's the other way around; you prefer a certain marque—for example, it's Harley or nothing—and you'll choose from what they have to offer, thank you very much. Or you want to buy from a dealer geographically close to you, so you'll make your choice from the brands available there.

Cruisers

The motorcycle market is awash in cruisers. Every major manufacturer offers several. In the case of Harley-Davidson, that's pretty much all it offers, with the possible exception of the somewhat-radical-for-Harley V-Rod. The market responds to what people want. Look at the parking lot outside any roadhouse. Why do so many people want cruisers?

Generally speaking, cruisers are long and low and heavy . . . and especially designed to look cool. This is what a lot of people think of when they hear the word "motorcycle." They come in all sizes, from Honda's 250cc Rebel (figure 4-9) to Kawasaki's enormous Vulcan 2000 (figure 4-10).

Fig. 4-9: The Rebel is Honda's smallest cruiser, with a 250 cc engine. This model has been around forever and is an ideal beginner's bike. You can always find good used ones in decent shape, as people often move up to larger machines when they gain more experience. Photo courtesy of Honda Motorcycles.

Fig. 4-10: Kawasaki's Vulcan 2000 cruiser has a 2053 cc engine and a dry weight of 750 pounds. Wowie kazowie! For more info, go to www.kawasaki.com/html/motorcycles/cruiser/vulcan2000_frame.asp.

Most of these bikes come with V-Twin engines, in the Harley tradition; one notable exception is Honda's Valkyrie (figure 4-5), with its six cylinders. People who buy cruisers seem to enjoy customizing them—this usually involves bolting on all sorts of aftermarket chrome accessories, of which there is no shortage. Browse through all the possibilities at a large online vendor site like CruiserCustomizing (figure 4-11).

Still, cruisers are popular for reasons that go beyond looks. I like my V-Star because it's an easy bike to ride, it's reliable, it requires little in the way of maintenance, and it's relatively comfortable on the

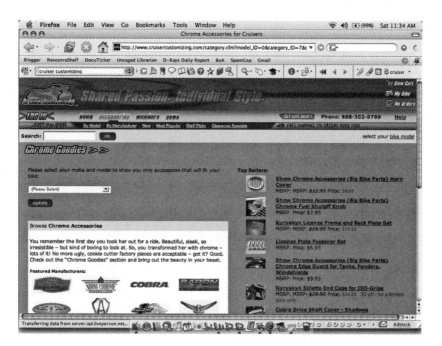

Fig. 4-11: Chrome, chrome, and more chrome. If you're into dressing up your cruiser, all it takes is money, money, and more money. Visit CruiserCustomizing at www.cruisercustomizing.com.

Savvy Tip

Because of their low center of gravity and relatively heavy weight for their size, cruisers in general are not known for nimble handling. It's easy for a novice to get into trouble quickly with a bike that is too heavy, too awkward, and too powerful. Yeah, you may have the bucks—these things can cost more than a small car—but it's probably not a great idea to choose a power cruiser like a Vulcan 2000, a Honda Valkyrie, a Triumph Rocket, or one of the bigger Harleys for your first motorcycle. Harley's entry-level Sportster, however, might work for you, although some riders have found it to be a somewhat top-heavy bike.

highway, especially since I added a windshield and a custom seat. Although the bike has an 1100 cc engine and weighs about 600 pounds and I am a five-foot, two-inch woman (on a good day), since it sits low and is generally well-balanced, I can get both of my feet flat on the ground when seated on it, which makes for secure handling at traffic lights, in parking lots, etc.

Sport Bikes

True story: A tall, thin young airman walked into my office. "The ladies at the front desk said you knew where I could sign up for the MSF class here on base," he said. "I got this new bike, and they won't let you ride it on the base until you take the class." He pulled a picture out of his wallet and handed to me. I looked. It was a yellow Ducati sport bike—so hot that the photograph smoldered in my hand. I said nothing, handed the picture back to him. He shrugged. "I know," he said. "It's my first bike. I probably should have picked something that wasn't so . . . " Mentally, I rolled my eyes and handed him a brochure with the base motorcycle rules and the phone number of the safety office. After he left, I called the base MSF instructor. "Someone," I said, "needs to get to this kid fast." (And the instructor said, "Hmmm . . . I wonder if he'd sell it to me. I've always wanted one of those." But that is another story.)

There's a reason the military pushes motorcycle safety and promulgates an ever-growing list of regulations for motorcycle riders: young GIs returning from overseas with large chunks of tax-free money and a need for the adrenaline rush that a sport bike can offer (OK, OK, and maybe also midlife-crisis civilian employees with deep pockets and a yen for power cruisers they can barely handle).

Sport bikes can be fun, no two ways about it. But by and large, these are not motorcycles for the novice, whether that novice is young and imbued with a sense of immortality or middle-aged, with eyes and reflexes that are not what they used to be. Twist the throttle on one of the higher performance models—Suzuki's Hayabusa (figure 4-12) or GXR 1000 come to mind—and the sensation is like being launched into outer space. If you don't know what you're doing, you can hurt yourself . . . badly.

Fig. 4-12: Suzuki says that's its high-tech Hayabusa GSX1300 is "the fastest production bike on the planet." This is a stunning motorcycle, but if you don't know what you're doing when you hop onto one, it could be the last ride you'll ever take. Photo courtesy of Suzuki Motorcycles.

Fig. 4-13: Not a Hayabusa . . . however, Suzuki's GS500F is a much better choice for your first sport bike. Photo courtesy of Suzuki Motorcycles.

The riding position is one key reason why these bikes appeal mostly to the "need-for-speed" demographic. The low handlebars, the rear foot pegs and the seat design pretty much force the rider to lean far forward. Those of us of a certain age are not going to find this riding position particularly comfortable—and people of any age who are planning any long-distance riding are not going to be happy on one of these things for very long. They are not ideal commuter bikes; their defining characteristics make them unsuitable for riding in traffic.

And yet . . . although you might be dissuaded from choosing a sport bike as your first bike, you may well end up on one later if you decide you want a fun bike to take to **track days** or out into the hills, valleys, canyons, or wherever you can go to get away from the urban congestion and twist the wrist a little bit. Some people do start accumulating a stable of bikes—different models for different types of riding. With a few exceptions, sport bikes come in 600 cc or 1000 cc sizes. But keep in mind that even a 600 cc sport bike can go 150 mph, and you'll want to start relatively tame here. Some frequently recommended sport bikes for beginners include the Suzuki GS500 (figure 4-13), Suzuki SV650, Ducati Monster, Buell Blast, and the smaller Kawasaki Ninjas.

Be aware that insurance premiums for sport bikes can go sky high, especially if your age is young and/or your driving record is spotty.

Touring Bikes

Here are your largest and heaviest machines, designed for hours and miles of comfortable long-distance riding, both for you and a passenger if you so desire. Although they typically have big engines, they are also hauling around a lot of weight, with features like hard touring bags and trunks, full **fairings** and windshields, large tires, and different types of body panels. You'll routinely find such comfort amenities as music systems, heated handgrips, seats with lots of cushioning (and backrests and armrests for your passenger), and electrical systems amenable to all sorts of add-on accessories.

A big touring motorcycle is a less-than-ideal choice for your first bike. As a group, they start slower, take longer to stop, and can be downright scary to maneuver at slow speeds and/or in parking lots. If a motorcycle this size starts to go over—whether you're on it or not—it's going to keep right on going. Then, good luck getting it upright again. But eventually, if long-distance riding is part of your agenda, you may want one. And you *can* learn to ride one proficiently. One of my MSF instructors, a retired moto-cop, had a fully decked out Honda Gold Wing (figure 4-14) that he whipped around the asphalt like a high-performance sport bike. It was truly something to see.

The Honda Gold Wing arguably owns this category, although Harley offers several heavy-duty, cruiser-style touring models—the Road Glide, the Electra Glide, and the Road King—and BMW's K1200LT top-of-the line tourer is an especially elegant motorcycle. See two of these in figure 4-15. Other options, Kawasaki's Vulcan Nomad and a couple of Yamaha's Royal Star models, are essentially large cruiser-style touring bikes like the Harleys.

Fig. 4-14: Honda's enormous Gold Wing is widely regarded as the gold standard in long-distance touring motorcycles. It abounds in creature comforts. Photo courtesy of Honda Motorcycles.

Fig. 4-15: Two BMW K1200LT touring motorcycles. Glenn Tussing, an MSF instructor for the U.S. Air Force and a friend of the author, sits on one. Its amenities include tons of storage space, a six-CD changer—Captain Tussing likes to listen to audio books—and a GPS system. Photo courtesy of Glenn Tussing.

Sport Tourers

Touring bikes are comfortable, but they are not the nimblest two-wheeled vehicles on the road. Sport bikes boast high-performance, responsive handling, but they're just not set up for long-distance riding. What has emerged as a compromise is the sport touring motorcycle. They offer more comfort and carrying capacity than a traditional sport bike—and are more suitable for riding **2-up** with a passenger—but they are certainly more agile than the enormous full-bore touring bikes. Generally, a windshield and/or a fairing will be standard equipment, along with hard bags. The riding position is not hunched over, as on a sport bike, and not laid back, as on a cruiser. Your feet are pretty much directly below you, and some people choose this style of bike mainly because they find this riding position most comfortable.

Harley-Davidson doesn't play in this market segment. BMW offers a number of impressive models; the new R1200RT, which replaces the venerable R1150RT, is a beautiful machine. Other bikes to consider: the Kawasaki Concours, a well-established model with a loyal following, Yamaha's FJR1300, Triumph's Sprint ST, Suzuki's V-Strom or SV models, and Honda's ST1300 (shown in figure 4-16).

Standard Bikes

This category contains a number of versatile motorcycles, several of which might be a good choice for your first bike. They are usually well-styled, not overengineered, relatively straightforward bikes that do a number of things well, although they may not excel at any one thing like long-distance touring or high performance. You won't find odd ergonomics and the included accessories are usually

Fig. 4-16: Sport touring motorcycles, like Honda's ST1300, lack the bulk of full-size touring machines but come with roadtrip-friendly accessories such as a windshield and hard bags. Photo courtesy of Honda Motorcycles.

Fig. 4-17: Suzuki's V-Strom 650 is a good choice for a first motorcycle. This model also comes with a 1000 cc engine. Photo courtesy of Suzuki Motorcycles.

minimal—maybe a windshield—although you can certainly add whatever you want after you buy one. Some have sporty good looks, but you won't get socked with the high insurance premiums that often accompany true sport bikes.

Many standard bike models have been around for a while. Especially worth your consideration: Suzuki V-Strom (figure 4-17), Honda Interceptor, and Yamaha FZ1.

What Else Is Out There?

Most folks in the market for a motorcycle are interested in street riding and will choose something from one of the categories discussed above. Off-road riding is beyond the scope of this book, which means we won't be talking about dirt bikes here. Some may be intrigued, however, by the possibility of a motorcycle that can run around town like a commuter bike yet still be functional off the beaten track, capable of being taken for a trail ride on the weekends. Such hybrids do exist, in the form of dual-purpose motorcycles or, at the higher end, adventure tourers. These bikes usually have knobbier tires than street bikes, and a higher suspension—which means a high seat height, making them a less-than-optimal choice for someone without long legs. Because they have all the equipment they need to be street legal, you can ride them through town to get to trails in outlying areas, rather than having to haul them in a truck or on a trailer, as you would a pure dirt bike.

The adventure tourers are like sport tourers for those who may be taking a long trip that will very

Savvy Tip

A dual sport motorcycle can be versatile if you can only have one bike and you know you'll be going off-road every once in a while. Around town, you'll be sitting up higher in traffic than on a more conventional machine, which makes for greater visibility, but a dual sport can be rather challenging for a short or average-sized rider in stop-and-go traffic.

likely include some off-pavement riding, or maybe bad road conditions. BMW's F 650 models fit into this niche and KTM, an Austrian manufacturer of several off-road models, has a few offerings here as well. The Japanese manufacturers—who rarely neglect a market niche—play in this space as well (figure 4-18).

Realistically, you probably won't be choosing a dual-sport or an adventure tourer for your first bike, but if you hear the call of the wilderness, you may eventually want to add one to your motorcycle collection.

Sure, we like to look at the cool bikes built by the Teutul guys on the American Chopper TV show, and these custom-built machines always attract a lot of attention at bike rallies and other gatherings. But you and I both know that something like this is not intended to be your daily ride. Because the front wheel is **raked** out so far forward, a chopper is a highly unstable thing to maneuver. And those high, **ape hanger** handlebars . . . well, they are likely illegal on the highways and uncomfortable for more than a few minutes everywhere else. We're talking about motorcycles as art here and not motorcycles as transportation. Enjoy, but custom builds like the ones in figure 4-19 are primarily for lookin' and not for ridin'.

Fig. 4-18: Honda's XR650L dual sport motorcycle. Fun, fun, fun . . . but not the best choice if you plan to do most of your riding on paved roads.

Fig. 4-19: Choppers and other custom machines—these were on display at the Leesburg, Fla., Bikefest in 2004. Look but don't touch.

AND IF YOU'RE AN ABSOLUTE NOVICE?

OK. After reading this chapter, you have a good idea of what you want for your own first motorcycle.

Or not. There are so many choices. Maybe you're just a little overwhelmed.

Since I don't know you and I don't know what kind of riding you plan to do, I can offer only the most general advice . . . and pass along what I've learned from experience and talking with other people. (See sidebar "Considerations for the First-Time Motorcycle Buyer.)

If you're an absolute beginner, you would be wise to put off buying anything until after you've taken a Motorcycle Safety Foundation Basic Rider Course. In most places, you don't need a motorcycle (or even a helmet) to enroll; the MSF people will supply small bikes and standard, approved motorcycle helmets for you to use. The basic course will not make you an expert, but it will expose you to the basics of riding and teach you some street survival skills. You will also have the benefit of your instructors' extensive experience—all MSF rider/coaches have been riding motorcycles for many years. They can make suggestions as to what would be a good first bike for you; several of the instruc-

Take advantage of quality online forums, such as those at Walter Kern's Motorcycles area on About.com. Novices are always asking the same question: What should I buy? Prowl through the forum archives and read the responses. Or have a look at Walter's suggestions at http://motorcycles.about.com/cs/beginners/a/beginnerbikes.htm.

tors in the class I took even offered to go look at motorcycles, new or used, with any student who wanted help and/or input.

Also, in most classes, at least a few of your fellow students will be more experienced riders who are taking the class to qualify for insurance discounts, for a knowledge refresher, or to be able to ride on a military base. All motorcyclists love to talk about their bikes. Pick their brains.

CONSIDERATIONS FOR THE FIRST-TIME MOTORCYCLE BUYER

- Don't buy more bike than you can handle, in terms of either weight or engine size. Start small and trade up when you have more riding experience under your belt. You will have learned a lot about yourself and your abilities and limitations by the time you are ready for your second bike. You may just decide to stick with the smaller bike you already have.

- A lot of people do start small and trade up . . . which means you can usually find beginner-friendly used bikes with low mileage at reasonable prices. Check the local paper, or see what trade-ins may be available at local dealerships.

- Visit all the dealerships you can and sit on all the different bikes you can. Even if it's a brand or model you doubt that you'd ever buy, the experience will give you more of a basis for comparison.

- Go to bike nights and bike rallies, look at the bikes, and talk to a wide range of owners. Almost every motorcycle owner is willing and eager to give you the benefit of his or her experience. (Getting them to shut up is often a larger problem.) You'll probably meet at least some folks who are a lot like you, and can offer practical advice, dealer recommendations . . . or you may encounter someone who has a good used bike to sell or knows of someone else who does.

- Don't let yourself be talked into something you don't like or feel comfortable with just because your spouse, significant other, or friends tell you it is just what you should buy. Women, in particular, often end up with bikes that are too large and/or powerful because the well-meaning guys in their lives either want them to have "the best" or make recommendations based on what an experienced male rider might want. If you end up with a new bike that overwhelms you, it can sour you on the whole experience of motorcycling. Not to mention the fact that you could get hurt.

- Use the Internet. Visit motorcycle manufacturers' Web sites, prowl through online forums, read bike magazines online, look at motorcyclists' individual weblogs. You'll find an extensive list of online resources in this book's bibliography.
- If you are inseam challenged, realize that a lot of bikes will not fit you well because they are just too tall. Sport and adventure tourers in particular are known for having high seat heights, as are many sport bikes. If you're a novice with a 28- or 29-inch inseam, you are not going to feel particularly secure on a bike with a 33-inch seat height because you will not be able to get both feet on the ground at the same time. Although you may be able to deal with a taller bike when you are more experienced, and some models can be lowered a bit by adjustments to the seat or the shocks, you will probably want a bike that you can "flatfoot" for your first bike. Don't worry. There are a lot of people, male and female, in the same boat. An Internet FAQ for inseam-challenged bikers, along with a recommended list of bikes, is available at Home of the Short Bikers, www.ki.org/sbl. It's a little dated but contains useful information nevertheless.

5 TIME TO LAY YOUR MONEY DOWN

◆ New or used? New or Used? Hmmm . . .

◆ A rose among the thorns; how to find a good used bike . . .

◆ If you think you may be better off buying new . . .

◆ All that chrome won't get you home: accessories for your motorcycle . . .

NEW OR USED? NEW OR USED? HMMM . . .

No matter what you buy—sport bike or cruiser, new or used, Harley or Honda—you will always remember your first bike. Even if you rode a motorcycle in your distant past, you still remember that machine, don't you?

If you last rode 25 years ago, you can't help but notice that bikes today are very, very different. In general, they are more powerful and require less maintenance. In particular, the motorcycle market has fragmented into niches. That bike you owned in the late 1970s or early 1980s was likely much more of a do-all machine—commuting, touring, sport riding . . . maybe even racing, if properly equipped. These days, motorcycles are much more specialized. You got a pretty good overview in the previous chapter of this book, and maybe now you have a good idea of what type of bike you'd like to buy.

The next question is, should you buy new or used? This may be purely a pocketbook issue for you if your budget is limited. But even if you have the financial wherewithal to buy a brand-new, top-of-the-line whatever, you may want to start smaller, cheaper, older.

There are so many opportunities to drop a motorcycle. See 101 Ways to Drop Your Bike, at http://medlem.spray.se/vikingatjejen/twodescphotos26.html.

Smaller, in particular, is a really good idea. An inexperienced rider on a heavy, powerful motorcycle is an accident waiting to happen, as National Highway Transportation Safety Administration data clearly demonstrates. As motorcycling has become more popular, there are more inexperienced riders on the roads. Many of these folks are over 40—with eyes and reflexes somewhat less sharp than when they were 20-somethings. And these are the people buying the big, powerful cruisers. Over the past 10 years, NHTSA data shows a more than 100 percent increase in fatalities among bikes in the engine size range of 1001 to 1500 cc. (And these are certainly not the largest engine sizes available in today's market.) Enormous bikes like this can be difficult to handle—cornering, braking, maneuvering in tight spots—especially for the older novice.

Cheaper and/or older bikes are also good ideas. As yet another motorcycling maxim goes, "Anyone who says he or she has never dropped a bike is either extremely gifted . . . or a liar." Figure that you *will* drop your bike, probably sooner rather than later. The highest risk, naturally, is in the steepest part of the learning curve, when you are just getting started (or restarted). Aside from the obvious fact that it's physically more difficult to pick up a large fallen bike, wait until you find out what it's going to cost to repair the body damage to your new $18,000 BMW sport touring machine that went down in a parking lot because you lost your balance while trying to get it onto its **centerstand**.

I've summed up the basic pros and cons and buying new and buying used in the sidebar "New or Used? We Report, You Decide." Once you've made that decision, let's forge ahead and learn how to buy that new or new-to-you machine.

A Rose Among the Thorns: How to Find a Good Used Bike

The many riders I know who have bought used bikes have found them in a variety of places: at dealerships where they were traded in, parked alongside the road with sale signs on them, in classified newspaper advertising, at work or supermarket bulletin boards, through a friend quitting riding or moving up, by "asking around" at bike nights and other gatherings, through motorcycle-oriented web forums, on eBay. We have a "lemon lot" on our air force base where people park vehicles they want to sell. There's usually at least one bike there, looking for a new owner.

True story: A guy I know spotted an old Honda Shadow in the garage of a house he drove past every day on his way to work. It looked neglected; it remained rooted to the same spot, month after month. One day, on a whim, he stopped, knocked on the door of the house and asked about the bike. Turns out it was there when the current homeowner bought the place; it had been abandoned by the previous owner. To make a long story short, $100 changed hands and the bike went home in the back of my acquaintance's pick-up truck. Numerous hours and several hundred dollars worth of parts later, a lovely old machine had been restored to roadworthy condition, and it is still being ridden regularly. There is something inherently spiritual about resurrecting an old motorcycle.

But that brings up a couple of questions you need to ask yourself. How mechanically inclined are you? And do you even have the time and the desire to **wrench** on a cantankerous older machine? It could be an ongoing process. And more than one weekend mechanic has gotten in over his or her head with a project bike. You could end up doing more wrenching than riding; for a few people, that's an optimal experience, but for most of you reading this book . . . not likely.

The Local Dealership

If you're not mechanically savvy in the least—your author falls into this category—your best bet may be to purchase a used bike from a reputable dealership. People are always trading in or trading up. (Or trading down; I once met a man at a local dealership who was swapping a large, almost brand-new bike for a smaller model. He'd bought this one for his wife and she would not ride it because she didn't feel safe on it.)

Particularly if a trade-in is not among the brands normally carried by a dealership, they are usually anxious to get rid of it. Before a used bike is taken in trade, a technician has had a good look at it. A machine with serious problems will likely not make it to the sales floor; more than likely, it will be disposed of via the wholesale market. Most dealers really do not want to put a lot of money into a used bike—or sell you something that is unreliable or downright dangerous. For one thing, they'd like you to come back to them when you are ready to buy a *new* motorcycle. And they know you'll be further opening your wallet for parts, accessories, gear, etc. They want an ongoing relationship with you.

Although you will not generally be allowed to take the bike for a test ride, a dealer will usually be willing to make minor adjustments for you so the bike fits you properly, and sometimes a limited warranty is available. When I bought my first used bike, I was afraid to ride it home in the rain through a couple of particularly treacherous intersections, so the salesman arranged to have it delivered right to my driveway—at no extra charge. And he also said that, if after a week or 300 miles I decided the bike was not for me, they would take it back and refund my money. (That was a pretty good gamble on their part; once I had the thing home, I couldn't stop staring at it, touching it, sitting on it . . . mine!)

NEW OR USED? WE REPORT, YOU DECIDE

Buying a New Motorcycle

ADVANTAGES

- Usually requires no hunting around. Just go to the closest dealership that carries what you want and lay your money down.
- Comes with a warranty—at least a year, in most cases—and you can often buy an extended warranty. Particularly for those who are not mechanically inclined, this is like an insurance policy.
- You can make sure, right from the start, that the bike is properly serviced at regular intervals recommended by the manufacturer. Some dealers offer a discount if you prepay service for a given period of time or mileage.
- Replacement parts are readily available for newer bikes, so you are less likely to be without your machine for an extended period when repairs are required.
- It is usually easier to finance a new bike; most manufacturers offer financing through the dealership, and special rates are often available if you shop around and/or time your purchase judiciously.

DISADVANTAGES

- All things being equal, a new bike will obviously cost more than a used bike of similar make and model. (For a while, used Harleys were carrying a premium because the manufacturer could not keep up with the demand for new ones and the waiting period could be extensive. These days, there are usually bikes sitting around at Harley dealerships that you can walk right in and buy.)
- If it's your first bike, you could end up with a costly mistake if it turns out to be the wrong machine for you. In most cases, you cannot try before you buy. For liability reasons, very few dealers will allow you to take a bike for a test ride. Except for some Harleys and BMWs, most motorcycles depreciate rapidly in value as soon as they leave the showroom floor.
- Do you really want to learn to ride on an expensive new motorcycle, given the high probability that you will drop the bike at least once, run into curbs, abuse the transmission, etc.?

Buying a Used Motorcycle

ADVANTAGES

- There are lots of well-priced, late-model used bikes around, given that people often decide rather quickly that motorcycling is not for them, or they trade up to more expensive/bigger machines.
- As a novice, you have much less to lose if you drop or otherwise damage a relatively inexpensive used motorcycle rather than learning on a brand new $20,000 Harley.
- Most modern motorcycles are well built and reliable. Unless the previous owner abused it badly, you are likely to have few serious problems with a late-model used bike.
- For some people, tinkering with a bike is part of the total motorcycling experience. Restoring an older machine to roadworthy condition can be immensely satisfying if you are mechanically inclined.
- Since the first owner has already taken the depreciation hit, you can usually sell it or trade it in and get something you like better without a huge financial penalty.
- If you are buying from a private party, you may be allowed to test drive the bike— or have a knowledgeable friend test drive it for you.

DISADVANTAGES

- It can be difficult to tell exactly what you are getting. You may be able to make an educated guess or have a mechanically savvy friend check it out, but there is really no way of knowing for sure how the machine was treated.
- The older the motorcycle, the more difficult it is to find parts for it.
- Unless there is still some time remaining on a transferable warranty for a fairly recent model, you will not have that insurance, although if you buy a used bike from a dealership, there may be some sort of warranty available for parts and service.
- You will probably have to pay cash or arrange for your own financing, especially if you are buying from a private party.
- Buying used requires more effort—locating a suitable bike, checking it out (and you'll almost always want to look at several, which means running around), researching prices, finding someplace you can have it serviced and/or fixed if this is something you won't be tackling on your own, etc.

Check out the Web sites of all the dealerships in your area. They usually have pictures of the used bikes that are currently available (provided someone updates the site regularly), along with some basic information. Don't confine your browsing only to those dealerships that carry the specific brand you think you want. Most dealerships take in a variety of makes and models in trade.

Classified Advertising

The tried-and-true method of buying and selling preowned vehicles of all types, newspaper classifieds in any major metropolitan area are usually loaded with ads for used motorcycles. Seems like every time I take a look, there are at least one or two Harleys that "must be sold immediately due to divorce." If someone is truly desperate, you may get a bargain. If someone is willing to hold out for the asking price, well . . .

You have to know what you're doing when you buy a used motorcycle this way. If you're not mechanically savvy, you'll definitely want to bring a knowledgeable friend along. When I took the Motorcycle Safety Foundation class, one of the instructors gave us his phone number and said he would be happy to check out a used bike that a student was interested in buying. Sometimes, a seller will let you take the bike to a mechanic for inspection. Private sellers are much more likely than any dealership to allow you to take a test ride, though you may have to provide a picture ID and/or leave your car keys as "collateral."

As you may already know, you have to kiss a lot of frogs before you find the handsome prince. Usually, you'll need to look at a number of bikes before you find one that you like at a price that is agreeable. Which involves a lot of running around. Some people think this is fun; they are into "the thrill of the chase," and they enjoy chatting with different motorcycle owners. Other people just do not have that kind of time or patience and may make a premature, potentially unwise decision just to be done with the whole ordeal. Know thyself.

Another caveat, especially when buying from a private seller: Make sure the motorcycle comes with a clear title, that the numbers, etc., on the title match what's on the bike. Pay particular attention when the bike is a Harley-Davidson, a marque with a high theft rate. Even if you unknowingly purchase a stolen bike, you could end up having it confiscated by law enforcement.

Cycle Trader, PowerSports Network

You've probably seen this family of publications in a rack at your local convenience store—*Auto Trader*, *Boat Trader*, etc. The dead tree version of *Cycle Trader* is fun to look at, but the Web site—

Virtually all newspapers put their classified ads online these days, and sometimes ads from several newspapers are aggregated at a single site, with a search engine to help you narrow down your choices. Craigslist (www.craigslist.com/) is a noncommercial online entity that offers free classified advertising in a number of different metropolitan areas. While it's much more popular—and content rich—in some localities than others, there are almost always a few postings offering motorcycles for sale.

shown in figure 5-1—is probably more useful, as the search tools allow you to hone in by make, model, age, price range, geography, etc. The database here—which also includes ATVs, "personal watercraft," and snowmobiles—contains thousand of listings from both private individuals and dealers. From what I can see, the prices overall look to be on the high side; as usual, you can figure that some sellers are going to be more flexible than others. Because there are ads from all over the country, you can get a good idea of the price ranges for different models and figure out whether your pocketbook will stretch to cover the type of bike you had in mind.

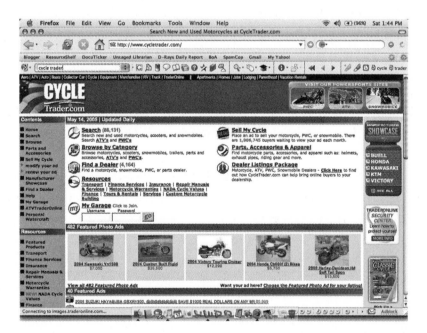

Fig. 5-1: The Cycle Trader Website (www.cycletrader.com).
Thousands of bikes for sale by dealers and private parties alike. A good place to check on what's available in your price range and to see pictures of many, many different used motorcycles.

Fig. 5-2: PowerSports Network (www.powersportsnetwork.com) offers used motorcycle listings, user-written reviews, goodies like downloadable motorcycle wallpaper for your computer, and a particularly useful database that aggregates the contents of a wide range of catalogs from part and accessory manufacturers and distributors (www.powersportsnetwork .com/enthusiasts/catalog.asp).

PowerSports Network, shown in figure 5-2, is another Web site offering a bunch of listings for used motorcycles. You'll find a lot of other stuff here as well, including reviews written by users. To read even more motorcycle reviews online, see sidebar "Where to Find Reviews of Motorcycles on the Internet."

eBay Motors

People buy and sell vehicles on eBay all the time (as well as a staggering variety of other merchandise, from the ridiculous to the sublime). But for the uninitiated, eBay Motors (figure 5-3) can be a minefield. Even serious gearheads, who know what questions to ask, may think twice about buying a motorcycle sight unseen over the Internet. And scammers of all sorts are omnipresent, waiting for an opportunity to fleece the unwary. That being said, it *is* possible to find a good used motorcycle on eBay at a fair price. But be prepared to do your research and take special precautions.

First of all, you may want to restrict your search of eBay's motorcycle inventory only to those machines located within a reasonable distance of where you live, so you can go have a look before

WHERE TO FIND REVIEWS OF MOTORCYCLES ON THE INTERNET

That used bike you're looking at was once a new bike that someone likely reviewed when it first came out. It's well worth your time to track down write-ups on the model or models you are considering for purchase.

- About.com Motorcycle User Reviews, http://motorcycles.about.com/od/roadtestsreviews/a/userreviews_m.htm

- Walter Kern, About.com's motorcycle guru, has also gathered links to other reviews that have appeared in magazines or online, from the year 2000 onward, http://motorcycles.about.com/cs/roadtestsreviews/a/testindx.htm.

- And he's collected specifications for virtually all makes and models of bikes starting with 2004—which saves you the time and trouble of hopping around to the various manufacturers' Web sites to track down this information, http://motorcycles.about.com/od/roadtestsreviews/a/modelprofilesyr.htm.

- MicaPeak.com Mailing List Roundup, www.micapeak.com/mailinglistroundup. Virtually every make/model of motorcycle has its own enthusiasts' e-mail list. See what present owners have to say about the bike you're thinking of buying. Are some years a better bet than others? Here you will find an alphabetical directory of "all known motorcycle-related mailing lists available via Internet electronic mail," along with contact information, directions on how to subscribe, and links to home pages where available.

- *Motorcycle Consumer News:* Model Evaluations, www.mcnews.com/mcn/model_eval.asp

- *Motorcycle Cruiser:* Road Tests, www.motorcyclecruiser.com/roadtests

- *Motorcyclist Online:* Road Tests www.motorcyclistonline.com/roadtests

You'd probably like to know whether the make and model of bike you're considering has ever been recalled by its manufacturer for a serious defect of some sort. The National Highway Transportation Safety Administration maintains a searchable recall database at www.odi.nhtsa.dot.gov/cars/problems/recalls/recallsearch.cfm. However, the indefatigable Walter Kern has already extracted all of the motorcycle recalls from the database, from 2000 onward. Have a quick look here: http://motorcycles.about.com/cs/motorcyclenews/l/blmotorecalls.htm.

Sometimes I wonder when Mr. Kern finds the time to sleep.

Fig. 5-3: eBay Motors: Motorcycles (http://pages.ebay.com/catindex /motorcycles.html). Not for the novice or the faint of heart.

you bid. The eBay Motors advanced search tool offers an option where you can choose to see results only within 500 to 2,000 miles of a particular zip code or city. Drill down until you get to the listings for the particular make and/or model of bike in which you're interested. Then click the "Advanced Search" link to the right of the search button at the top of the listings, as shown in figure 5-4.

Scroll down the advanced search page. Toward the bottom, as seen in figure 5-5, you'll find a check box that allows you to restrict your search by geographic proximity, as explained above. Alas, it is not possible to search within a smaller geographic area than a 500-mile radius—probably because there would be too few or maybe zero listings.

If you're lucky enough to have a knowledgeable friend or relative located in a different geographic area, you can look on eBay for bikes there, too—provided the person is willing to go check it out for you. Remember, though, that if you win your auction, you'll then have to deal with the problem of getting your new treasure home. If you are up to it, of course, you can fly and ride. Or maybe your friend/relative wouldn't mind a road trip. If all else fails, there are plenty of services that will ship the bike. (We take an extended look at shipping motorcycles in chapter 9.) You'll almost always foot the bill for this, but many sellers are willing to work with you to make it happen.

People selling vehicles on eBay Motors often include a "reserve price" in their listings—that is, the

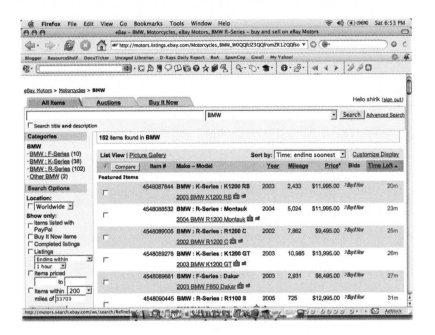

Fig. 5-4: You can refine your search using the variety of options available on eBay's advanced search form. To get to it, click the "Advanced Search" link which you see to the right of the search button.

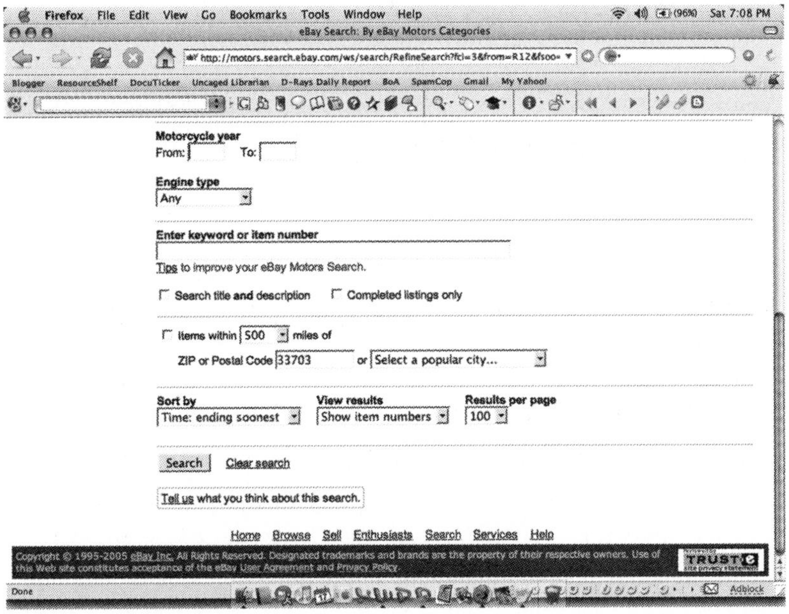

Fig. 5-5: Toward the bottom of eBay's advanced search form, you'll find an option to restrict your search to a particular geographic area.

smallest amount they are willing to take for the item. You could find the bike of your dreams and be the high bidder when the auction ends, but the seller does not have to let it go unless his or her reserve price was met. If your high bid was not too far off the mark, however, you'll often hear from the seller by e-mail, seeking to work out a compromise deal.

Many listings also contain a "Buy It Now" price. This is usually the top dollar the seller hopes to get for the item. If you absolutely, positively must have a certain bike and money is a secondary concern, you may not want to chance losing the auction. If you're willing to ante up the "Buy It Now" price, click the link to stop the auction—keeping in mind that you've just entered into a contract to purchase the vehicle at the seller's "Buy It Now" price. See figure 5-6 for an example.

Other caveat emptor stuff when buying a motorcycle on eBay:

- Look at the seller's feedback rating to see if there have been prior complaints.
- Know the value of the bike on which you're bidding. It's easy to get carried away in the excitement of the auction and end up paying way too much.

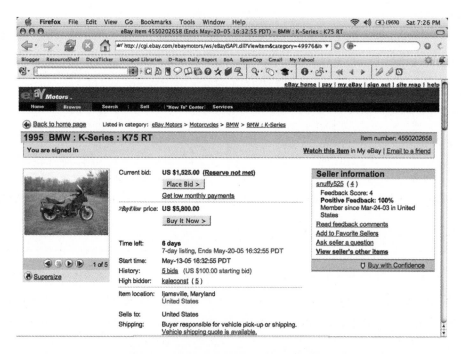

Fig. 5-6: Here is a nice 1995 BMW K75RT. The seller's reserve price has not yet been met, but someone lusting over it who was willing to pay $5,800 would have been able to "Buy It Now" and stop the auction. Had it been in Florida, your author would have been sorely tempted.

- Know in advance how you are going to pay for the bike; some sellers will only accept certain forms of payment, and if financing is required, it's best to have it lined up ahead of time.
- If you have any questions about the bike, ask before you bid. It's possible to retract a bid at the discretion of the seller, but it's considered bad eBay etiquette to get yourself into this situation. If you bid, be prepared to buy if you should win.
- Make sure the bike has a clear title. If it's not stated in the auction listing, ask the seller.
- Get some insurance quotes ahead of time so you won't have any unpleasant surprises after you buy the bike and try to get it covered.
- If you're buying an older bike that may need some work, it's worth taking a browse through eBay's motorcycle parts and accessories listings to see if you can reasonably expect to find what you need to make the repairs. The older the bike, the harder it is to find parts—although eBay Motors has made this a lot easier than it used to be.
- Know in advance how you are going to get the bike from the seller's location to your home. Will you need it to be shipped? Get some quotes in advance. (Shipping a motorcycle is not cheap.) Are you fortunate enough to have a friend who is savvy about transporting motorcycles and has a trailer or a truck? You can't just toss the thing into the back of a pickup truck and take off. It must be properly secured. Ask around—someone may be willing to help you out for the price of gas and lunch. Motorcyclists are like that.
- If you're planning to pick it up and ride it home but can't get away from work for a couple of weeks, find out in advance if the seller would be willing to hold it for you in a safe location.

Checking Out a Used Bike

I am not the person you want to take along with you when you go to look at a used bike. Better you should rely on the expertise of someone who is much more knowledgeable about these things. If you

Savvy Tip

What's that used bike worth? You can find out on the Web; check these sites: (1) Kelly Blue Book (www.kbb.com—Click on "Motorcycle Values" in lower left-hand corner.) (2) NADA Guides (www.nada.com—Choose "Motorcycles" from the navigation bar at the top.) (3) Motorcycle Consumer News: Used Bike Value Guide (www.mcnews.com/mcn/usedbike.asp). Also, the advanced search form on eBay Motors offers a checkbox for "Completed Listings Only." A good reality check, this option allows you to see what different makes/models actually sold for (or did not sell for) on eBay during the past 15 days.

are not mechanically inclined yourself—or even if you are, but have no experience with motorcycles—find a friend/relative/neighbor/coworker who can help out. If you don't know what you're looking at, it's often difficult to discern between a serious problem and something that is easily remedied—or no big deal because "they all do that."

Of course, even if you don't know your way around machinery, you can elicit much useful information from a seller over the phone (or via e-mail) before you even see the bike if you know what questions to ask. Some of this is pretty basic.

- What is the bike's general condition? (If the ad or listing included mileage, confirm the number with the seller.)
- Has the bike ever been dropped?
- Are you the first owner? If not, where did you get it and how long have you owned it?
- Is it ridden regularly or has it been sitting idle for a long time?
- How has it been ridden? For daily commuting? For weekend recreation only? Have you taken any long trips with it?
- Do you have all the paperwork that goes with it—title, tags, owner's manual, receipts for maintenance and repairs performed?
- What, if any, repairs have been made to it?
- What, if any, repairs does it need right now?
- Does it have any accessories such as a windshield, bags, engine guards, etc.?
- How much are you asking for it? (If a price was mentioned in the listing, ask if the seller is "flexible.")
- Why are you selling the bike?

If you're going to be inquiring about a number of bikes, you may want to use a form on which to record the information you receive. MotorcycleBeginners.com offers a comprehensive one that you are welcome to use "as long as you don't alter it." I've gotten permission to include a copy in appendix B.

As far as the nuts and bolts of what you should be scrutinizing, Adam Glass's excellent *Used Motorcycle Evaluation Guide* (www.clarity.net/adam/buying-bike.html) is a frequently recommended Internet resource. Glass pretty much covers the whole used motorcycle buying experience, with advice and tips in an easy-to-read bullet point format. You'll also find helpful pictures, recommended reading, and links to other useful Web sites. The entire guide is available on a single page so you can print it out and take it with you when you go around looking at bikes.

Answers to Questions about Used Bikes from Someone Who Knows

Richard Emerson, a friend mine who is both mechanically savvy and no stranger to the used-bike market, offers some words of wisdom here. He owns—and rides almost daily—the 1981 Honda CB900 shown in figure 5-7.

I'll talk mainly about bikes from the 1970s and 1980s. It's what I know. Newer bikes are approached about the same way you approach buying a used car. You buy used cars because you want to let someone else take the hit for driving it off the showroom floor.

Why buy used?
Since we're talking about bikes from the 1970s and 1980s, this seems like a dumb question. It's hard (but not impossible) to buy a new 1980 bike. I'd be very suspicious of someone offering a brand-new bike from the period I'm interested in. But every so often a bike either still in its crate or stored "from new" for some reason may show up on the market. Or it may be claimed to be new—rule number one of smart buying is, "If it seems too good to be true, it probably is." Shop wisely.

How/why do you select a particular make and model?
Much of the appeal of riding is not tied to the logical and reasonable. This also applies to choosing a bike.

Nostalgia plays a big part. Maybe we chose a bike because it's like the first one we rode on, or because a friend had one that looked so cool, or maybe it was a bike that we owned and sold later, to our regret.

The sad truth is the era of the bargain bike is basically over. Auction Web sites and collectors with more money than common sense have raised the prices of bikes, and parts for bikes, to levels that verge on the absurd. Replacement exhaust systems, for example, can cost well over half of the purchase price of some bikes. Bargains will, of course, show up, but they're getting harder to find. So the choice may be based on what can be afforded as much as what appeals to us emotionally or aesthetically.

Where do you find good used bikes?
As with many things, the Internet makes bike hunting both easier (so many more ads to look at) and harder (so many more people looking at the same number of bikes). Nonetheless, the Internet will probably offer the highest chance of finding a particular bike with the right features. Auction sites (notably eBay) are geared to letting prospective buyers interact with sellers easily. "For sale" Web sites such as Cycle Trader or Craigslist often lack the channels to find out if a particular bike is worth pursuing. Usually the only choice is to spend time on the phone, trying to reach the seller.

Many newspapers now put their classified ads on a Web site and this makes browsing the ads much easier than hunting through the physical newspaper. However, again, the most likely way to reach the seller is by phone.

The last place *I'd* look for a bike is at a dealer. Reselling an older bike is, in general, not attractive to a dealer, so either they'll encourage a prospective trade-in to sell the bike privately or, to cover overhead, the bike will have a relatively high price tag. Still, it never hurts to check with dealers. Who knows what surprise could be waiting for the adventurous buyer?

Coupled with *where* to look for a bike is *when* to look for one. It should be no surprise that bike prices vary with the time of year. On the first warm day of spring, prices will rise with the thermometer. When fall comes and the temperature drops, so do prices. The end of summer marks the start of school and more than one good bike has come on the market at a low price because of a need to raise tuition money in a hurry. Of course, there are sellers who are aware of the variability in bike prices and who'll hold back a bike until the market heats up.

Would you buy a bike sight unseen?

If you remember the 1970s and 1980s, you probably remember Clint Eastwood saying, "Do you feel lucky, punk? Well? Do you?" The same thing applies here. I think it's safe to say that most bikes sold on eBay are sold sight unseen. There's no real measure of how the buyers fare after their prize arrives or is picked up, but if the experience were usually negative, the market would dry up, and it hasn't.

The biggest obstacle here is communication. What the seller means by "in excellent condition" may actually be "collection of parts staying together out of habit." It's not that the seller is dishonest; he

Fig. 5-7: Rick Emerson on his 1981 Honda CB900. Photo by Barbara L. Harms.

or she has just gotten used to things that a new owner may well find objectionable. Once the money changes hands and the title is signed, the buyer is stuck with the machine.

If it's impractical for the buyer to look at a bike, it may be possible to find someone near the seller that the buyer can send in his or her place. But again, communications may lead to disappointment. The buyer's friend may miss details that matter to the buyer. For all these reasons, it's best to at least look at, and listen to, the bike before committing to buy it. And if a test ride is possible, so much the better.

What are the major things to look for—for example, "no way" deal breakers?

Where is your personal pain threshold? If you've got experience with resurrecting dead machinery, a junker may have a lot of appeal. If you're expecting to lay your money down and then ride home, even something as trivial as needing new tires or brakes could be a deal breaker.

It also helps to know a bike's quirks and faults. The early Kawasaki 500 triples, for example, have a well-earned reputation for being lighting fast in a straight line and having disappointing handling in turns. A test ride on one of these bikes would show they don't corner well and need to have the throttle and clutch treated with respect. It doesn't mean the bike is "broken"; it's acting as it did when new.

British bikes have a deserved reputation for leaking oil and having less than fully reliable electrical systems. Finding a bike with a light coating of oil or a small spot under the motor isn't immediate cause to reject the bike. By comparison, however, most Japanese bikes should be oil-tight and have working electrical systems (with notable exceptions like the Suzuki GS models that have had problems with their alternators).

In the end, what is a deal breaker is tied to the buyer's abilities and desires. A bike with the front forks bent back from an accident might deter one buyer while another sees an opportunity to get an otherwise desirable bike at a very low price (plus, of course, the cost of repairs).

What are minor things that you shouldn't get your shorts in a knot about?

We're talking about used bikes and use means wear. Expect to find some rust somewhere. Expect to find the odd bit of chipped paint or scrape on a light. It's even reasonable to expect the bike's engine and brakes will be due or past due for maintenance. None of this is major work in itself. (Keep in mind that signs of abuse or neglect may provide clues to a bike's overall condition, though.)

How difficult it is to find parts for old bikes?

How common was the bike when it was made? Bikes that were obscure when new will be hard to repair now; more popular bikes will be less difficult, but expect surprises.

Some early models of bikes or bikes that had short production runs are now prized by collectors willing to pay amazing amounts of money for parts. The same reason why these bikes aren't bargains to buy applies to their maintenance.

In many cases, parts may still be available directly from manufacturers. Keep in mind, though, that the prices are often "modern" prices even though the parts may be "old." Happily, there are sources of both routine consumables (e.g., oil filters) and more unusual parts (an Australian firm, for example, is now making exact replicas of tank and side cover badges). Places like Bike Bandit and even J. C. Whitney carry a surprising number of replacement parts. And don't forget eBay and other auction sites for both new and used parts. Even if parts aren't available in new form, there are "bike breakers" or bike "bone yards." The parts may come from wrecked bikes, bikes that are just plain tired out, or even perfectly sound bikes. A bike that may bring $1,000 intact might well net five or ten times that if "parted out." It's sad to see a perfectly good bike torn apart just for profit, but when it's that or no parts at all . . . As with buying a used bike, ask lots of questions before buying used parts.

How valuable are online forums where you can ask questions?
The advice is worth what you pay for it. If you're lucky, you'll come out ahead. But it's also very easy to get incredibly bad advice that sounds good. Here's a little sample of the latter: "My throttle cables are sticking. What's the best way to lubricate them?" "I always squirt some WD-40 on the cable at one end and pull it back and forth." It sounds like good advice and may even work briefly. But WD-40 isn't a lubricant; it's used to free rusted parts and to displace moisture. The residue will turn into a sticky mess.

What can you do? Ask questions and question the answers. Clymer and Haynes both produce detailed manuals about most major bikes. These are not factory shop manuals (which may turn up on eBay in any form from new to used to CDs with scanned copies), which you should buy if possible, but these aftermarket manuals are also a good source for detailed information.

Beyond that, watch a forum to see whose replies seem reasonable and whose replies are often either ignored or marked as wrong. Sample a few forums; the first one you find may seem like a dead end, but there may be a better one around the corner.

IF YOU THINK YOU MAY BE BETTER OFF BUYING NEW

Common sense tells you that buying a new bike—given a similar make and model—is certainly going to be more expensive than buying a used bike, especially considering the depreciation hit you'll likely take just as soon as it leaves the showroom. On the other hand, it is a whole lot less complicated just to walk into the dealership of your choice and pick out the motorcycle you want. (See

Fig. 5-8: "Give chrome a home." Photo courtesy of Keith Syvinski, a photographer (and motorcyclist) in Franklin, Ind.

figure 5-8.) It will come with a warranty—for added peace of mind you can usually buy an extended warranty—and often, easy financing is available.

All Dealerships Are Not Alike

And that is not just in terms of the brands and/or merchandise they sell. On a smaller scale, it's pretty much the same thing as with car dealerships—there are good ones and there are bad ones. Go to bike nights and local establishments that are popular with motorcyclists. Track down people who are riding newer models of the same brand you've been looking at and ask where they bought—and why. Local motorcycle clubs or chapters of national clubs can be an excellent resource—particularly those organized around specific brand ownership. You can pretty well assume that these folks have the lowdown on every dealership in the area that sells what they are riding.

Some general considerations when choosing a dealership:

- Visit several dealers carrying the same brands if at all possible. In a large metropolitan area, obviously, you're going to have more choices.
- Keep in mind that you'll almost certainly be bringing the bike back to the dealership for maintenance and warranty work. All things being equal, you're better off with a place that is convenient to your home or work.

- You will usually get better treatment from the service department at the dealership where you bought your bike. For example, they may try harder to "squeeze you in" than they would if you had purchased your bike elsewhere.
- Is it a motorcycle-only dealership? If it's sideline business for a car dealership, you may not receive the attention you want. If it's a large establishment carrying a variety of "powersports equipment"— boats, "personal watercraft," snowmobiles, ATVs—seek out a salesperson who knows and is enthusiastic about motorcycles.
- There is something to be said for longevity. If a dealership has been around for a while—like the one in figure 5-9—it obviously enjoys some degree of support from the local motorcycling community.

How to Deal with the Dealer

True story: I went back to the dealership to look around several times before I bought my latest bike. I told the salesman that I refused to be pushed into a premature decision. "I want to make up my mind based on logic and not emotion," I said. He laughed at me. "Come on now," he said. "Logic? You're in a *motorcycle* showroom."

When you get right down to it, nobody really *needs* a motorcycle. Yes, it's transportation, but most of us already have at least one set of wheels at home. To a greater extent even than a highly impractical sports car, a motorcycle is a toy and an object of outright lust. Yes, you're giddy with pleasure about that new Boxster, but how likely are you to go out and load up on merchandise festooned with its logo or have its brand name tattooed into your flesh. On the other hand, have you visited a Harley dealership lately?

Still, you owe it to yourself not to get totally carried away and make a bad and/or costly decision at the dealership. As with any other major purchase, you want to do your homework first. The Web is an amazing tool; use it. Visit manufacturer, dealer, and bike magazine Web sites. Peruse online

Fig. 5-9: Barney's (www.barneysstpete.com) has been selling motorcycles on Gandy Boulevard in St. Petersburg since 1953. This image is part of the Florida Photographic Collection,www.floridamemory.com/PhotographicCollection.

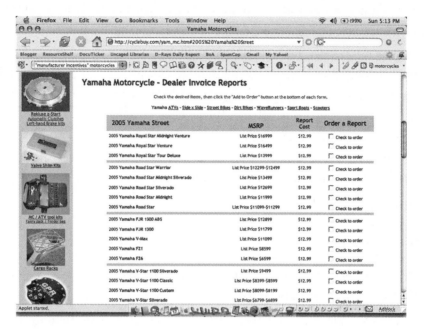

Fig. 5-10: Whereas you can find dealer invoice information for cars and light trucks in a number of places for free, you'll have to pay for this data on motorcycles. CycleBuy appears to have a lock on the market; according to its FAQ, "The auto industry has made this information freely available, but it is a lot of hard work to keep things current in the motorcycle industry." http://cyclebuy.com/faq.htm

forums. If the make and model of bike you're considering has any idiosyncrasies, you want to know about it in advance so you can quiz the salesperson. Maybe you're trying to decide among several models. Decide first what features are most important to you and be prepared to ask about them

Your power to negotiate has a lot to do with what you're negotiating over. If it's some highly desirable top-of-the-line H-D for which there is an 18-month waiting list . . . good luck. Otherwise, you may be able to work a deal, sometimes just by asking, "Is that the best you can do?" As with cars, it's helpful to know the dealer's invoice price—what the dealership paid for the bike. Alas, this information is not widely available for motorcycles in the same way it is for cars. But it is out there—for a price. CycleBuy (http://cyclebuy.com)—see figure 5-10—offers dealer invoice reports for Harley-Davidson, Honda, Kawasaki, KTM, Polaris, Suzuki, and Yamaha. As of mid-2005, these were going for $12.99 per model (with a $5 discount for every additional report purchased at the same time). Each report includes "information on dealer holdback and any available dealer rebates or sales incentives." Other things worth knowing:

The Better Business Bureau's database is now nationwide. You can look up reliability reports for businesses all over the United States and Canada from a single location. So check out that dealership before you enter into a sizable financial transaction with them. And after you've got your bike and you're thinking about buying parts, accessories, or gear from an online vendor, look them up here first. If there's a pattern of unresolved complaints . . . danger, Will Robinson. http://search.bbb.org/search.html.

- You may be able to play dealerships off one another, as in car buying (e.g., "Can you beat the price I got at . . . ") if there are enough dealerships selling the same brand within a reasonable geographic area.
- Can you pay cash? If you put the new bike on a credit card, the dealer will have to pay a transaction fee. Ask if there is any discount for an all-cash payment.
- Depending on the dealership, certain fees may be unavoidable, such as destination charges, setup fees, doc prep fees, assembly fees. There is a profit margin built into at least some of these fees, however, and you may be able to negotiate.
- You will usually be offered such items as an extended warranty, a prepaid service place, roadside assistance. If you buy, the dealership makes a small profit. But if you don't want them, don't be pressured into them.
- You may get a good deal on a leftover bike from an earlier model or model year. It costs the dealer money to keep these around, and there is usually a strong desire to move them off the sales floor.
- According to various sources consulted in the research for this book, a dealership usually tries to make a profit of around 10 percent on every new bike it sells.

ALL THAT CHROME WON'T GET YOU HOME: ACCESSORIES FOR YOUR BIKE

Yes, you bought it. But it's not really yours until you add accessories to make it at least a somewhat unique machine. Generally speaking, accessories fall into two categories—things you attach to your bike to make it safer or more comfortable or more practical, and things you attach to your bike to make it look and/or sound cool.

Cool, of course, being a highly subjective term. See figure 5-11.

Fig. 5-11: This highly accessorized machine was spotted at the Leesburg, Fla., Bikefest in 2004. Definitely not for everyone.

Windshields

If your motorcycle didn't come with one, you'll probably want to add one, especially if you've got a bike with a laid-back riding position like the typical cruiser. Take it from someone who rides a long bridge across a large body of water to get to and from work every day. Fighting the wind without some sort of protection is exhausting and can leave your shoulders, neck, and back all knotted up. Even a full-face helmet is not enough; the wind will keep trying to push you backward.

Most manufacturers offer a few different windshields to fit their bikes, but the selection available in the aftermarket is truly staggering—wide, narrow, tall, short, color-coordinated, leather-trimmed . . . Memphis Shades (www.memphisshades.com) and National Cycle (www.nationalcycle.com) in particular make a wide range of styles that will fit almost any bike.

But looking at a windshield in a catalog and trying to imagine what it would look like on *your* bike is difficult. So once again, go to places where lots of motorcyclists gather and look around. Or find an enthusiasts' Web site catering to the make and model of your bike. These usually include some sort of online "gallery" where people post pictures of their rides. If you see a bike with a windshield you really like, contact the owner and ask about it.

Motorcycle Luggage

Most touring or sports touring motorcycles come with hard luggage—side bags, and/or a top case. These are usually waterproof and can be locked. The bags can usually be detached fairly easily from the bike and carried with you. This is a good solution not only for people who take long trips, but also for commuters who ride in all sorts of weather and typically carry a variety of items back and forth to work. If your bike didn't come with hard luggage, its manufacturer may have some available that you can add later. Or look to the aftermarket. Givi (givi.it) an Italian company, and Touratech,

Fig. 5-12: Your author chose this set of National Cycle Cruiseliner hard bags for her bike.

(www.touratech-usa.com/shop/index.lasso), a German company, make attractive hard luggage to fit a variety of bikes. I have a set of National Cycle Cruiseliner hard bags like the ones shown in figure 5-12. Hard luggage tends to be expensive, and it has a certain high-tech, rigid look to it that not everybody likes. LeatherLyke (www.leatherlyke.com) offers a popular line of ABS polymer hard bags that are styled to look like traditional leather motorcycle bags.

Many motorcyclists, especially those who own cruisers, prefer the look of traditional leather (or faux leather) saddlebags. These are available in a wide range of sizes, styles, and prices; if this is what you want, there is almost certainly something out there that will fit and look good on your bike. Some folks prefer a relatively plain set of bags, while others go in for studs, fringe, metal ornaments of various types, often to match their seats or other accessories. Take a look at the bike in figure 5-13 and then flip back to chapter 4 and look at my bike in figure 4-7. They are both Yamaha V-Star 1100s.

As with motorcycle gear—which we explore in detail in chapter 6—motorcycle luggage is also available in heavy-duty textile fabrics such as Cordura. These are tough, durable and often come with expansion zippers, rain covers, and integrated bungee-type tie-downs. You can often mix and match shapes and sizes, or buy yourself a whole set that fits together and can be loaded onto your bike up for a long trip.

Cordura tank bags and tail bags are popular; they are especially useful for sport bike owners. The exhaust pipes on these machines are mounted high, so that traditional hard luggage or saddlebags will not work. A tank bag sits on the motorcycle's gas tank, secured by strong magnets or other mounting systems. It's small enough not to get in your way, but large enough to hold what you need

Fig. 5-13: This Yamaha V-Star 1100 Silverado belongs to Joseph R. Meece, who spends part of the year in Florida and part of the year in Pennsylvania (and rides in both places). Joe's V-Star has that traditional "biker look," while your author's V-Star 1100 Midnight Custom is quite austere by comparison. Particularly if you own a popular model of bike, an endless array of aftermarket accessories is available.

when, say, you are out running around town. Some have a clear plastic sleeve on top in which you can display a map.

A tail bag sits behind you—on the **pillion** seat or rear fender. I have one of Tourmaster's Cortech sport tailbags, shown in figure 5-14. It is held on with integrated bungee cords and large plastic hooks that do not pose a threat to the bike's painted surfaces. It's bigger than a tank bag, and can be expanded horizontally via zippers and comes with a shoulder strap and a rain cover, as does the matching tank bag. You can also get a pair of matching saddlebags.

If you want to browse a variety of motorcycle luggage options, start with webBikeWorld's motorcycle luggage page, www.webbikeworld.com/motorcycle-luggage.

Chrome Stuff

How many chrome accessories you attach to your bike is purely a matter of personal preference (as well as the size of your bank account). Some folks like the look of lots and lots of chrome, while oth-

Fig. 5-14: A Tourmaster Cortech tailbag exactly like this one has traveled roughly 15,000 miles with your author, on three different motorcycles.

ers are less enthusiastic about it. One thing you need to know is that chrome is high maintenance. It gets nasty if it's neglected; in humid climates particularly, rust is quick to settle in. The more chrome on your bike, the more time you'll spend polishing it. (You'll learn how to care for the chrome on your bike in chapter 8.)

Most chrome accessories—such as replacement controls, foot boards, pieces of trim, covers for various parts of the engine, etc.—are decorative rather than functional. Engine guards (**crash bars**) and aftermarket exhaust systems (**pipes**) are two possible exceptions.

Engine guards are often found on cruiser-style bikes and, in spite of what their nickname would have you believe, they will not really protect you in a crash. They can, however, protect your bike from expensive damage if it falls over when you're moving at slow speed or not moving at all. As we discussed earlier, bikes do fall over. The novice motorcyclist is more likely than not to drop his or her bike at least once. When I first started riding, more than one experienced rider recommended that I install engine guards. Most manufacturers make them to fit their own line of cruisers, but the aftermarket fishing hole is also well-stocked.

What you'll see most often are the large "hula hoop" style engine guards—U-shaped bars that are mounted on the front part of the frame, behind the front wheel. You can see a typical example on my neighbor's old Harley Police Special, in figure 5-15. I decided I wanted something different for my bike, so I got a Lindby Custom Lindbar (www.lindbycustom.com), which you can see in figure 5-16. Note the rows of O-rings on the top of each side. These are integrated footpegs; in theory, I can rest my feet on them and stretch out—usually when doing some long-haul freeway riding. In practice, my legs are too short, and so this is just a "look-cool" feature for me. If you have long legs,

Fig. 5-15: My next-door neighbor owns this older Harley Police Special, which has enormous front engine guards. (The snoozing cat is definitely an aftermarket accessory.)

Fig. 5-16: I wanted something out of the ordinary when I bought engine guards for my bike. These are made by Lindby Custom (www.lindbycustom.com)for a number of different makes and models.

you can buy bolt-on "highway pegs"—also sometimes referred to as "highway bars"— that will fit most standard engine guards.

You can also see, in figure 5-16, that I have added a light bar—the two extra lights on either side of the headlight—to the front of my bike. Where motorcycles are concerned, more lights are almost always better than fewer lights. As one MSF instructor told me, "If you only have one headlight, oncoming drivers may think you are a car with one highlight out. If you've got three lights up there, you're a motorcycle." There is no end to the aftermarket selection of accessory lighting you can add. Some riders install a "modulating headlight" that alternates high beam, low beam, high beam, low beam during the day, for a flashing effect that is hard to overlook. A guy I know who has this on his Gold Wing says it sometimes makes other motorists think he is a **LEO** (cop) and they slow down "and stop acting nuts."

Savvy Tip

If you're thinking of adding accessory lighting to your bike, check your state laws first, as there may be restrictions on certain types of vehicle lights. If you're not sure where to find this information, call the local highway patrol office.

Loud Pipes . . . Yada Yada Yada

Here's another topic that generates almost as much controversy in the motorcycling community as do helmet laws. Some riders firmly believe in the hoary old maxim, "Loud pipes save lives." In other words, if the cagers are assaulted by the throaty roar of your bike, they are less likely to run into you. Other riders think that adding loud aftermarket exhaust systems just further alienates the nonmotorcycling public, and that if you have to rely on loud pipes to insure your survival on the road, you're doing something wrong. On the other hand, I've heard from riders in rural areas that loud pipes provide a heads-up to wildlife on the roads, giving them a chance to beat feet out of there before they get hit—which may cause injury or death to the motorcyclist. You really, really do not want to hit a deer, let alone a moose or an elk. And even something as small as a squirrel can cause you to go down.

Of course, in some places, the decibel level of your exhaust system is regulated by law or local ordinance. Loud pipes will get you a ticket, at the very least. In states that require an annual inspection, an edgy exhaust system may cause your bike to fail.

All of that being said, there is something deeply satisfying about the sound of well-tuned pipes. For some people, it is a key part of the whole motorcycling mystique. So maybe those **stock** pipes—the ones that came with your bike—look and sound somewhat wimpy to you. Once again, the aftermarket runneth over with choices that will attract attention (hopefully not from law enforcement) and even increase performance. Aftermarket racing pipes are available for sport bike owners. (Unless you know your way around a motorcycle engine, you'll probably want to have the installation of any aftermarket exhaust system done by a professional.)

Your local dealer has accessory catalogs that you can look through, and the parts department will order whatever you want. The advantage of buying locally, besides supporting the local dealership, is that the parts folks will make sure that whatever you are yearning to buy is something that will fit your bike. Alternately, the back pages of every bike rag are filled with accessory ads. And of course, the Internet is like one huge aftermarket bazaar for the motorcyclist. If you know what you're doing, try your luck on eBay Motors. Or have fun browsing through the online catalogs of some of the larger accessory vendors such as:

- Bike Bandit (www.bikebandit.com)
- CruiserCustomizing (www.cruisercustomizing.com)
- Dennis Kirk (www.denniskirk.com)
- JC Whitney (www.jcwhitney.com)

Remember that before you open your wallet, it's always a good idea to check out online or mail order vendors in the Better Business Bureau database or via online motorcycle forums.

Dennis Garner
COO of a software company
Woodruff, S.C.
1996 Harley-Davidson Road King

I graduated from high school in 1979 and was very interested in motorcycles. My mother and father were very adamant that bikes were dangerous and I would get killed if I got close to one. Any time I mentioned it, they flatly refused to listen, so all I could do was dream. During my second year in college, I was working full time and going to school full time. A friend of mine mentioned that his dad had a "nearly new" 1973 Honda CB350 Four that he wanted to sell. Long story short, I went to see it and bought it. I convinced my girlfriend's father to take me to pick it up in his truck and keep it at his house. I rode 50 miles sitting in the back of a pickup holding the bike.

I had never ridden a motorcycle before so I started riding it around my girlfriend's yard to get the feel of it. Several weeks later, I wrote my parents a letter about why I felt I needed a bike. I left the note on the counter, headed to school and stopped on the way back to ride my bike home. My girlfriend followed behind me in a car. It was great until I came to the first curve. Steering in the yard was easy. Turn right, go right. Since countersteering was a foreign concept, that first 25 mph curve was very treacherous. I did make it home and very slowly learned to ride. After patching things up with my parents, I was on my way. I loved the freedom of riding.

My girlfriend and I got married after college, and she was very nervous about my riding. When I would come home one minute late, she would be in a panic. I loved her very much and could not stand hurting her, so I sold the bike. I really missed riding, and 10 years later, I couldn't stand it anymore. My first cousin was getting married and her husband-to-be was told he had to sell his bike. I was happy to come up with the money. So after a brief but loud discussion with my wife, I was riding again. After a couple of years, kids came along and the anxiety returned. My wife was concerned that something would happen to me and leave her alone with small kids. I loved her and the kids and did not want to hurt them, so I sold that bike.

Fast forward another 10 years. The kids are older, the job is more stressful, and one spring day my wife said, "You really miss riding, don't you?" I guess she could tell by the way I drooled when a bike would go by. I told her that I did. She responded, "Why don't you see if you can find a new bike?" Well, I may be slow, but you don't have to tell me twice. Now, five years and three bikes later, I have my first Harley. It is a 1996 Road King and I love it. Riding is a great stress reliever for me. When I ride, the cares just drop away. Over the last year or so, my wife has begun riding with me. After 20 years, we have a girl who is 17 and a son who is 13 and they both love motorcycles. We have been richly blessed, and if God allows, I hope to be riding as long as I am able.

6 GEARING UP: A CRASH COURSE IN PERSONAL PROTECTIVE EQUIPMENT

◆ Dress for the crash, not for the ride

◆ The helmet wars

◆ Brain Buckets 101

◆ Buying a helmet

◆ Caring for your helmet

◆ Black leather jacket . . . or textile . . . or mesh

◆ Protect your hands

◆ Protect your feet . . . and ankles . . . and . . .

◆ But what if it rains?

◆ More cool stuff

◆ Finding reviews of gear

DRESS FOR THE CRASH, NOT FOR THE RIDE

When it comes to personal protective equipment (PPE)—especially helmets—we hit one of the great philosophical divides in motorcycling. Some of us would never think of venturing out without full PPE. Some of us reject it entirely. Some of us wear bits and pieces. And some of us . . . well, I'm only running down to the store to pick up a half gallon of milk, so maybe I don't really need . . . (although statistically, something like 90 percent of all accidents occur within five miles of home).

Full PPE (which you see on the G.I. in figure 6-1) includes the following:

- A helmet manufactured to meet U.S. Department of Transportation (DOT) standards (at minimum).
- Eye protection (face shield, impact-resistant goggles, etc.).
- Jacket and pants especially designed for motorcycle riding (or a one-piece riding suit).
- Full-fingered, reinforced gloves.
- Sturdy, over-the-ankle footwear.

Fig. 6-1: Uncle Sam insists on full personal protective equipment for motorcyclists (www.apg.army.mil).

By and large, folks, this stuff doesn't come cheap. It's been my experience that buying motorcycle gear is one of those "you get what you pay for" experiences. But if you know what you're looking for and you're not obsessively fashion conscious, it is entirely possible to stay out of debtor's prison. Bottom line: The price of proper equipment is one part of your Total Cost of Motorcycling.

Now, let's tackle the controversial stuff first.

THE HELMET WARS

A helmet is far more than just a key element of PPE. It is probably the biggest emotional flash point in motorcycling. Many of us look at the statistics churned out by government agencies and other organizations and make the decision to always wear a helmet, completely independent of whether we live in a state that requires one. Other riders absolutely do not like helmets and will not wear one except if required by law—and even then, may choose a flimsy beanie-like helmet that provides virtually no protection.

Some of the reasons riders give for not wearing a helmet include:

- They block peripheral vision.
- They impair hearing.
- They increase the odds of a neck injury.

The Motorcycle Safety Foundation says all of these so-called helmet myths have been repeatedly disproved by various studies. And yet, the arguments go on. The bottom line here is that some people just like riding without a helmet; it represents freedom to them. And even those of us who always wear helmets and, in general, advocate their use . . . well, some of us are uncomfortable with the idea of Big Brother mandating a choice we feel that each adult should make for him- or herself. Some even foresee a slippery slope that will eventually lead to motorcycles being banned outright.

Whenever the topic of mandatory helmet laws rears its controversial head, letters to the editor come pouring into the newspapers on both sides of the issue. As you read these, you can see that many of those writing in support of helmet laws are people who do not ride. On the other hand, many of these advocates are police officers and medical professionals—those who have to deal with what happens after there is an accident in which a rider goes down (or goes flying).

The American Motorcyclists Association (AMA), which calls itself "the premier defender of motorcyclists' rights in the United States," recommends the use of helmets and has no problem with laws requiring minors to wear them. However, as an organization, "it maintains a long-standing fundamental belief that adults should continue to have the right to voluntarily decide when to wear a helmet." (You can read AMA's "Position Statement on Voluntary Helmet Use" at www.amadirectlink .com/legisltn/positions/helmet.asp). AMA has a prepared set of responses to several of the claims made repeatedly by mandatory helmet law advocates. To wit:

Claim: Injured motorcyclists are uninsured and disproportionately rely upon the public to pay for their injuries.

Response: Motorcyclists are just as likely to be privately insured as any other road user.

Claim: The costs associated with unhelmeted motorcyclist injuries and fatalities compel the enactment of mandatory helmet laws to save taxpayer dollars.

Response: The costs associated with the treatment of motorcyclist injuries account for less than 0.001 percent of total U.S. health care costs. Only a portion of these costs are attributable to unhelmeted motorcyclists, the majority of which are paid by privately purchased insurance. The remainder, spread across the taxpayer base (which includes millions of motorcyclists), is insignificant.

Claim: Mandatory helmet laws are the most effective way to reduce motorcyclist injuries and fatalities.

Response: The most effective way to reduce motorcyclist injuries and fatalities is to prevent crashes from occurring in the first place. Helmets and helmet laws do not prevent accidents.

These responses are all supported by statistics—but we all know how malleable statistics can be. Consider these statistics, from the U.S. Department of Transportation's National Highway Transportation Safety Administration (www-nrd.nhtsa.dot.gov/departments/nrd-30/ncsa/AvailInf .html):

- In 2003, 52 percent of fatally injured motorcyclists were unhelmeted.
- Two-thirds of unhelmeted fatalities were in states without a universal helmet law.
- In potentially fatal crashes, helmets have an overall effectiveness of 37 percent in preventing fatalities.
- In 2002, helmets saved an estimated 1,005 lives.
- At 100 percent use, an additional 579 lives could have been saved in 2002 alone.
- Only 58 percent of motorcyclists were observed to be wearing helmets, according to the 2002 National Occupant Protection Use Survey (http://troy.tamu.edu/safety/Webnews/ 4thquarter/occprotec.htm).

As of December 2004, according to the Insurance Institute for Highway Safety, all but four states require some (e.g., minors) or all motorcyclists to wear helmets. Some 20 states have universal laws, requiring all motorcyclists to wear a helmet. See *History of U.S. Motorcycle Helmet Laws and Changes in Coverage* (www.iihs.org/laws/state_laws/helmet_history.html); and, in figure 6-2,

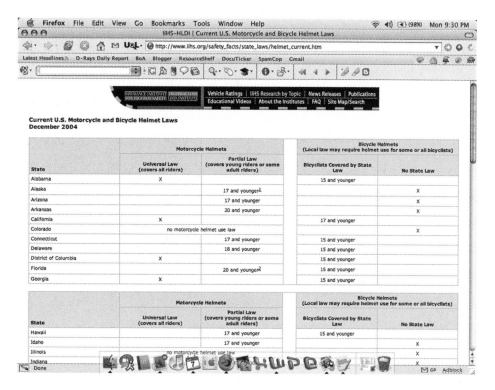

Fig. 6-2: The Insurance Institute for Highway Safety keeps an up-to-date chart of motorcycle (and bicycle) helmet laws nationwide. See www.iihs.org/laws/state_laws/helmet_current.html.

Current U.S. Motorcycle and Bicycle Helmet Laws (www.iihs.org/lawss/state_laws/helmet_current.html).

When you decide to ride a motorcycle, you are automatically assuming a higher risk level than any automobile driver. According to National Highway Transportation Safety Administration statistics for 2002, motorcyclists were about 27 times more likely to die in a motor vehicle accident than passenger car occupants, and six times as likely to be injured. But we also know that risk can be managed. Wearing a helmet when you ride is one element of motorcycle risk management. We'll look at some of the others in chapter 7.

Will wearing a helmet while riding a motorcycle guarantee that you will stay alive? No. Will it increase your chances of staying alive? Lots of people think so. I do, which is why I wear one. But I am not you. I'm guessing, however that since you're the kind of person who laid your money down for a book like this (or borrowed it from a library), you're probably going to buy a helmet anyhow, so let's go ahead and make sure you choose a good one.

Fig. 6-3: Shoei manufacturers high-quality helmets. You can see how they are designed and put together. (Photo courtesy of Shoei Helmets.)

BRAIN BUCKETS 101

A motorcycle helmet is a classic example of the whole being greater than the sum of the individual parts, as you can see in figure 6-3. The individual parts, in this case, are:

- Outer shell
- Impact-resistant lining
- Comfort padding
- Retention system

The **outer shell**, of course, is the Hard Stuff—made from such materials as fiberglass, molded plastic, or polycarbonate composites, but designed to compress when it takes a hit, so the negative energy gets spread out.

The **impact-resistant** lining—for example, Styrofoam-type material—provides cushioning and shock absorption when the helmet suddenly stops moving but your head wants to keep right on going.

The **comfort padding** is the soft cloth and foam that touches your face inside the helmet. On some helmets, this is removable so you can wash it.

The **retention system** is a fancy phrase for the chinstrap that holds the helmet on . . . if you are zealous about remembering to fasten it correctly every time you ride.

To get a helmet that meets minimum safety standards, you need to make sure it is manufactured to standards established by the U.S. Department of Transportation (DOT) and/or the Snell Memorial Foundation. We all know what DOT is; its standard applies to all helmets intended for use by motorcyclists and other motor vehicle users. For more information, see www.fmcsa.dot.gov/rulesregs/fmcsr/regs/571.218.htm. The Snell Memorial Foundation is a nonprofit organization completely and totally "dedicated to research, education, testing and development of helmet safety standards." For more information, visit www.smf.org. To peruse DOT helmet testing data, see www .nhtsa.dot.gov/cars/testing/comply/fmvss218. For a list of helmets certified by the Snell Foundation, see www.smf.org/certlist/std_M2000_M2005.html.

It's worth noting that two European standards in particular are making inroads into the American market for protective gear, including helmets. Read a comparison among Snell, BSI British Standards, and ECE (European Union) helmet testing at www.helmetharbor.com/snell/comparison.htm.

Helmets come in several styles. For street riders, the Motorcycle Safety Foundation recommends a **three-quarter** (open-face) helmet or a **full-face** helmet.

A full-face helmet, like the one in figure 6-4, offers the most protection since it covers your entire head and face. Most come with a flip-up face shield; these are often interchangeable so you can wear a tinted one for sunny day riding and a clear one for gloomy days or night riding. Glasses or sunglasses can easily be worn underneath, although you'll have to remove them to put the helmet on or take it off.

A three-quarter/open-face helmet (figure 6-5) is made from the same components as the full-face helmet but doesn't offer the same face and chin protection. You will need separate eye protection, either a snap-on face shield or riding goggles. Regular sunglasses or eyeglasses won't cut it; they

Savvy
Tip

Motorcyclist magazine explored these standards in depth and reports on its own comprehensive helmet tests in the June 2005 issue. Basically, you do not have to spend an arm and a leg to get top-notch protection. Some of the highest rated helmets were also some of the least expensive. This is a must-read: http://motorcyclistonline.com/gearbox/hatz. At least two helmet manufacturers were annoyed enough about this article that they canceled advertising contracts with the magazine, according to an editorial note in the August issue.

Fig. 6-4: You can't go wrong with one of Arai's highly rated Quantum series full-face helmets. But dig deep into those pockets, as this is most assuredly a high-end brain bucket. (Photo courtesy of Arai Helmet Americas, Inc.)

Fig. 6-5: If you prefer an open-face helmet, Arai's Classic/m is an excellent, if somewhat pricey, choice. But what's your brain worth, anyhow? All of Arai's helmets meet or exceed both DOT and Snell standards. (Photo courtesy of Arai Helmet Americas, Inc.)

could shatter or fly off, and they don't fit tightly enough around the eyes to keep out wind and junk like gravel, bugs, and other flying objects.

Other helmet styles include:

- *Modular/flip-up helmets,* where the entire front of the helmet flips up so you can eat, drink, smoke, talk understandably, and put on/take off your glasses without removing the helmet, as with a full-face model. By various reports, the degree of protection offered by flip-up helmets varies widely; for example, the chin guard locking mechanism may be weak. For more information, see *Motorcycle Consumer News's* "2004 Modular Helmet Update" (part 1, (www.mcnews.com/mcn/model_eval/HelmetA04.pdf), (part 2, www.mcnews.com/mcn/model_eval/HelmetB04.pdf).

- *Half helmets,* which cover only the top half of the head. That means no protection for your ears, face, or chin, although many are manufactured to DOT standards, so do offer some brain protection. Keep in mind, however, that according to a widely quoted German study by Dietmar Otte and Gunter Felton, most hits to the helmet in accidents are in the left and

Fig. 6-6: The Washington State Patrol wants to make sure you you choose a helmet that provides adequate protection. (www.wsp.wa.gov/traveler/helmet3.pdf)

right chin area. ("Requirements on Chin Protection in Full-Face for Motorcyclist Impact and Injury Situations," *Proceedings of the 1991 International Motorcycle Conference*).

- *So-called novelty helmets*, which are small beanie-type helmets that generally consist only of a shell, with no inner layers. These offer virtually no protection and are bought by riders because they like the style and/or they represent minimal compliance with helmet laws. The Washington State Patrol offers an informative brochure about these *Bogus Helmets*— www.wsp.wa.gov/traveler/helmet3.pdf. See figure 6-6.

BUYING A HELMET

Helmets are not one-size-fits-all. As a matter of fact, it's critical you get one that fits correctly if you expect it to protect you. Also, if the fit is uncomfortable, it might be a little too tempting to leave it home, no?

If you're purchasing a helmet for the first time, there's no way around the fact that you have to visit one or more local dealerships and try on different models by different manufacturers. Certain brands will be more compatible with the shape of your head than other brands. If you're lucky, you'll find a knowledgeable salesperson who can answer all your questions and help you get a good fit, in which case you should support the dealership by buying locally instead of hunting around for the cheapest price on the Web, especially for your first helmet. Once you find a brand and model that suits you well, it's probably worth venturing online to see what's available when you're in the market for a spare or second helmet.

Standard sizes for motorcycle helmets range from XX Small to XX Large. Although you'll find generic sizing charts, each individual manufacturer has its own specifications. In general, there are certain things you'll want to keep in mind when trying on helmets.

It should fit snugly—maybe even feel a little too tight initially, since the padding inside will eventually conform to your face and head. On the other hand, it should not be too tight. If, when you take it off, you feel sore anywhere or see red spots on your forehead, you may want to choose a larger size or try something from a different manufacturer. Those pressure points could turn into a headache during a long ride.

What color helmet should you buy? Well, that's basically up to you. Some are relatively sedate while others feature eye-popping graphics. Many people like to get a helmet that matches their bike, and sometimes a dealer can help with this. If you're buying primarily with safety in mind, choose a white or light-colored helmet. According to a 2004 study done in New Zealand, riders who wore a white helmet instead of a black one had a 24 percent lower risk of crash-related injuries. Read the study, "Motorcycle Rider Conspicuity and Crash Related Injury: Case-Control Study," published in the *British Medical Journal* in 2004, at http://jeff.dean.home.att.net/white-helmets.pdf.

Helmets are available in a wide range of prices, but spending more doesn't necessarily mean getting better protection, at least beyond a certain level. While you don't want to totally cheap out here, a $75 helmet that meets DOT and Snell standards will protect you just as well as a $600 helmet of the same type and rating. So what *does* more money buy you? Perhaps a lighter, more comfortable helmet with more efficient ventilation, removable padding (for washing), designer graphics, and easier face-shield removal/replacement.

Whatever you end up buying, know that your first helmet will not be your last helmet—not if you stick with motorcycling over an extended period of time. For one thing, the padding in the crushable inner liner becomes less effective; at minimum, you should replace your helmet at least once every three to five years, depending on how much use it gets. But helmets deteriorate even when just sitting on a shelf. This is something to keep in mind if you're buying a brain bucket online; there are bargains to be had in past-season merchandise, but can you find out how long it's been hanging around? Every helmet made for sale in the United States has a label inside showing the month and year it was manufactured. Ask the vendor about this.

Another reason for replacing your helmet at regular intervals is that the technology keeps getting better, and you'll likely get more protection and enhanced comfort.

Where accident protection is concerned, helmets are good for one-time use only. When you're in a crash, you'll need to buy a new one. In all likelihood, that inner line did absorb some shock impact, even if the accident was minor and the visible damage negligible. Some manufacturers will inspect and possibly repair the helmet, but don't wear it again until you have it checked.

Caring for Your Helmet

As a matter of fact, if you drop your helmet from even a few feet, you may well have damaged it to the point where it can no longer be counted on to protect you. This is why you want to be careful where you put it. Don't set it on the seat of your bike; it's too easy for it to fall off. (Don't ask me how I know this.) It's better off sitting on the ground next to the bike or on some other flat, secure surface. Keep it away from hot exhaust pipes and engine parts. (The outer shell may look fine while the inner crushable padding has gone into meltdown.) If you're carrying a spare helmet on your bike, make sure it's securely tied down and protected, and not banging around as you ride. (All of which are very good reasons to be wary of buying a used helmet. You just don't know how it's been treated.)

At home, don't store your brain bucket where it will be exposed to gasoline, household cleaning products, exhaust fumes, or constant heat, all of which may cause the inner liner to deteriorate without your being aware of it. Follow the manufacturer's instructions for cleaning the helmet—generally only with mild soap and water, which is also fine for a face shield. Do not, however, use paper towels; over time, these will create minute scratches on the surface and your vision will be impaired; at night, in particular, you'll be subject to prismatic-like effects. Soft cloth is always the best choice. Go through your bureau drawers and weed out your rattiest T-shirts, which make excellent cleaning rags. After all, you'll surely be accumulating new ones at bike nights, bike weeks, bike rallies . . .

Oh . . . and a few words here about do-rags. Yeah, some bikers wear them instead of helmets and yeah, they do have "the look," if you are into that, like the dude with the Ducati in figure 6-7. But appearances aside, it's not a bad idea to wear a do-rag *under* your helmet. For one thing, they absorb perspiration, hair oil, etc., and you can just toss them in the wash regularly, which saves wear and tear on the inside of your lid and keeps it from getting nasty quite so fast. Special helmet liners, such as the ones from Sliks (www.cyclegadgets.com) or American Roadrider (www.americanroadrider .com) are an alternative for those who cannot picture themselves in a do-rag. You can get plain ones that look like skullcaps.

Not only do these things protect your helmet, but they also protect your hair from being badly mangled *by* your helmet. While helmet hair is never totally avoidable, you can mitigate the effect to a certain extent by wearing a do-rag or a helmet liner.

Fig. 6-7: Do-rags—always appropriate. (Photo courtesy of Fairchild Sports/FirstGear)

Good advice about helmets is available from the Motorcycle Safety Foundation (www.msf-usa.org/downloads/helmet_CSI.pdf), *Motorcycle Cruiser* magazine (www.motorcyclecruiser.com/streetsurvival/howtobuyhelmet), and David Hough, author of the well-regarded Proficient Motorcycling books (www.soundrider.com/archive/safety-skills/crash_padding-pt2.htm).

BLACK LEATHER JACKET . . .

The black leather motorcycle jacket emerged as an American cultural icon back in 1954 when Marlon Brando came roaring across the silver screen on what was, indeed, his own 1950 Triumph Thunderbird in *The Wild One*. Black leather motorcycle jackets have always been cool; it's an enduring style that never drifts very far from fashion consciousness, although there is a heck of a difference between a "fashion" leather jacket and a high-quality leather motorcycle jacket.

In truth, there is a lot of practicality in the traditional motorcycle "look" that is regarded by many as an affectation. Black is an eminently practical color when you are exposed to road grime, oil, grease, etc. Jeans not only provide some leg protection (although you can do much better, as we will see), but standard styles fit close to the body; you can't wear loose, floppy clothes on a motorcycle. Black biker boots not only look great, but they provide good protection; sturdy, over-the-ankle footwear will shield you from a painful burn, courtesy of the hot exhaust pipe. And, let's face it, you use your feet a lot more on a motorcycle than you do in a car—to shift, to brake, and to hold your balance while stopped at a traffic light. Do-rags and bandanas, as noted above, absorb sweat and hair oil (and you can take them off and wipe your face with them—or wipe those fingerprints off your glossy gas tank).

Fig. 6-8: The black leather motorcycle jacket is an American classic. But make sure you get one that is designed for motorcycling riding, like FirstGear's Powercruiser style, and not a flimsy fashion wanna-be. (Photo courtesy of Fairchild Sports/FirstGear)

If you are looking for the ultimate in protective gear and have the bucks to spend, nothing beats leather; high-performance motorcycle racing types will wear nothing else. But you don't want to go looking for a leather jacket (and pants or chaps, if that floats your boat) down at the local mall. You want one that is meant specifically for motorcycling—preferably one with state-of-the-art armor built into it, like the one in figure 6-8. Motorcycle clothing is cut to fit you best when you are seated in a riding position (as opposed to hanging around at bike night, trying to look cool). The sleeves are cut longer and are slightly curved, the shoulders are fuller and often have gussets to facilitate freedom of movement. You'll find flaps, fasteners, zippers, etc.—all designed to keep out the wind.

For a really excellent overview of what's available in different price ranges, as well as useful information and lots of good links, check out the Leather Motorcycle Clothing page at webBikeWorld (www.webbikeworld.com/leather-motorcycle-clothing). But do consider that this may be the kind of thing you don't want to buy without trying it on first—if it's too tight, you will be uncomfortable; if it's too loose, the protective armor won't be where it needs to be—so perhaps a tour of the local dealerships is in order.

. . . OR TEXTILE . . .

Yes, leather looks great and provides fantastic protection. But—and take this from someone who lives in Florida and rides year-round—it tends to be very hot and very heavy. Even though good leather motorcycle jackets come with a series of vents that can be unzipped to allow for some airflow, they are still . . . very, very hot. Fortunately, there are some excellent synthetic alternatives. And some of them have clear advantages over leather. Better living through chemistry.

Fig. 6-9: Textile jackets are available in a wide range of styles, colors and price ranges. FirstGear's Kilimanjaro style is waterproof, has a full-sleeve zip-out liner, foam armor in the shoulders and elbows, and comes in five colors. (Photo courtesy of Fairchild Sports/FirstGear)

So-called textile riding clothes are made from materials like Kevlar or Cordura nylon. With armor in all the right places, these fabrics have gotten to the point where they can protect you almost as well as leather, in the event of the unthinkable. And there are all-weather models with zip-in liners to keep you warm and dry when it's cold and wet. See figure 6-9.

You'll find a vast array of styles and colors here. You may want something that matches your bike. You may want red because you look good in red. You may want black because . . . well, it's black.

From a safety-conscious point of view, however, you might want to think about our old friend conspicuity. Pick something that makes you as visible as possible to the unwashed, motorized hoards out there—reflective or fluorescent material being your first choice. If, like your author, you ride a bike on a military base, you will have to wear a "reflective upper garment" in addition to all the other mandated PPE. Some riders wear things like this all the time, particularly at night. The alternative is to choose gear that incorporates a sizable amount of reflective material. (You can also buy reflective/**retroreflective** tape, stick-on patches, etc.)

You can buy textile riding clothes as a one-piece suit or separate jacket and pants. Look for those designed to zip together in the back; they will stay together and protect your tender flesh from the elements—or worse, in the event of a crash. Adjustable straps at the waist, wrists, and collar (and ankles, for pants, like the ones in figure 6-10) will allow you to get in and out of your gear without a struggle, while still allowing you to tighten things down so the wind can't get in. Keep in mind that at certain times of the year, most of us welcome some airflow when we are riding. Look for strategically located vents that you can zip open. I have jackets that incorporate these on either side of the chest, both upper arms, and near each of my shoulder blades.

Fig. 6-10: You could wear FirstGear's HT Overpant with the Kilimanjaro jacket in figure 6-9. (Photo courtesy of Fairchild Sports/FirstGear)

By and large, textile garments are made to be worn over your street clothes, so they are a good choice for commuters. For less-than-optimal weather, you'll need a zip-in waterproof liner (or full rain gear, as we'll see below) and/or a quilted liner for cold weather; if these don't come with the jackets, you can usually purchase them separately. Some materials are heavier than others; consider where you live, and where and how you will ride.

Start your browsing at webBikeWorld's Motorcycle Clothing page (www.webbikeworld.com/ Motorcycle-clothing/Motorcycle-clothing.htm). Then take a day and visit as many local motorcycle dealerships as you can, since most of them carry at least a small selection of gear. Try on different items, read the hangtags, ask questions. Again, it's up to you whether or not you buy online. But it's not a good idea to buy this stuff without trying it on first—especially if this is your first foray into motorcycle gear. And if you can find apparel that you like locally . . . well, there is something to be said for keeping your money in the community, no?

. . . OR MESH

Right off the bat, you need to realize that mesh riding gear will never provide the same level of protection as leather or the close-weave, heavier textile fabrics. But the technology is getting better here, too, and for those of us who live where it's hot most of the year, mesh offers an alternative to the obviously less desirable choices of going without gear or not riding at all during the worst months. (Of course, some riders eschew gear altogether; here in Florida, it is not *that* uncommon to see people riding around in bathing suits.)

Fig. 6-11: FirstGear's Mesh-Tex jacket is available for both men and women. (Photo courtesy of Fairchild Sports/FirstGear)

OK, so maybe you're settling for a bit less protection here, but under the circumstances, you'll take what you can get. And what you can get is a mesh jacket that comes with some sort of armor—at the elbows, shoulders, and down the back, if at all possible. Sometimes, this is our old friend Styrofoam. Sometimes you'll find Kevlar or ballistic-quality nylon. If you live where the nights get cool, some of these jackets come with a zip-in liner. See figure 6-11.

Motorcycle Cruiser magazine offers a nice rundown of hot weather riding gear: http://motorcycle cruiser.com/accessoriesandgear/hotwxgear.

PROTECT YOUR HANDS

When we start to fall, our survival instincts kick in. What is the first thing we do? We extend one or both of our arms to break our fall. What this means is that if you fall from a motorcycle, your hand may well be the first thing that hits the ground. This, alone, is an excellent reason to wear gloves when you ride. But they will also protect your hands from the elements and, if they fit snugly enough, will improve your grip on the handlebars. By the way, you want full-fingered gloves and not those open-fingered styles designed for driving a car or lifting weights.

There are plenty of choices in all styles and price ranges here. Again, what you need depends on where and how you ride. You can rarely go wrong with leather; perforated leather works well for warm climates, but you'll get more use out of heavier gloves (some have a Thinsulate lining) in other places. Look for adjustable wrist straps you can tighten to seal out the wind.

As you might expect, most leather gloves are made from cowhide (and the dye used to color them—

Fig. 6-12: High-tech gloves provide a lot of protection, but they may feel a bit bulky—especially if you are just starting out and you need to get used to the feel of the hand controls. Plain leather might be a better bet. (Photo courtesy of Fairchild Sports/FirstGear)

usually black—will indeed come off on your hands when the gloves get wet). Many experienced riders prefer gloves made of deerskin, elkskin, or goatskin, which are more flexible. Elkskin, in particular, retains its softness and shape even after getting wet repeatedly, and can stand up to a lot of abuse.

Synthetic materials have made inroads here as well—particularly the by-now-familiar Kevlar and Cordura—for insulation, waterproofing, protection, etc. Sometimes these materials are used in combination with leather; other gloves are wholly synthetic. See figure 6-12.

When it starts to get really cold, you may want gauntlet-style gloves that extend up your forearms. Be aware, however, that some of these are rather bulky and may interfere with your ability to operate the hand controls. Then again, if your hands get too cold—and it's been my experience this is the first place you really start to feel the cold—they'll go numb and you'll have trouble operating the controls anyhow. Gerbing's Heated Clothing—their Web site is shown in figure 6-13—is a company that makes electric gloves especially for motorcyclists (www.gerbing.com); they are pricey, but if you live where it gets and stays cold and you ride every day, well . . . you'll likely get your money's worth. (Note: If you're interested in electric gloves, you'll probably also want an electric jacket liner or vest. See "More Cool Stuff," page 130.)

Some of the higher-end touring bikes come with heated handgrips. Aftermarket solutions are available. Check with your dealer or at a few of the larger online vendors that cater to motorcyclists. You can find a few user reviews on MotorcycleGearReview.com (www.motorcyclegearreview.com).

Browse through the links on webBikeWorld's Motorcycle Gloves (www.webbikeworld.com/motorcycle-gloves) page to get an idea of what's available. Visit dealers and try them on. It's a good idea to bring your jacket with you so you can see how well the glove fits over or under the cuff. Gloves that

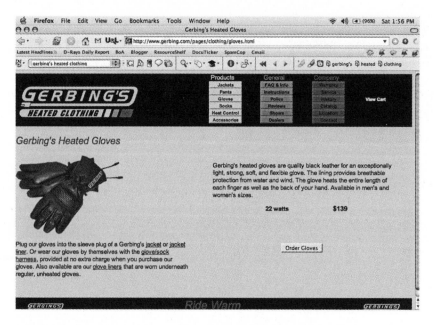

Fig. 6-13: "Gerbing's heated gloves are quality black leather for an exceptionally light, strong, soft, and flexible glove. The lining provides breathable protection from water and wind. The glove heats the entire length of each finger as well as the back of your hand. Available in men's and women's sizes." Sound like something you could use? (Photo courtesy of Gerbing's Heated Clothing, Inc.)

are too tight will impair your circulation, but leather gloves do have a tendency to stretch out with use, so keep this in mind.

PROTECT YOUR FEET . . . AND ANKLES . . . AND . . .

"Sturdy over-the-ankle footwear" does not mean Converse High Tops, people. Leave the athletic shoes in the gym bag. What you're looking for here is good-quality boots—and that usually means leather uppers and some sort of a heavy composite sole.

Your feet are not just along for the ride when you take to the open road on your bike. They are major players. You use them to shift and operate the rear brake. You stand on them to keep the bike up when you're stopped at an intersection. Good boots can shield you from exhaust pipe burns on the lower legs, and they will deflect stones and other debris that fly up from the road. And if you should go down and do a little asphalt surfing, they will protect your feet and ankles.

What you end up buying will, as with all gear, depend on where you ride and how you ride. For example, if you commute on your bike, will you change out of your boots at work, or do you need something you can walk around in all day? Comfort can be a very big issue. Do you need something that would not be grossly out of place in your office? Resist the temptation to buy those big clunkers with the silver buckles, the studs, and the medallions and settle for the plain black touring boots instead.

What you want:

- A composite sole; leather soles are very, very slippery and you need your traction.
- A low heel; flat soles make it difficult to keep your feet on the pegs.
- A low heel; ladies, leave the high-fashion stiletto boots at home.
- Some degree of waterproofing; even if you don't want to ride in the rain, sooner or later you *will* ride in the rain . . . or step in a puddle.
- Insulation; although you can probably skip this if you're not doing much riding in cold weather.
- Pull-on or zippered boots; laces can come undone and get tangled in moving bike parts.

In all likelihood, if you ride pretty much year round, you'll probably end up with several pairs of boots; my collection is on display in figure 6-14. Good boots can be expensive, but with proper care, they will last for years and years. Start browsing at webBikeWorld's Motorcycle Boots page (www .webbikeworld.com/motorcycle-boots), but footwear is something you really do not want to buy without trying on first, unless you're purchasing something with which you've had prior experience.

Fig. 6-14: Your author's boot collection.

But What If It Rains?

Yes, sooner or later, you *will* ride in the rain. Maybe that wasn't what you had in mind when you left the house in the morning, but somewhere along the line, the sky opened up and here you are. We'll discuss wet-weather riding techniques in the next chapter. Right here, right now, we are going to attempt to make you reasonably comfortable.

As with textile riding suits, you have your choice of one- or two-piece rain suits. It's more or less up to you which style you'll have less trouble struggling into when the magic moment arrives and you suddenly have to pull off the road under that overpass and rummage through your bags to find the thing. Some of the one-piece styles are kind of nifty, as they can be folded up inside themselves, into an integrated fanny pack. Bulky old PVC plastic rain gear has been largely supplanted by synthetic materials that are not only waterproof but also light and breathable.

If you can, buy rain gear that is specifically designed for motorcycling, as it will more likely be cut to go over your heavy jacket and pants, with adjustable zippers, Velcro, and/or elastic. Also, some rain gear has retroflective material sewn in, for greater visibility. However, if you really want to be seen out there on the roads in inclement weather, get yourself bright orange or yellow gear, like the good-looking example in figure 6-15. You may also want to consider waterproof rain covers for your boots and gloves.

Read reviews of different brands of rain gear at MotorcycleGearReview.com (www.motorcyclegearreview.com). *Motorcycle Cruiser* magazine reviewed 10 different rain suits in 2002; while the review is a bit dated—technology and, certainly, styles change—there is good advice on choosing rain gear (www.motorcyclecruiser.com/accessoriesandgear/rainsuit).

More Cool Stuff

ICON Mil Spec Vest (www.rideicon.com)

If you ride on a military installation, you will need a "reflective upper garment." Most of what is available in this category is fairly primitive. But here's a relatively new alternative. When I started seeing these on motorcyclists at my base, I was motivated to buy one as well. It even has a front pocket for your Department of Defense ID card so you won't hold up the line at the security gate in the mornings while you fumble through your jacket pocket trying to find the darn thing. See figure 6-16.

Fig. 6-15: There's something to be said for a bright yellow rain suit. It increases the odds that you will be seen. (Photo courtesy of Fairchild Sports/FirstGear)

Fig. 6-16: Says ICON: "Jumping through hoops trying to get that new bike onto base? While we can't help you bypass military regulations, we can help you meet them without looking like a construction worker." (Photo courtesy of LeMans Corporation)

Draggin' Jeans (www.dragginjeans.com/jeans.html)

What I don't own: leather, mesh, or textile riding pants. Why? It's difficult to get a good fit if you're short, and they are . . . hot. And when you get right down to it, what looks better than a black leather jacket and blue jeans? Except regular jeans really don't provide much in the way of protection. You go asphalt surfing, they're gonna shred right quick. Here's a compromise: Kevlar-lined jeans. Realize that you're compromising somewhat on protection, but something is better than nothing. They look like regular jeans and they're available in several styles, in a wide range of sizes, and in both blue and black denim. See figure 6-17. KBO Clothing Company, a Canadian firm, offers something similar: www.kboclothingcompany.ca/prod01.htm.

Gerbing's Heated Clothing (www.gerbing.com)

The last thing a Florida motorcyclist needs is a heated jacket liner, right? Well, that's what I thought—until my next-door neighbor (who owns a big old Harley cop bike) watched me pull into

Fig. 6-17: Jeans . . . with something extra. (Photo courtesy of Fast Company)

the driveway all bundled up one chilly January day, and hollered, "Have I got something for you! Hang on a minute!" He ran into his house and emerged with this quilted . . . thing that had wires protruding from it. He told me it was a heated jacket liner. "You may as well take it," he said. "I don't ride when it's cold anymore." He attached a wiring harness to my battery and I slipped the jacket liner on, plugged it in, put my leather jacket back on top, and started the bike. In about a minute, I was seriously warm and toasty. See figure 6-18.

FINDING REVIEWS OF GEAR

First, for a good overview of what to look for when buying gear, read David Hough's take on suits, boots, and gloves (www.soundrider.com/archive/safety-skills/crash_padding-pt1.htm).

Virtually every viable Internet motorcycle forum hosts discussions about gear. Read what your fellow riders have to say. Or if you are thinking of buying something specific, post a message asking if anybody owns one and would like to share information. Other places to look:

- CruiserCustomizing (www.cruisercustomizing.com), a large online vendor, posts reviews of products by customers.

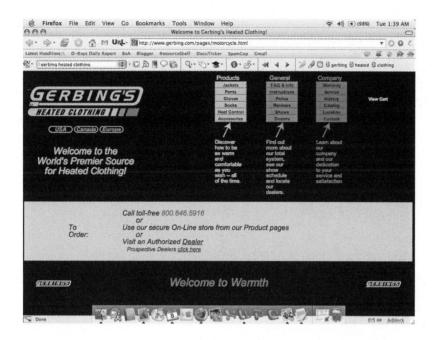

Fig. 6-18: Especially if you live in a cooler climate, you can stretch your riding season by opting for gloves, socks, jacket liners, etc., that plug into your bike's electrical system to keep you warm and toasty. Gerbing—www.gerbing.com—is a leading vendor.

- NewEnough (www.newenough.com), an online vendor specializing in motorcycle gear, offers very informative write-ups about the products it sells, including information about cut and fit. They carry merchandise from many different vendors. Note for those of you who have trouble finding things because you don't wear a mainstream size: NewEnough has a well-stocked "Hard to Fit" section (www.newenough.com/product_group_category _hard_to_fit.htm).
- *Motorcycle Cruiser* magazine has a nice collection of reviews: http://motorcyc lecruiser.com/accessoriesandgear/gearfinder/.
- *Motorcycle Consumer News* (www.mcnews.com/mcn/) is regarded as a good, unbiased source of information since it doesn't accept advertising. Some gear reviews are available, along with their motorcycle model evaluations (www.mcnews.com/mcn/model_eval.asp).
- *MotorcycleGearReview.com* (www.motorcyclegearreview.com/) offers user reviews of a wide range of products.

For women motorcyclists, it used to be a challenge to find decent riding gear that fit well. Well, as we learned in chapter 1, women now own about 10 percent of all the motorcycles out there, and that number is growing. We are a desirable market, ladies. Browse the Women's Motorcycle Clothing page at webBikeWorld and see just how desirable (www.webbikeworld.com/women-motorcycle-clothing). On the other hand, some of us may still do better with men's sizes—speaking as one who usually ends up buying men's size small—so don't ignore what's available on *their* racks. If you like it, try it on and don't worry about the size label. And check out some of the woman-focused Web sites in the bibliography for more gear reviews.

Marni Sorrick
St. Louis, Mo.
Retail bank manager
2004 Harley-Davidson XL 883 Sportster

One day two summers ago, my husband casually asked me to go with him to look at Harley-Davidson motorcycles. A couple of weeks later, after we had visited no less than three Harley dealers, I asked him if he had plans to actually buy one. He admitted that he did, indeed, plan to buy a motorcycle. I said, "You know, you're having a midlife crisis." He replied, "Yeah, I guess so." (My hubby is a man of few words.) I said, "Well, if I have a choice between buying a motorcycle or letting you run off with some 20-year-old floozy with a bad dye job, wait here just a minute while I run and get my checkbook so we can buy a motorcycle!"

Darrell ordered a touring seat with passenger pillion and backrest so I could ride with him without feeling like I was going to slide off the rear fender. He also made sure I had proper riding gear—a helmet, leather jacket, chaps, boots, and gloves. I was actually terrified to ride with him but refused to admit it publicly. I decided I had better learn to enjoy riding or else I was going to be sitting at home alone a lot during the summer months. But I soon became comfortable on the back of the bike, and the poor man couldn't get his helmet to go for a ride without my begging to go with him.

About six months after Darrell had purchased his bike, I was watching a television demo of Harley-Davidson's new 2004 Sportster. The rubber-mounted engine and easy-pull clutch were features that appealed to me. The price also seemed reasonable for an entry-level bike. I said, "I might like to have one of those sometime." My jaw nearly hit the floor when Darrell replied, "So let's go buy one for you." Within a week we had purchased a 2004 XL 883 Sportster.

Darrell started me out on the bike in a church parking lot across the street from our house, learning to control the clutch and throttle and riding figure eights. Then I graduated to riding the streets in our neighborhood. I was hooked! I passed the Motorcycle Safety Foundation Basic Rider Course and received my "M" endorsement for my license. After that, it didn't take me long to start riding alone and riding the bike to work. I rode more than 5,000 miles that first year, including a 1,000-mile road trip.

All our vacation this coming year is planned around motorcycle rallies and road trips. We ride often with friends from our HOG chapter, and this year brings our first ladies-only overnight ride for the Ladies of Harley from our chapter. My life has changed forever, and I never dreamed that middle age would be so much fun!

7 STAYIN' SAFE, STAYIN' ALIVE

◆ Behold the urban warrior!

◆ Rules of the road

◆ Different types of rides

◆ Health issues

There are old motorcyclists and there are bold motorcyclists, but there are no old, bold motorcyclists. (Which is the same thing they say about pilots.)

—Old saw

BEHOLD THE URBAN WARRIOR

My motorcycle, for better or worse, is transportation rather than recreation. I commute to work on it every day that the weather is reasonable (e.g., no hurricanes) unless I need the car to transport other people or bulky objects. There is really only one good way to get from where I live to where I work, with minor variations in side streets, etc. And in using this route day after day, week after week, I am quite intimate with the range of hazards that it presents. Just a few examples:

Just after I leave my neighborhood, there is a extensive school zone with a crosswalk monitored by a crossing guard. I usually pass this location about five minutes before the final morning school bell, so I am aware of parental time-anxiety behind the wheel, which sometimes results in aggressive and/or brain-dead maneuvers, and child time-anxiety, which sometimes results in a child darting into the street on foot or bicycle, without using the crosswalk where the guard will stop the traffic. I ride at 15 mph, on hyperalert, with my right hand covering the brake and my left hand covering the clutch.

Once I get out onto the causeway and bridge I use to cross Tampa Bay, there are two immediate hazards:

- A very busy service station that has the lowest prices in the area, so drivers are sometimes overwhelmed by the sudden desire to gas up, and they dart across four lanes of fast-moving traffic in order to slake their thirst for petroleum products;
- A large condominium complex under construction, where workers park on one side of the causeway and hotfoot it across the road to the worksite on the other side, trying to dodge oncoming vehicles.

This area is easily the scariest part of my trip, coming and going, even if I am in the car rather than on the motorcycle.

The bridge itself presents several unique hazards:

- This is a main route to the port and the area fuel tank farm, which means a lot of big rigs and tank trucks, always coming and going. Sometimes it is difficult to find a safe spot in which to place myself.
- There always seems to be a lot of debris in the roadway—"**road gators**" from retread tires on the big trucks, plastic drywall buckets, bags of sand that have split open (very bad news), rolls of carpet padding. A guy at work who commutes on his Honda VTX 1800 told me he ran over a beach umbrella on the bridge. I once saw a whole, dead fish in the middle of the left-hand lane, obviously dropped there by some unfortunate water bird.
- With all of this aggro, it is still a beautiful ride. I have to force myself to pay attention to the road and the traffic rather than looking at the water, the osprey on the light pole, the boats, the downtown Tampa skyline, and the interesting flying objects sometimes emanating from the Air Force base where I work.
- The winds can be very unpredictable on the bridge. Sometimes, it's downright hard work to handle the bike. (Read more about riding in the wind below.)
- At certain times of the year, I am looking directly into a very, very bright ball of sun when I am both coming and going, since I go east in the a.m. and west in the p.m. If my vision is impaired, I assume everyone else's is as well. Extra vigilance is required.

- A **LEO** with a radar gun likes to hide on the Tampa side of the bridge, trying to nab drivers who come flying off at a high rate of speed. People who use the bridge frequently are aware of this and will often slow down abruptly, which causes other drivers to slam on their brakes.

There is a large public boat ramp on the right-hand side as I come off the bridge. Trucks and SUVs pulling humongous boats will often cross the busy road regardless of the traffic flow, figuring all the other drivers will make an effort to avoid them. I am on high alert again, as I do not want to T-bone some enormous fishing boat.

Merging onto the busy road that terminates at the base gate is often a challenge. On some mornings, traffic is backed up from the gate beyond that intersection, and it is stop-and-start all the way to the gate. My left hand goes numb from the need to keep the clutch constantly squeezed in. In the heat of the summer, sitting in the middle of all this traffic, breathing everyone's exhaust fumes while the cagers luxuriate in air conditioning, I sometimes question my sanity for riding a motorcycle.

I stop at the gate so the security GI can check my sticker and ID. It is like stopping at a toll booth, with the same sorts of hazards—particularly the oily strip in the middle of the lane from all the vehicles that stop there, day in and day out. I am careful not to lose my footing when starting up again; I test the ground tentatively with my right foot before pushing off and riding through. And then I watch for drivers in the other lanes who decide, having passed through security, that they would rather be in my lane than the one they are currently occupying.

Although I made it sound somewhat harrowing, my commute is actually not all that bad compared to what many people go through. And yet I cannot allow my attention to lapse for even a few brief seconds. It's easy for a novice motorcyclist to get in over his or her head before acquiring the competence needed to cope with the wide range of hazards he or she is likely to encounter. Do not let yourself be pressured (and do not pressure yourself) into riding in traffic or other situations—bridges, toll booths, freeways, etc.—that you know you aren't ready to handle. Don't try it for the first time at rush hour. And certainly don't try it until you are thoroughly familiar and comfortable with your bike and its controls, so you don't have to think about what you are doing and can direct all of your attention to what is going on around you.

And don't try it at all if it isn't what you want to do. Many—maybe even most—people never commute on their motorcycles, reserving them for weekend recreation only. They have no desire to be two-wheeled urban warriors, or their occupation or work location makes motorcycle commuting impractical or impossible.

You may not care to ride your motorcycle to work on a daily basis, but do consider riding, if at all possible, on the annual Ride to Work Day, always the third Wednesday in July. Ride to Work Inc., is a nonprofit organization that "advocates and supports the use of motorcycles for transportation, and provides information about transportation riding to the general public." Ride to Work Day is intended to demonstrate: (1) the number of motorcyclists to the general public and to politicians; (2) that motorcyclists are from all occupations and all walks of life; (3) that motorcyclists can reduce traffic and parking congestion in large cities; (4) that motorcycles are good for transportation as well as recreation; and (5) that motorcycling is a social good. Get the whole story—and download photos, logos, and other supplementary materials at www.ridetowork.org. Organizer kits for employers, motorcycle dealerships, clubs, and groups of all sizes are available for purchase. See figure 7-1.

RULES OF THE ROAD

Can I teach you everything you need to know to operate a motorcycle safely on the roads? I cannot. Can I provide you with a rundown of some "best practices" recommended by experienced motorcyclists and safety instructors? Yep. Unlike helmet laws and loud pipes, established safe-riding practices are largely noncontroversial in the motorcycling community.

Intersections

The infamous Hurt Report (*Motorcycle Accident Cause Factors and Identification of Countermeasures* [www.clarity.net/~adam/hurt-report.html]), a detailed study of factors causing motorcycle accidents and injuries published in 1981 and still regarded as the most authoritative source of information on this topic, found, "Intersections are the most likely place for the motorcycle accident, with the other vehicle violating the motorcycle right-of-way, and often violating traffic controls." In other words, the most common type of motorcycle accident involving another vehicle occurs when an oncoming vehicle turns left directly in front of a motorcyclist. Which usually takes place at an intersection.

Be that as it may, there's really no way to avoid dealing with intersections unless you intend to spend all your time riding off-road or in empty parking lots, never venturing out onto the public streets. Fortunately, there are measures you can take to minimize the chances of Something Bad happening to you at an intersection.

Fig. 7-1: Maybe you can't wait to ride your motorcycle to work, maybe you want to but can't, or maybe you're not all that enthusiastic about the idea. Every motorcyclist should at least consider commuting once a year, on Ride to Work Day, the third Wednesday in July. It's an excellent way to demonstrate that motorcyclists are just ordinary folks — your neighbor, your child's teacher, your boss, the tech who fixes your computer, the hygienist in your dentist's office.... It can also show how motorcycles are an efficient, economical form of transportation. (Source: Ride to Work, Inc.)

- Dress for conspicuity. We discussed this briefly in chapter 6. I can't say that I'm crazy about the look of the orange reflective vest that the Air Force makes me wear when I'm riding on base, but there is a reason for that rule. That flash of orange makes me a whole lot more visible to the cagers than I would be in my usual black jacket, with black gloves and boots and jeans . . . and dark helmet . . . on a black motorcycle.

- Slow down. You'd think this would be a no-brainer, but there's also a tendency to want to get away from an especially bad intersection as quickly as possible. So we tempt fate by twisting the wrist and praying silently that the oncoming cagers don't misjudge our speed or location. By slowing down, however, we can take control of the situation—scope out the intersection for potential problems and consider potential evasive maneuvers. And when you drop your speed, you also cut down on your stopping distance.

- Cover the front brake lever with your right hand and the rear brake pedal with the right foot when traveling through an intersection. And cover the clutch lever with your left hand. If you have to make a panic stop, you will be ready.

- Try to stay away from other vehicles as much as possible. You'll be better able to see and be seen, and have more room to spare should you need to execute an evasive maneuver. Not that you'll always have control over this.

- Be completely sure that the intersection is free of other vehicles before proceeding through. An oncoming vehicle may be turning. Someone approaching the intersection on the cross street may be absorbed in a cell phone conversation and fail to notice that the light is red. (This has happened to me.)

- Yellow lights present an additional set of hazards since most drivers regard them as a signal to put the pedal to the metal in an attempt to beat the change to red. If you're waiting to make a left turn, don't count on being able to go when the light turns yellow; we've all seen how many vehicles will continue through the intersection after the light turns yellow . . . and even red. Be extremely careful yourself if you decide to "run the yellow," since oncoming drivers will be attempting to turn left, but also recognize the need to be cautious if you choose to stop for the yellow light instead. The cager behind you may have already decided that he or she is going to floor it on the yellow, and you could be mowed down from the rear. Use your mirrors to assess the situation. Flash your brake light to signal your intention before actually stopping.

- Watch the front wheels of other vehicles. This is the best clue you will have as to the actual intentions of other drivers, since using turn signals appears to be a dying practice in America. For example, if the front tires on that minivan in the left oncoming lane are pointed slightly to the left when stopped on red, you can figure that the driver is getting ready to make a left turn. And he or she may try to do it the second the light turns green, in an attempt to beat out the oncoming traffic.

Speaking of green lights . . . Don't proceed through an intersection the second the light turns green. Wait for things to "calm down" first. Make sure the left-turners and red-light runners have cleared the intersection first, and take a good look around to make sure no one else is doing something stupid. You may have to edge out slowly to get the full picture. If the impatient cager behind you starts honking the horn—and it *will* happen, sooner or later—just ignore it. Don't be pressured into doing something unsafe.

Sooner or later, you're going to end up at one of those intersections that is controlled by an electronic sensor and learn that your bike is not heavy enough to activate the thing. So there you sit, fruitlessly waiting for the left turn signal or the green light, with the choice of either cooling your heels until another vehicle comes along, or taking a chance and running the red light. Is there anything else you can do? Well, maybe.

- Get off your bike and push the "walk" button on the traffic signal, if one is available.
- Position yourself directly over the sensor(s) in the road if you can see the strips. Roll your bike back and forth if necessary.
- If you're waiting for a left turn signal, consider proceeding straight through the intersection on green and then making three successive right turns, which obviously works best when streets are laid out in a standard urban grid.
- Some suggest that after sitting through one light cycle, you try putting down your side stand, under the assumption that some actual metal touching the road will activate the sensor.
- If you look through the backs of the bike rags, you'll find ads for devices to install on your motorcycle which emit an electromagnetic field that is supposed to trigger the sensor. I don't know anyone who has one of these, so I can't vouch for their efficacy. White Horse Press carries such an item, and it's only $14.95, so the gadget-minded may want to give it a try. See figure 7-2.
- If all else fails and you have no option but to run the light, be very careful and make sure the intersection is completely clear before you go. In the future, if there is any way you can avoid an intersection like this, it is wise to do so.

Lane Position

Positioning yourself properly within a lane can help you avoid windblast from other vehicles, help you see and avoid roadway hazards, and help you create and maintain a space cushion between yourself and other traffic. Don't hide among other vehicles. Position yourself so that drivers ahead can see you in their mirrors. Choosing a position that helps you see potential problems ahead can also help drivers see you sooner.

—Motorcycle Safety Foundation

The epigraph is from Motorcycle Safety Foundation, *Basic RiderCourse Handbook,* www.msf-usa.org/CurriculumMaterials/BRCRiderHndbk_2005v6.pdf.

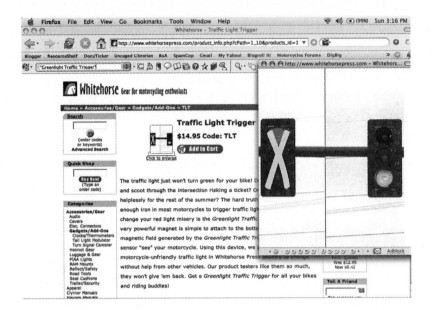

Fig.7-2: White Horse Press offers the Greenlight Traffic Trigger in its catalog, at www.whitehorsepress.com/product_info.php?cPath=1_10&products_id=118. Does it work? I've never tried it myself, so I couldn't tell you. Let me know if it does.

Lane position is a two-part issue. Which lane will you ride in, and which part of that lane will you ride in? The choices you'll make are highly dependent on the circumstances in which you find yourself, but there is one big no-no. You'll always want to avoid riding in the center of any traffic lane. Can you guess why? It has to do with that dark strip down the middle, which comes from all the yucky stuff that drips from the bottoms of countless automobiles and trucks. It's nasty, it's slippery, and it can deprive your tires of traction.

The basic rule of thumb for lane position is to ride where you have the best view of what is ahead of you. Depending on the traffic situation, that could be any lane and any position in that lane. In theory, the leftmost lane is for passing, but in practice, people tend to sit out there indefinitely and not move over. Where you definitely do not want to be is behind a large vehicle—truck, van, enormous SUV, etc. Besides completely obscuring the forward view for you, their odd aerodynamics create an air disturbance that can sometimes destabilize your motorcycle if you get too close and/or if and when you decide to pass. Also, stuff falls off trucks; you read my diatribe about road debris a little earlier in this chapter. Where do you think it comes from?

Actually, other traffic can be used to your advantage. Once you've found yourself a spot with good

Most experienced motorcyclists recommend riding a bit faster than the flow of traffic. Not 20 or even 10 miles over the speed limit, mind you, but just fast enough to keep you ahead of the "pack." This cuts down on the amount of time you'll spend in the blind spots of other vehicles and it reduces the amount of attention you need to give to what is going on behind you. Speed can also be your friend at traffic signals, if you are at the head of the line; when the red light changes to green, after scanning the intersection carefully for cross traffic, left turners, etc., accelerate rapidly to put some distance between you and the pack of cars moving slowly away from the light behind you.

visibility, other vehicles going in the same direction can shield you from oncoming drivers making left turns in front of you.

You cannot ride timidly in traffic. You have to control your lane or you may end up with some cager trying to share it with you. And you have to keep up with—or maybe even ride a little faster than—the flow of traffic. This will keep the impatient from tailgating or otherwise bothering you from behind, so you can concentrate more on what is on up ahead. And if you are keeping pace with the car ahead of you and maintaining just the right space cushion, it's less likely that other drivers will cut in ahead of you, something they are quick to do if you start dropping too far behind. A friend with many years of urban street riding experience once told me, "It takes an odd combination of extreme caution and controlled aggression." And that about sums it up.

Other things to know about lane position:

- Never allow yourself to get so boxed in by other vehicles that you have no space cushion should you have to execute an emergency maneuver.
- Stay out of other drivers' blind spots. When you're out riding around in your car, pay particular attention to where your own blind spots are and use this knowledge to position yourself safely in relation to other drivers when you're on your bike. Remember that trucks and buses have extensive blind spots.
- On freeways, avoid the right-hand lane, since that is where vehicles are entering and exiting the highway. You're probably best off in the left-hand lane, which eliminates traffic concerns to your left.
- Riding in the right-hand track of the left lane usually allows for the best forward view, in terms of keeping tabs on what the cagers ahead of you in your lane and other lanes are doing. It provides you with a space cushion to the left, and discourages lane intrusions from the right.
- When changing lanes, signal your intentions clearly and make sure the surrounding drivers all see you. (Try attracting attention by dropping back a bit behind the car in front of

you and moving from side to side in your lane if you think you are not seen.) On multilane highways, make sure someone is not trying to merge into the same lane from the other side.

Curves

> Crash studies show that running off the road, usually in a curve, accounts for over 40 percent of total motorcycle fatalities. This is the primary situation in which motorcyclists have single vehicle crashes.
>
> —*Motorcycle Safety Foundation*

Negotiating curves on a motorcycle is all about traction . . . and control. The reason curves are trickier on a motorcycle than in a car is that there's less rubber on the road—two wheels instead of four wheels being the most obvious difference. And since the motorcycle leans when it turns, your **contact patch**—the sections of your two tires that are actually touching the road—is smaller than when you're riding straight. The smaller the contact patch, the less traction you have. And traction is your friend.

Size up the curve before you get there. How sharp is it? What is its radius? What is the slope of the road? What is the road surface like? Can you see the entire curve or is your visibility limited? What's around the other end of the curve? Is there much other traffic? Take in all this information and plan a strategy in terms of entry speed and location—that is, an optimal lane position.

How you accelerate, decelerate, and handle braking in a curve can further complicate the situation. In a nutshell:

- Get on the brakes, slow down, and get off the brakes before heading into the curve. In other words, use the brakes while the motorcycle is still standing upright, when you have the maximum amount of traction available. If you brake when leaned over, you are more likely to skid and/or **low side**. If you absolutely have to slow down while in a curve, try first to get the bike upright by reducing the lean angle as much as possible.
- Maintain a steady engine speed—use the throttle smoothly—to maintain maximum control over your bike. If you feel the bike start to lean over a little too much, fight your instinct to brake. Instead roll on the throttle gradually. A bit more speed will stabilize the motorcycle and, at the end of the curve, allow you to exit proficiently.
- Refrain from sudden acceleration while in a curve, which will upset the bike's chassis, causing instability. For the same reason, you don't want to shift gears in a curve.

The epigraph is from Motorcycle Safety Foundation, *Basic RiderCourse Handbook,* www.msf-usa.org/CurriculumMaterials/BRCRiderHndbk_2005v6.pdf.

When you get to the point that you're really proficient in the "twisties," you may want to give Deal's Gap—U.S. Highway 129 in North Carolina—a try. Known by motorcyclists as The Dragon, this 11-mile stretch of road features 318 curves. If you're not quiet up to the challenge yet, you can enjoy it vicariously via this QuickTime movie: http://homepage.mac.com/terry_m/iMovieTheater6.html.

David Hough, in his Proficient Motorcycling series, has written extensively about a concept he calls the delayed apex—"an apex imagined to be farther around the curve than where the rider believes the sharpest part of the curve actually is" (*More Proficient Motorcycling*, p. 252). Basically, he maintains that if you point your bike toward the sharpest part of the curve too soon, your path for the rest of the curve will be too wide—which may run you off the road or cause you to wander over the centerline. He recommends entering a curve more from the outside and head for an apex that is slightly further along the curve than where the actual sharpest point is.

Rain . . . and Wind

Sooner or later, if you ride regularly, you're going to end up riding in the rain. And you know what? It's not that bad . . . if you have proper gear and if you know what you're doing. I keep rain gear at my house, on my bike, and in my office. Of course, I live in Florida, and if you absolutely, positively do not want to ride in the rain here, you'll spend most of the year not riding at all.

Now mind you, I'm not foolhardy. If Jim Cantore from the Weather Channel is hanging out on any of the beaches around where I live, I am not riding. I don't like lightning, thunder . . . or hurricanes. And frankly, if the weather dude on TV says that it's going to rain all day long, I'll probably opt for the cage, especially if I have errands to run during or after work.

When I was first starting to ride and was timid about the weather, a more experienced motorcyclist told me, "The only way to learn to ride in the rain is to ride in the rain." True enough.

- Avoid riding for the first half hour or so after the rain starts, particularly if it hasn't rained in a while. That's when the grease, oil, and other yucky stuff in that dark center lane strip rises to the surface and makes the road extremely slick.
- As with a car, you'll need to allow for increased braking distances and, especially if visibility is decreased, try to put more space between you and the vehicle in front.
- Be especially smooth with the throttle, the shifter, and the brakes. Jerky, erratic actions are more prone to cause a loss of traction on wet roads.

Savvy Tip

You are always using eye protection, aren't you? As you might imagine, it's particularly important in the wind. You'll want to be wearing a full-face helmet with the face shield down, or close-fitting, shatter-resistant sunglasses or goggles. (Though if it's really dismal out as well as windy, you may not want dark sunglasses; an MSF instructor I know recommends the yellow-lens "BluBlocker" glasses for heavily overcast days.) And make sure your jacket is zipped up, with the snaps completely fastened, etc. You do not want to contend with the distraction of flapping clothing on top of having to control your motorcycle in windy conditions.

- Are your tires up to wet weather? If they're too worn, the lack of tread can be hazardous to your well-being. And make sure they are inflated to the proper pressure.
- We discussed raingear briefly in chapter 6. It can't hurt to reiterate here: If at all possible, choose a high-viz color, especially if your bike is a low-viz color.
- If your motorcycle's final drive is a belt, make sure it's in decent shape. Rain can cause belt slippage, which results in excessive wear.
- Manhole covers, railroad tracks, bridge gratings, painted road markings, and leaves are all very slippery when wet. Ride with care.

Wind presents its own set of challenges. A motorcycle can be difficult to control when it's windy, especially in strong crosswinds. A tall windshield, for example, can act as a sail, pushing you off balance if you don't know how to compensate. Gusts that catch your arms can interfere with your steering.

Basically, you need to steer your motorcycle into the wind as much as possible, which can require no small amount of effort. In a left crosswind, push forward on the left handgrip to lean the bike to the left. In a right crosswind, push forward on the right handgrip to lean the bike to the right. Should the wind suddenly abate, you may have to do some quick **countersteering** to regain stability.

Riding in the wind, like many things, gets easier with experience. When I first started riding to work, my bridge commute was a white-knuckle trip as often as not; bridges are windy by nature. But it became second-nature after a while. I got used to the way my bike handled, and I became acutely aware of the places where the wind was particularly problematic—for example, exiting the bridge on the west side, where beach areas on both sides of the road provide no windbreak whatsoever—and learned to automatically adjust for it.

Construction Zones

> Every year, thousands of motorcyclists drop their bikes in work zone accidents. But it's hard to find any meaningful statistics about motorcycle accidents and fatalities in work zones. Motorcycles are such a small minority of vehicles on the road that highway departments and contractors don't seem to have much interest in how work zone hazards affect two-wheelers.
>
> —*David Hough,* More Proficient Motorcycling *(p. 75)*

Sand. Loose gravel. Enormous, slow earth-moving machinery. Uneven road surfaces. Detours, flagmen, and confused cagers. Flying dust and dirt. Orange cones that have been knocked down and blown into your lane of travel. What's not to like about construction zones?

Pretty much everything.

But there's usually no avoiding them, particularly if you live in one of those regions of the country with two seasons—winter and road repair. Some things to remember:

- Slow down! Those reduced speed limit signs are there for a reason. A construction zone is dynamic; things change. Even if you travel through that area every day, you can't be sure of what you'll find. Stay safe *and* avoid a ticket—an expensive one, too. "Fines are doubled when workers are present."
- Those steel plates they sometimes use to temporarily cover a hole? They're slippery . . . and they may not cover the entire hole properly.
- David Hough defines an "edge trap" as "the raised edges of bumps or cracks in a paved surface that can catch a motorcycle's tire and cause the bike to lose balance" (*More Proficient Motorcycling,* p. 252). You'll often find these where there are temporary lanes, for example, or where the pavement has been ground down in preparation for new surfacing. Don't try to gradually ease your way over from one side to the other. If you have to cross a raised pavement edge, do it at the greatest possible angle—at least 45 degrees.
- Loose gravel abounds in construction zones, and of course it is hazardous to your traction. Don't be going so fast that it catches you by surprise. If you have to ride through it, slow and steady does the trick. Keep the bike upright, keep the throttle smooth, don't shift gears or brake suddenly.
- It's particularly nasty when a road contractor takes the quick-cheap-dirty route to road resurfacing, putting down a layer of tar and then scattering loose gravel over it, the idea being that passing vehicles will eventually press everything down and seal it up. In the meantime, it makes for poor traction and causes bits of gravel (and tar) to be thrown around, which mars the finish on your bike and can cause injury if you are not wearing full body protection.

- "Tar snakes," those lines of sticky stuff remaining after a quick road patch job, can remain slick for longer than you might think. Likewise, if you spot a dark patch of fresh asphalt that signals a pothole repair, keep in mind that it may still be soft, especially in warm weather.
- A construction zone can be especially hazardous after it rains. You may encounter slippery mud, and what looks like a mere puddle may turn out to be a deep, water-filled pothole.
- If it's an extensive, hazard-filled construction project that is destined to go on indefinitely, you may want to explore alternate routes of travel, even if they are less convenient.

Animals

If you hit a dog or cat in your car, it's sad . . . but you'll almost certainly escape injury or significant vehicle damage. If you hit a dog or a cat while on your motorcycle, you could crash and die. Given that so many people apparently think it is a good idea to let their pets run free, you'll always need to be alert, especially in residential areas.

Dogs, in particular, often enjoy chasing motorcycles. It can be startling at best and frightening at worst to have one take off after you. The danger, of course, has less to do with being bitten and more to do with having the animal get caught in your wheels, bringing you down.

What should you **not** do? Kick out at the dog, since it can destabilize the motorcycle and make it difficult for you to keep control. The MSF recommends slowing down to give the dog the idea that he's almost got you, and when he slows down, rapidly accelerating past him. Since dogs pretty much max out at 30 mph, you should be able to outrun him. Note, however, that most dogs are clever and will actually catch onto this after a while, something to keep in mind if you deal with the same dog on a regular basis.

Cats will not chase you, but they will run into the street in front of you—especially at night, as they tend toward the nocturnal. This is also true of other smallish critters like raccoons and opossums. If you hit one wrong, you could go down, or maybe veer off the road and strike a tree or a guardrail. You need to be aware of those areas where you are most likely to encounter these animals—which have adapted quite nicely to urban environments—and watch accordingly. My own older suburban-type neighborhood is crawling with raccoons, and that is likely true of yours as well.

True story: My regular commute takes me past a nature preserve. When I was riding home one night, an opossum emerged from the brush alongside the road and ran right between the two wheels of my motorcycle to get to the other side. It hit the heel of my boot as it passed beneath the bike. Obviously, this is a species with no survival instincts whatsoever.

The deer population is booming, and deer are a huge problem for motorists as well as motorcyclists. If this were not true, there would not be a need for an organization such as the Deer-Vehicle Crash

Information Clearinghouse (http://deercrash.com), funded by the Wisconsin Department of Transportation, "to find better ways of dealing with the problem of deer-vehicle crashes." A cornucopia of "countermeasures" are discussed here—fencing, repellants, reducing the deer population, etc.—but there doesn't appear to be a good solution. According to the Insurance Institute for Highway Safety (IIHS), fatal crashes involving animals jumped 27 percent from 2002 to 2003. The IIHS notes that "65 percent of those killed riding on motorcycles weren't wearing helmets" (www.hwysafety.org).

Knowing something about deer and their habits can at least serve to heighten your awareness of times and places where you might encounter them. *Motorcycle Cruising* magazine columnist Art Friedman has done some deer-related research (www.motorcyclecruiser.com/streetsurvival/critt ercrashes), and informs us that:

- Deer and other wild animals are designed to be hard to see. Aside from the flickering white tail of some species or reflection from an eye, they simply disappear. However, this absence of reflected light can also tip you off.
- Deer travel in groups. One deer means there are probably more, so even if the one you see is off the road and going away, slow down immediately.
- The Wisconsin DOT says that deer collisions peak in October and November, with a smaller peak in May and June. Such crashes between April and August are most likely to occur between 8 p.m and midnight. Between November and January, 5 to 10 p.m. are the danger times.

Friedman offers some suggestions about getting deer to move—honk your horn, flash your headlights—and strategies you can take to avoid hitting one or to ameliorate the consequences if you do. He also discusses larger animals—buffalo, moose, elk, mountain lion, bear . . . Long story short: You *really* do not want to hit one of these.

DIFFERENT TYPES OF RIDES

Every type of riding environment presents a unique set of challenges. Let's have a look at the pre-eminent ones.

Urban

I learned how to drive in a large city, so I've never been too intimidated by urban riding once I was confident in my ability to handle my bike. But some folks will never, ever venture into city traffic on a motorcycle, and that's OK, too. There are days when I am just not up to it myself. You have to be completely and totally alert, and have your wits about you at all times. As David Hough points out in *Proficient Motorcycling*, "The traveling motorcyclist's greatest hazard—most anywhere in the world—is motor vehicle traffic" (p. 99). And in cities, of course, there is plenty of that. Hough advises motorcyclists to stay out of cities, but knows this caveat is unrealistic.

- Get in the habit of looking way, way out ahead of you. There is a lot going on in the city, and the sooner you spot a potential hazard, the sooner you can start thinking about how to deal with it.
- All of the caveats about intersections, discussed above, apply in spades in the city. Remember that alleys, driveways, parking lot entrances and exits . . . all of these are intersections, in terms of how the motorcyclist should approach them.
- Make sure your collision avoidance skills are up to par. Practice panic stops and swerving. (But never brake and swerve at the same time; choose one evasive maneuver or the other.)
- Try to keep away from large vehicles—trucks, buses, etc. They impede your vision and prevent other motorists from seeing you.
- Be conspicuous in your dress. As we've already noted, yeah, black may look cool, but bright colors enhance your visibility and are more likely to keep you alive.
- Be constantly "reading" other motorists for clues about what they may or may not be ready to do. Body language can be instructive, and you'll certainly want to watch out for those drivers who are distracted by cell phones, food, etc. Keep an eye on the front wheels of vehicles to anticipate sudden left turns.

Suburban

The suburbs are so built up these days that it can be just as bad or worse to ride there as in the city. And the same caveats apply. But there are a few other things to think about:

- In residential areas, you must be alert for free-range children and pets.
- Commuting motorists are often preoccupied with other things besides driving, may be in a particular hurry because they're running late, or may not be paying attention to the road because they're so familiar with the area that they zone out. Be especially vigilant during morning and evening rush hours.
- Many heavily-trafficked suburban roads—mile upon mile of strip malls, "big box" stores, chain restaurants, etc.—have shockingly poor or nonexistent signage. As a result, you'll encounter drivers creeping along looking for a particular address, drivers making sudden lane shifts or turns because what they want is on the other side of the road, and drivers making (often illegal) U-turns because they've inadvertently driven past wherever it was they were headed.

- Cars parked along the curb on side streets may suddenly pull out in front of you, or the driver may throw open the door without looking. Watch for heads in those parked vehicles and/or indications that the vehicle is sitting there idling for some reason.

Rural

Many motorcyclists are really only comfortable riding in lightly trafficked rural areas; some will transport their bikes there to avoid riding in city and/or suburban traffic. And even the most hardened urban warrior will likely choose a more bucolic or scenic environment when he or she is riding for recreation. (See a vintage World War II rural warrior in figure 7-3.) The sport bike crowd in particular is much happier in the **twisties** than, say, going up and down the rows, looking for a parking space at a shopping mall. When we plan a motorcycle vacation, most of us prefer to minimize urban riding. But rural and scenic areas have their own set of challenges:

- Where there are farms, there may be livestock escapees wandering the road. You really don't want to come zipping around that blind curve and have a full-grown black-and-white cow be the last thing you ever see.
- Ditto for slow-moving farm machinery. (And make sure you have a clear view way up ahead before you decide to pass one of these things on a narrow, two-lane road.)
- "Interesting" things may be on the road—grain, cow pies, fuel or oil that has leaked from a tractor, etc. And fallen rocks in mountainous areas.

If you're in a scenic area that happens to be a popular tourist location, watch out for drivers who are

Fig.7-3: This soldier, participating in war games at Ft. Knox, Ky., during World World II, did not have to cope with some of the hazards you and I are likely to encounter today when out riding in the country. Photographer: Alfred T. Palmer, June 1943. Library of Congress, Prints & Photographs Division, FSA/OWI Collection, LC-USE6-D-006155.

more interested in sightseeing than in paying attention to the road. You'll also encounter motorhomes, trailers, campers, etc., being driven or towed by people who really don't have a great deal of experience doing this. (True story: A military retiree came up to my desk at the base library and asked if we had any books that would show him how to tow a trailer—how to park, back up, etc. Scary. You're a nice man—and thank you for serving our country—but I don't think I want to share the road with you and your trailer.)

The Superslabs

When I first began riding, I was scared to death of the freeways. I found them even more frightening than riding in traffic. Statistically, however, you are less likely to die riding your bike on the freeway than almost anywhere else. For one thing, with the exception of the occasional impaired motorist, all the traffic is headed in the same direction on your side of the divided highway. And since these are "limited access" roads, you won't be faced with the number one cause of motorcycle accidents—drivers turning left in front of you. Unless you are in a construction zone, the road is wide, smooth, and gently graded, with no sharp curves. And unless it's a freeway in an urban area, there's usually no traffic congestion.

All of that being said, things move much faster on the freeway, which means bad things can happen much faster on the freeway. And when bad things happen at 75 mph, the end result is almost always very ugly. When the traffic is moving that fast, you need to be scanning for problems that much farther ahead—and not be riding so fast that you don't have time to react if, say, another vehicle suddenly moves into your lane up ahead.

Getting on and getting off the freeway are the most dangerous parts of **superslab** riding. Entrance and exit ramps often involve negotiating sharp curves. Because you can only lean your motorcycle over so far, you may have to proceed more slowly than you would in a car—and the impatient motorist behind you may try to pass you. And fluids from other vehicles often build up on these ramps, as drivers are slowing down, so they can be very slick. Merging into high-speed traffic is a challenge requiring good eyes and a lot of moxie; the average street motorcycle is more than up to the task when it comes to acceleration. But get your speed under control quickly when leaving the freeway; if you take one of those sharp turns a little too fast, you could easily run right off the road.

True story: A friend who is an experienced and very skillful rider had his first and only accident on a freeway on-ramp. The car in front of him stopped short, apparently having decided there wasn't enough room to merge into traffic. My friend managed to stop short as well. But the driver behind him wasn't paying attention and ran into him from behind. End result: a broken leg, ongoing back

Savvy Tip
What in the world do you do if your tire blows out when you're flying down the highway? Well, if your bike has tubeless tires, the odds of this happening are very small—but it's not impossible. If a blowout does occur, the Motorcycle Safety Foundation advises keeping a firm hold on the handgrips and not fighting any wobble or weave. You should not brake or downshift until your speed is under control, but if you must brake, use the brake on the good tire. In other words, if your front wheel blows out, use the rear brake pedal. According to the MSF, the most common reason for a blowout is riding with the tire pressure too low, which is why you are supposed to check your tires regularly and keep them inflated to the manufacturer-suggested pressures.

---

problems . . . and a totaled motorcycle. Fortunately, the driver wasn't moving that fast or it could have been much worse.

Other things to know about the superslabs:

- As soon you merge onto the highway, get out of the right lane as soon as possible. You don't want to be close to where people are getting on and off. Be especially wary of the daydreaming motorist who suddenly realizes that he or she is about to drive by their desired exit, so he or she suddenly darts across three or four lanes of fast-moving traffic in order to get there.

- You are probably safest in the extreme left-hand lane, even though it's usually the fastest lane. For one thing, you've immediately eliminated the need to concern yourself with traffic problems on one complete side of you.

- When changing lanes on freeways where there are three or more lanes, be especially careful that someone in another lane—or the driver behind you—doesn't have exactly the same intention.

- Always use your turn signal to let other drivers know when you want to change lanes, and turn it on well in advance of your exit ramp so other drivers will be aware that you will be slowing down, but never assume it is being seen by other motorists.

- For some reason, vehicles tend to travel in packs on the freeway. If at all possible, avoid the crowd by either backing off a bit or riding a bit faster to place yourself where you'll have a better space cushion.

- Regularly scan your mirrors to see what is going on behind you. You can usually spot the aggressive or otherwise troublesome driver in advance, and plan on how you will avoid a problem with that particular vehicle.

HEALTH ISSUES

Eyes

You can be in denial for a long time about the fact that your eyes are not what they used to be. I certainly was. Having been blessed with excellent vision my entire life, I was not prepared to accept the changes that come with the passage of time. At first, when books, magazines, newspapers, etc., started looking Not So Sharp, I blamed it on shoddy typography and slipshod printing jobs. Then I got to the stage where I was willing to admit that the problem was with my eyes—went out and bought my first pair of reading glasses—but of course it had nothing to do with aging. *My* eyesight was deteriorating because *I* spent too much time staring at computer screens.

At this point, I've more or less come to terms with the fact that I cannot read without glasses. I have a large and varied collection of reading glasses, and I keep at least one pair stashed in each room. I have several pairs in my office, and I frequently lend them out to my customers who are having trouble reading the phone book or the dictionary and have left their own glasses at home.

Maps are a problem. In the car, when I have number two son with me, I don't worry much about it. He's a living, breathing GPS system who loves maps and has been able to read them proficiently since the age of three. On the motorcycle, by myself, well, I have to pull over, fish a pair of reading glasses out of my pocket or one of the side bags, raise my face shield, take off my sunglasses, put on the reading glasses . . . you get the picture. And it's a blurry one.

Maps aside, what do you do when your eyes have gotten to the point where you can no longer read the smaller gauges on your motorcycle?

Actually, I did find something that helps. And unlike so many things connected with motorcycling, it's cheap. "Cheaters," distributed by LessLight Inc., are wrap-around riding glasses with built-in bifocal reading lenses. They come in powers from 1 to 2.5, in half-power increments, and you can buy them as sunglasses, or with clear lenses for nighttime riding. At only $15 a pair, you can afford one of each. See figure 7-4.

Yet another thing that happens to many of us as our eyes age is that we no longer see as well at night as we used to. I sorta don't think I'm here yet, and my distance vision is still good. But if you know that this is an issue for you, think twice about riding at night. If you've never thought much about this, it's probably a good idea to schedule yourself for a thorough eye exam. If you already wear glasses on a regular basis, make sure that your frames do not interfere with your peripheral vision. You may want new frames—and possibly new lenses, if your current lenses do not conform to ANSI standards for safety glasses. Check with an optical professional.

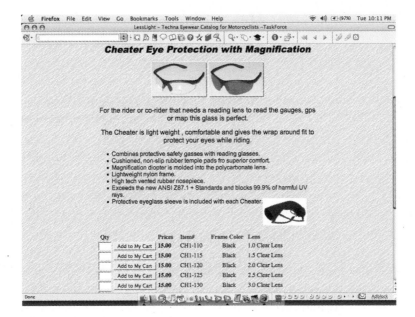

Fig. 7-4: Cheaters, distributed by LessLight, Inc., are riding glasses with built-in bifocal lenses. Even the ones with clear lenses block 100 percent of UV radiation, and their wrap-around design will protect your eyes from the wind, dust, bugs, gravel and other debris. Lightweight and flexible, each pair comes with a neoprene protective sleeve that has a clip you can fasten to your belt. Only $15 a pair—such a deal; www.lesslight.com.

The Motorcycle Safety Foundation offers additional tips for older motorcyclists. See the "Tips for Older Motorcyclists" sidebar.

Ears

While some motorcyclists insist that "loud pipes save lives," those high-decibel exhaust systems certainly will not enhance the long-term prospects for your hearing. Many of us are already starting to cope with hearing problems before we even take up motorcycling. We liked . . . and may still like . . . loud music. All those rock concerts where we sat next to humongous speakers. All those hours cruising around in cars with the sound system volume cranked up to the max. Hearing specialists are seeing younger and younger people who are starting to lose the ability to make out sounds that are in particularly high or low ranges.

A friend who took her elderly father to an audiologist for a hearing test told me that the man blamed the beginning of hearing problems in the relatively young on the invention of the Sony Walkman—

TIPS FOR OLDER RIDERS FROM THE MOTORCYCLE SAFETY FOUNDATION

- Get eyes checked. Vision clarity and peripheral vision diminish with age.

- Keep a greater following distance. Reacting to a hazard may take twice as long for a rider age 40 to 54, and three or four times longer after 55.

- Avoid complicated and congested roads. Input overload makes it difficult to process information accurately.

- Pay special attention to blind spots. Traffic research shows that older drivers do not check blind spots as well as younger drivers.

- Keep fit. Riding a motorcycle can be physically demanding, and without training, people begin losing muscle mass starting around age 30.

---

people walking around with headphones or earphones on, the volume cranked up to full-tilt boogie. And now, of course, we are walking around, or riding public transit, or exercising while plugged into our iPods.

Most of the serious motorcyclists I know regularly wear some form of ear protection. Frankly, it's the wind noise rather than the rumbling from the exhaust system that will do in your hearing. Some folks have good luck with the cheap, disposable foam plugs you can buy in the drugstore. I've never quite gotten the knack of using those; I think my ear canals may be too narrow. You can go top-of-the-line and get yourself a pair of custom-molded ear plugs; I saw someone offering these at a booth at a motorcycle rally for about $45.

Aerostich Rider Wearhouse offers a sampler set of ten different pairs of reusable earplugs for $25. (See figure 7.5.) I bought these, and I'm still trying out different styles. Haven't found nirvana yet. For those who prefer disposable earplugs, Aerostich offers a sampler set of 12 pair for $10.

If you're not used to ear protection—and most of us don't have the sort of job or avocation where this is necessary—they take some getting used to. I was initially afraid I would not be able to hear traffic noises, but that hasn't been the case. I also had to adjust to the muted sound of my own engine; I've always relied on the sound of the engine to let me know when to shift gears—even in a car with manual transmission, before I started riding a motorcycle regularly. With earplugs, the sounds are still there, but they are "different." After a while, they will become "normal."

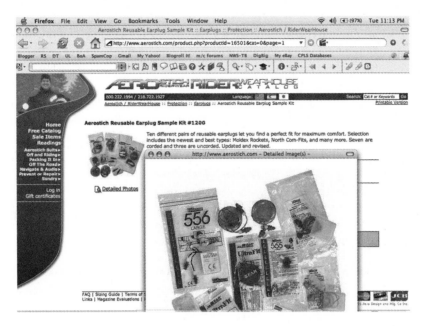

Fig. 7-5: Aerostich Rider Wearhouse offers relatively inexpensive sampler sets of both disposable and reusable earplugs. With any luck, you'll find a pair that works for you. Warning: the Aerostich catalog can be hazardous to your wealth. They sell high-end street rider clothing and touring accessories, and way too many other things that you "need," including inflatable rubber snakes for camping pranks. It's a very cool wish book and the writing is witty. Order one at their Web site, www.aerostich.com. Click on "Free Catalog" and wait with one hand on your wallet till it arrives.

University of Florida researchers cranked up 33 different motorcycles to full throttle and found that "they produced noise levels above 100 decibels—the equivalent of a loud rock concert or chainsaw." According to the National Institute for Occupational Safety and Health, exposure to noise levels of 100 decibels is safe for only 15 minutes, and prolonged exposure to noise levels of 85 decibels can cause permanent hearing loss. Motorcycle helmets do not provide much noise protection, but the use of cheap foam earplugs can reduce the noise level to 20–25 decibels. "A ringing sound in the ears immediately after exposure and muffled hearing are warning signs of noise-induced hearing loss, which is permanent" (www.healthfinder.gov/news/newsstory.asp?docID=52017).

The Impaired Motorcyclist

When we hear that someone is "impaired"—behind the wheel of a car or sitting astride a motorcycle—we immediately think "booze." And for good reason; alcohol is ubiquitous in this society and inextricably linked, for better or for worse, with "having a good time." And there is no denying its role in motorcycle culture—cruising from bar to bar as a recreational activity, hanging out at taverns on "bike nights," **poker runs**, where each stop along the route is at a pub . . .

I'm not your mother and I'm not in a position to take away the key to your bike if you've had one too many. Just let me point out that the first things to go after you start drinking are your alertness, judgment, coordination, and vision—all of which you desperately need to be in top-notch condition when you ride a motorcycle. (See table 7.1 for a take on the progressive effects of alcohol.) And let me remind you that, according to the National Highway Traffic Safety Administration, 40 percent of fatally injured motorcycle operators in 2003 tested positive for alcohol; 32 percent had a blood alcohol level of .08 or higher (www-nrd.nhtsa.dot.gov/pdf/nrd-30/NCSA/RNotes/2004/809-734/images/TSF-CrashStats.pdf).

Cruising and boozing—and dying—used to be done mostly by "stupid young kids." But times have changed. Now it's stupid middle-age baby boomers who are drinking and riding—and dying. According to the Center for Disease Control and Prevention's cheerfully titled newsletter, *Morbidity and Mortality Weekly Report* ("Trends in Motorcycle Fatalities Associated with Alcohol-Impaired Driving—United States, 1983–2003," December 3, 2004), "Among alcohol-impaired motorcycle drivers, the mortality rate was highest among persons aged 20–24 years in 1983 and among persons aged 40–44 years in 2003. In 1983, 8.2 percent of alcohol-impaired fatally injured motorcycle drivers were aged 40-plus years; by 2003, 48.2 percent of such drivers were in this age group." In its analysis, the MMWR noted:

> Mortality rates might be increasing among motorcycle drivers aged >40 years, not only because more persons in this age group are riding motorcycles, but also because older motorcycle drivers might now be more likely to consume alcohol before driving than younger motorcycle drivers. Older drivers might be more likely than younger drivers to limit their riding to recreational trips on weekends under circumstances that might involve alcohol consumption.

It's probably not necessary to discuss why you would not want to hop on a motorcycle after ingesting illegal substances like marijuana, cocaine, or whatever scary drug is currently leaving its mark on the "club scene," etc. But you can be just as quickly done in by what your own doctor is prescribing for you—or even that box of over-the-counter allergy capsules that you picked up at the local phar-

Table 7-1: The Progressive Effects of Alcohol

Blood Alcohol Concentration	Changes in Feelings and Personality	Brain Regions Affected	Impaired Activities (continuum)
0.01–0.05	Relaxation Sense of well-being Loss of inhibition	Cerebral cortex	Alertness Judgment Coordination (esp.
0.06–0.10	Pleasure Numbness of feelings Nausea, sleepiness Emotional arousal	Cerebral cortex + forebrain	fine motor skills) Visual tracking Reasoning and depth perception
0.11–0.20	Mood swings Anger Sadness Mania	Cerebral cortex + forebrain + cerebellum	Inappropriate social behavior (e.g., obnoxiousness) Slurred speech
0.21–0.30	Aggression Reduced sensations Depression Stupor	Cerebral cortex + forebrain + cerebellum + brain stem	Lack of balance Loss of temperature regulation Loss of bladder
0.31–0.40	Unconsciousness Death possible Coma	Entire brain	control Difficulty breathing Slowed heart rate
0.41 and greater	Death		

Source: National Institutes of Health, National Institute on Alcohol Abuse and Alcoholism, http://science-education.nih.gov.

macy. Did you ever really *look* at the fine print on some of those boxes . . . or bother to read the stickers the pharmacist attached to that bottle of pills?

- May cause drowsiness or dizziness.
- This drug may impair the ability to drive or operate machinery.
- When using this product, avoid alcoholic beverages.

Be especially careful if you're taking something you've never taken before, since you don't know how your body will react. According to a National Safety Council publication from September 2004

> **Savvy Tip**
>
> It seems that a week cannot pass without yet another story in the local press about an injury or death due to "road rage." This is an emotion you absolutely cannot afford to give in to when you are riding a motorcycle. You are just about the smallest thing out there and you are vulnerable. As a friend who has been riding a lot longer than I have once told me, "You can't occupy the same place in the time-space continuum as another vehicle. If you try, you're going to lose. Badly."

(www.nsc.org/issues/drugimpaireddriving), 37 states and Washington, D.C., currently have laws on the books against drug-impaired driving. It's a growing problem; as the population as a whole is aging, more prescription and nonprescription drugs are being ingested. If you think this may be an issue for you, talk to your pharmacist or health care provider. There may be alternatives to something you're currently taking that is causing reduced alertness, or maybe just taking it at a different time of the day—for example, before bed—could make a difference.

While drugs and alcohol are the most obvious causes of impairment and get the most attention, there are other insidious things that can be equally deleterious to your ability to operate a motorcycle, like not getting enough sleep—or taking sleeping medication before you go to bed and finding that when you get up in the morning, it hasn't quite worn off and you are groggy. Or you feel like you "might be coming down with something."

The MSF (www.msf-usa.org/CurriculumMaterials/BRCRiderHndbk_2005v6.pdf) points out that your own emotions can get in the way of a safe ride; "feeling angry, troubled or stressed" can rob you of the concentration you need to operate a motorcycle on the busy public streets. Are you anticipating a rotten day at work? Did you have a breakfast table argument with your significant other? Did your child bring home an abysmal report card? Maybe it's a good idea *not* to ride.

8 YOU BROUGHT IT HOME, YOU TAKE CARE OF IT

◆ Adjustment phase

◆ Pre-ride checkout

◆ Stuff you gotta know

◆ The winter of our discontent, the spring of our hope

◆ Kaona—Keeping it clean

If you're settling in to read this chapter so you can learn about motorcycle maintenance and repair, stop right here. Flip to the bibliography in the back of the book, where you'll find several excellent titles that can provide detailed information.

For some people, working on their bikes is part of the total motorcycling experience. (See figure 8-1.) Then there are the rest of us . . . who'd rather be riding than wrenching (and wouldn't feel particularly secure riding a bike that we've wrenched on ourselves). Heck, on the bike I have now, I can't even change the oil by myself because you have to drop the exhaust pipes to get to the oil filter.

No, thank you. I sucked it up, opted for the extended warranty and prepaid all the scheduled maintenance when I bought the thing, and so the service department at the dealership changes the oil . . . and does all the other stuff I can't even imagine doing—valve adjustments and whatnot. They have tools and trained technicians. I have . . . no illusions about my lack of mechanical ability.

Not that such things are gender-linked in any way, shape, or form. As you will see, when you meet the Wrench Wench later in this chapter.

Fig. 8-1: "Sneezy," my friend Rick Emerson's bike, spends a fair amount of time in various states of repair in Rick's garage. A 1981 Honda CB900, Sneezy needs a lot of TLC. Fortunately, Rick is knowledgeable enough that he doesn't have to outsource the work. Motorcycle labor around where I live is roughly $70 an hour. Ouch!

All of that being said, you can't allow yourself the luxury of complete ignorance about how your motorcycle works . . . and what it needs to keep running safely and well. If the tire pressure gets too low, you could have a blowout. If you don't change the oil on a regular schedule, you could ruin your engine. Light bulbs burn out and fuses blow. Spark plugs get gummed up. Brakes wear out. Chains—if your bike has one—need lubrication and maintenance. And if something works its way loose and starts vibrating, it's not going to suddenly tighten up on its own. You really, really don't want to be riding down the highway and have parts flying off your motorcycle.

ADJUSTMENT PHASE

Any new relationship has some awkward moments, but they can be lethal if they happen on a motorcycle in traffic.

—Art Friedman

The epigraph is from Art Friedman, "Skills Exercises to Familiarize Yourself with a New Motorcycle," *Motorcycle Cruiser,* June 1999, www.motorcyclecruiser.com/streetsurvival/familiarize.

Well, you got it home. Whether you rode it, hauled it, or had it delivered, it's now part of your life . . . and your responsibility. If it's a brand-new machine, you probably didn't even get to take it for a test ride before you laid your money down; most dealers don't allow this, presumably for liability reasons. If you bought used, you may have been able to take it out for a spin, and you may even have had it checked over by a mechanic or a knowledgeable friend. But it's still a new-to-you bike, and even if you've been riding for a while, you're dealing with a whole 'nother kettle of fish in terms of feel and handling. Which is why, as Art Friedman points out, in the article from which the quote at the beginning of this section was taken, "Riders are more likely to crash a new motorcycle than the old familiar one." If your riding experience is really limited, the situation becomes even more precarious.

In his article, Friedman recommends that you "accelerate the familiarization process" by taking the Motorcycle Safety Foundation's Experienced Riders Course (ERC). However, if you haven't been riding all that long—maybe not at all since you took the MSF's Basic Rider Course—you're not ready for the ERC. Captain Glenn Tussing (this book's technical editor), who is an MSF instructor for the Air Force, recommends that you spend a minimum of six months or 3,000 miles on a new (or new-to-you) bike before taking the ERC. You may want to find a local MSF instructor to speak with about this.

Friedman recommends slow speed exercises—you do get a lot of that in the ERC—to familiarize yourself with a new bike. Try some tight circles and figure-eights in an empty parking lot and get a feel for the bike's **friction zone**, center of gravity, and steering sensitivity. Try cornering at different speeds and lean angles. And don't forget panic stops; you want to get a feel for those brakes, especially if you've moved to something completely different, like **ABS**.

For a good set of practice exercises, check out Jerry Paladino's Ride Like a Pro Web site (figure 8-2). Paladino is a "motorman" in Pasco County, Florida, with many years of riding experience. His Ride Like a Pro video series (see bibliography) draws on motor officer training to teach precision riding techniques—notably, the type of slow-speed maneuvers that tend to be difficult for novice motorcyclists. You'll see men and women just like you doing cone weaves, and tight figure-eights and U-turns—sometimes on enormous, heavy cruisers. Don't miss Paladino's wife, Dr. Donna, on her tricked-out Honda VTX. We should all look this good in leathers.

Breaking in a new motorcycle is an ongoing subject of debate in the online world (and probably offline as well.) Basically, most recommend taking it easy at first. The owner's manual for my V-Star says:

> Since the engine is brand new, do not put an excessive load on it for the first 1,600 km (1,000 mi). The various parts in the engine wear and polish themselves to the correct oper-

Fig. 8-2: Learn to "Ride Like a Pro" from motorman Jerry Paladino. A practice guide on his Web site offers an excellent set of exercises to familiarize yourself with a new bike . . . or brush up your techniques. You can also read motorcycling articles written by Paladino, and browse through a lot of interesting pictures. I own a couple of these DVDs and they are worthwhile; Captain Tussing borrowed them and hasn't given them back yet. (Hint, hint . . .) Visit www.ridel ikeapro.com.

ating clearances. During this period, prolonged full throttle operation or any condition that might result in engine overheating must be avoided.

Yamaha advises, "Avoid prolonged operation above one-third throttle" for the first 600 miles, and "avoid prolonged operation above one-half throttle" for the next 400 miles.

On the other hand, Pat McGivern, who calls himself "MotoMan," recommends in a *Power News* article that you "run it hard" so that the piston rings will fully seal (www.mototuneusa.com/break_in_secrets.htm). There are a lot of links to this article around the Web, so MotoMan (who warns you right up front, "This is a very controversial topic!!") apparently does have a following. (I'll warn you right up front that this page gets rather geeky, in a gearhead sort of way.)

My gut feeling is that you're better off going with what the manufacturer recommends, but if this is a topic of great interest to you, there's plenty of fodder for debate on the Web. Do a Google search for "break in motorcycle" or "breaking in motorcycle".

Savvy Tip

When you buy a new motorcycle, it comes with an owner's manual—sometimes referred to as MOM (for Motorcycle Owner's Manual). You'll want to read this thing cover to cover and keep it close at hand for reference. If you buy a used motorcycle, even from a dealer, you may not get an owner's manual, which is a very useful thing to have. Sometimes, if you go to the manufacturer's Web site, you can find owner's manuals for the different models online—dating back several years, if you're lucky. They also turn up for sale on eBay Motors. If worse comes to worst, you may be able to find somebody in an enthusiasts' group online who owns one and is willing to make a copy for you.

PRE-RIDE CHECKOUT

If it's a new bike—or even a used bike you bought from a dealership—you kind of cross your fingers and hope that the service department has checked it out thoroughly before you leave the premises with it. However, if you're a novice at this sort of thing, you may want to do whatever it takes—beg, plead, whine, offer a bribe—to get a knowledgeable friend to go with you so you can make your own inspection. (See figure 8-3.) It's not that you can't take it back to be fixed if something is not right after you get it home—you've probably got a warranty of some sort, and any reputable dealership will take care of a problem with something you just bought there (unless, possibly, it's an older bike that was sold as-is). It's just that if something is really wrong, you may not get the bike home at all. If you're lucky, you'll only get stranded. If you're unlucky, well . . . let's not go there.

STUFF YOU GOTTA KNOW

Now that this bike is a member of your family, you are responsible for its well-being. If you take care of it, it will take care of you. Ideally, you will perform a pre-ride check that covers all major parts and systems before every ride. The Motorcycle Safety Foundation uses the acronym T-CLOCKS to help you remember what you need to look at during a pre-ride inspection. See figure 8-4. Your owner's manual may provide information on how to do these various checks; in my manual, there is a "Pre-Operation Checks" chart with a list of items to inspect, along with the page numbers in the manual where you can read about each thing.

Dino Juice or . . .

What kind of gasoline does your bike need? Most use regular grade but a fair number of models require high-octane premium. Your owner's manual will tell you; in the absence of one, check with

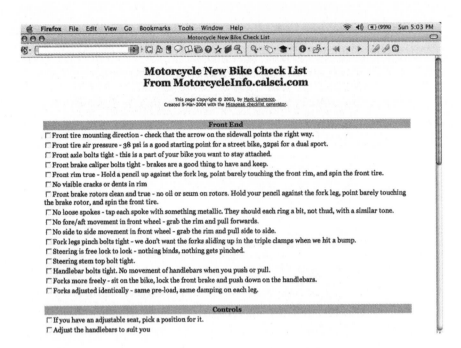

Fig. 8-3: There are a zillion things to check out on a new bike before you leave the dealership with it. You probably don't even know what a lot of this stuff is, which is why you really want to take the iconic "knowledge-able friend" along. http://motorcycleinfo.calsci.com/NewBikeList.html.

the dealership. One anal-retentive BMW owner I know, whose bike requires premium, will not purchase gas from any station where all three grades are dispensed through a single hose, his reasoning being that the last person to use the pump probably bought regular, which means there is still regular left in the hose that will end up in his gas tank before the premium starts flowing. He may have a point; motorcycle gas tanks are much smaller than automobile gas tanks, so any remaining regular gas in the line represents a larger percentage of what he puts into his bike. The subject of "gas pump dilution" has been discussed in *Motorcycle Consumer News* and probably elsewhere. The consensus seems to be that if your bike does require high-octane fuel, you probably *should* avoid gas stations with single-hose pumps. So anal retention is relative, I guess.

You probably change the oil in your car regularly. Your bike deserves at least the same consideration, no? You want its engine to have a long, trouble-free life. Your owner's manual will tell you what kind of oil you need—and how much. Many motorcyclists change the oil in their bikes more frequently than the interval recommended by the manufacturer. Generally speaking, you should use motorcycle-specific oil; some of the additives in many regular automobile oils are not good for your bike.

Should you use synthetic oil or should use you use dino juice—regular, out-of-the-ground "mineral"

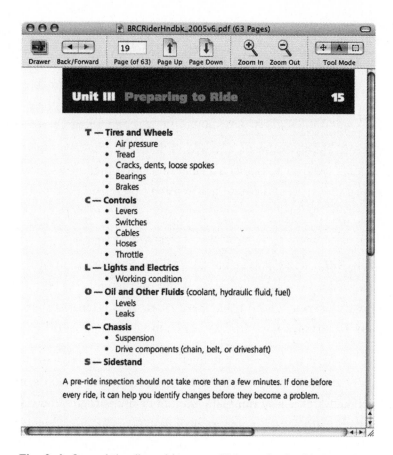

Fig. 8-4: One of the first things you'll learn in the Motorcycle Safety Foundation's Basic Rider Course is the recommended T-CLOCKS pre-ride inspection. www.msf-usa.org/Curriculu mMaterials/BRCRiderHndbk_2005v6.pdf (page 19).

oil from decomposed dinosaurs? Here's another topic that gets debated frequently. Synthetic oils are more expensive, but they are said to hold up better in high-stress conditions such as extreme heat, hard use, and extended periods between oil changes. Some riders feel that higher-end mineral-based oils do just as well, and certainly for a bike ridden regularly under normal conditions, dino juice will do just fine, especially if you are diligent about changing it. You should, of course, use synthetic oil if the manufacturer recommends it, but unless specified otherwise, it's usually recommended that you break the engine in on mineral oil so that the piston rings seal properly.

Where the Rubber Meets the Road

Tires on a motorcycle are a bigger deal than tires on a car, at least in terms of the attention you'll give them. The major reason, of course, is that a motorcycle only has two wheels. If a tire on your

If you're changing your own oil, make sure you warm up the engine first. The oil will be less viscous and will drain out more readily, but be careful not to burn yourself on the oil or on hot engine components. Your owner's manual will tell you where to find the drain plug and the oil filter if it is not immediately obvious. The location of these items has a direct effect on how difficult of a job this is. (Most filters simply screw on and off.) I had no trouble changing the oil and the filter on my Suzuki Savage because they were readily accessible. On the V-Star, as I mentioned earlier in this chapter, you have to drop the exhaust pipes to get to the oil filter and that is something I prefer not to tackle.

---

car wears out, blows out, or goes flat, you've got three others and you can probably get control of the situation and bring the vehicle to a stop without getting into trouble. On a motorcycle, if one of the tires goes, you're left with just one . . . and that ain't good. This is another situation where Very Bad Things can happen. Quite literally, your life depends on your tires. And that is why I will go on at some length here.

You're concerned mainly about three things with tires: air pressure, tread depth, and general condition. When your bike is new, or if you've bought a new set of tires for an older bike, you probably won't have to worry about the condition of the tread for a while. (You will have to worry about traction, however, as brand-new tires need to be ridden on very carefully for the first hundred miles or so until they are "scuffed in.") But you'll want to keep tabs on the general condition; anyone can run over a nail or glass, something could fly up from the road and damage the sidewall . . . you get the picture.

You can check your tires over when you check their pressure, which you should do frequently. Motorcycle tires are subject to a lot more stress than car tires, and improper inflation takes a great toll on them. If your tires are chronically underinflated, you'll be dealing with increased instability, sluggish handling, and the possibility of sudden blowout. If your tires are overinflated, you'll have less traction and they will wear out faster. I use one of those cheap, pencil-type gauges to check my tire pressure; Captain Tussing—another anal-retentive BMW owner—shelled out for the nifty gizmo from Brookstone in figure 8-5.

There is one gas station convenient to my house that actually offers free air. It is a great place to meet other motorcyclists on Sunday mornings, as everyone seems to know about this place and everyone has the time and inclination to check their tire pressure on the weekends.

How long do motorcycle tires last? It's hard to say, since it's so dependent on your bike, your riding style, the conditions in which you ride—and the quality of the tires to begin with. From what I can gather, they last a lot longer than they used to; the technology has gotten much better. Figure 10,000

Fig. 8-5: Here's a slick twist on the standard, cheap, boring tire pressure gauge. This gadget has a bleeder valve so that if you overfill, you can easily release some of the excess air.

miles or maybe 15,000 if you are lucky, but I've had some riders tell me they've never gotten more than 8,000 miles out of any set of tires.

It's not hard to see when a tire's tread is getting thin, and its colored "wear bars" will let you know when a tire is really circling the drain. But it may well be on its way around the bend before that, depending on the pattern of wear it has gotten. For example, tires on cruisers typically wear out faster in the center since their relatively low ground clearance means they don't lean over as far in curves as other types of bikes.

I've also heard that you should replace any tire that is three years old or older. Even if the tires have not been used that much, the sidewalls deteriorate—potentially a dangerous condition—and the rubber hardens up, so they are less pliable and you get less traction. How do you tell when your tires were made? Check the code on the sidewall—a string of numbers starting with DOT (and you know what that stands for—your tax dollars at work). For tires manufactured in the year 2000 or later, the last four digits tell the story—the week and the year of manufacture. For example, if the code is DOT817AD472503, that tire was made in the 25th week of the year 2003.

Motorcycle tires come in two basic flavors—tube and tubeless. The tubeless ones are a little safer, as tires with tubes will blow out if punctured. If your bike has spoked wheels—many cruisers do—it's almost certainly got tube-type tires, which keep air from leaking out from around the ends of the spokes. Bikes with solid or cast wheels are usually fitted with tubeless tires.

Should you patch or plug a punctured tire or should you just go ahead and replace it? Depends on whom you ask. Personally, the thought of riding on a patched or plugged tire makes me kind of uncomfortable; my bike has tires with tubes. But Captain Tussing—who is certainly no daredevil—has plugged one of the tubeless tires on his touring Beemer using a kit like the one in figure 8-6.

Replacing a motorcycle tire, by the way, is one of those jobs that is not for the faint of heart. Specialized tools make it easier, but it's still an ordeal if you're inexperienced and fairly aggravating even if you know what you're doing. Also, you'll need to take it to a dealer or other service facility anyhow to get it balanced—highly recommended for even wear—since I'm fairly sure that no one reading this book has a tire balancer at home in the garage. But if you want to see what's involved, check out *Dan's Online Motorcycle Repair Course: Tires and Tubes* (www.dansmc.com/tires1.htm). Not only is there a lot of wrench-head stuff at this site, but Dan is also a taxidermist and he can teach you how to do that online, too. You gotta love the Internet …

More advice about motorcycle tires:

- Remember that your recommended front and rear tire pressures will be higher when you are carrying a passenger and/or cargo.
- It's often not easy to check the condition of the tires on a cruiser. Few have centerstands, and many have fenders, extended exhaust pipes, and other things that make it difficult to see the tires. If you don't have your own workstand to keep the motorcycle upright while you turn the tires, you may have to get a friend or neighbor to roll the bike while you check out the sidewalls and the tread.

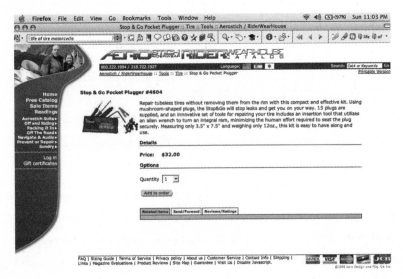

Fig. 8-6: Aerostich and other vendors sell kits like this that you can use to plug a leaking tire . . . which may or may not be a good idea. If nothing else, it may buy you time to get to wherever you need to go to replace the tire. www.aerostich.com

- Make sure to replace the valve caps after putting air in your tires or you're going to have a slow leak. Keep them from disappearing in the first place by putting them in a safe place like your pocket when you're using an air station.
- Keep the tires clean with soap and water only. Certain "protectants" may cause them to deteriorate faster than normal. Be sure to wipe off any gas, oil, or other deleterious fluids that drip onto the tires.
- Don't mix and match—mount two different types of tires on your bike at the same time. Make sure they are both either tube or tubeless, radial or bias ply. And if you have tires with tubes, don't cheap out; make sure you replace the tubes as well as the tires.

Bright Lights, Dead Battery

Unless you really know what you're doing, you should probably not be messing around with the electrical system on your bike. (See figure 8-7.) Even installing accessories that come with clear instructions—a light bar, heated handgrips, etc.—can be dicey, since it's very easy to overload the electrical system and start blowing fuses. The owner's manual for my V-Star warns, "Use caution when adding electrical accessories. If electrical accessories exceed the capacity of the motorcycle's electrical system, an electric failure could result, which could cause a dangerous loss of lights or engine power."

The good news is that there are really only five basic electrical problems: no circuit, short circuit, an absence of power, too much power, or a component that's gone bad. The bad news is, they manifest themselves in similar ways, and if you're unfamiliar with electrical system troubleshooting—if you don't know your way around a wiring diagram or don't possess the equipment you need—you're looking at an exercise in frustration.

Not that you can't try some simple things. If you know where your fuse box is—check the owner's manual—you can at least check to see if there is a blown fuse, replace it, and see if blows out again, which would indicate a more complicated problem. If the headlight, taillight, or turn indicator lights are out, replace the bulb with an identical one. It could be an easy fix.

And then there are battery problems. Most new motorcycles today come with sealed batteries that require zero maintenance. If you have an older bike that needs a battery replacement, the extra money you spend for a sealed battery is worth it.

That being said, you do need to know where your battery is; it's not always obvious from looking at the bike. Check the owner's manual. Even no-maintenance batteries can run down—say, if you don't turn the ignition key all the way off and your lights stay on for an extended period. (Don't ask me how I know this.) Also, if the bike sits idle for an extended period of time, the battery can lose its charge.

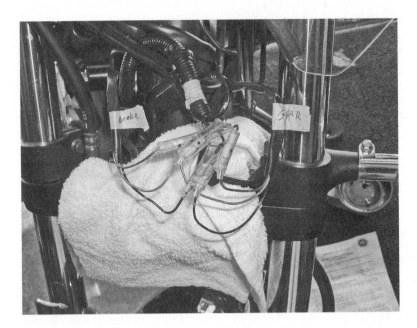

Fig. 8-7: It's good to have a knowledgeable person who is at least somewhat anal retentive doing work on your bike's electrical system. Captain Tussing installed the light bar on my bike and relocated the rear turn signals to accommodate my hard bags. Note how the wires are labeled.

True story: I rode to work one day and, as I was parking, taking off my helmet, gathering up my stuff, a colleague walked over and engaged me in a conversation. Since I don't multitask well, I neglected to turn the ignition key to the Off position and left the bike sitting there with its lights on. When I came out later to try and start it—nada. If you've done this with your car, you have some idea of what an awful feeling it is. Fortunately, I work on a military base, and assistance of some type is usually available. I got on the phone and hollered for Captain Tussing, figuring he could help me jump start the bike. When he arrived, he looked at the key in the ignition and said, "Have you tried turning it completely off, and then turning it back on and trying to start it up again?" I shook my head and did what he suggested. Lo and behold, the bike came to life! Apparently—with most newer bikes anyhow—there is just enough charge left in the electrical system to get the machine started once after the battery runs down. Mirabile dictu! Then, of course, you have to ride around for a while to recharge the battery.

Tough Brakes

Here's the least you need to know about your brakes. Almost all newer motorcycles have disk brakes in the front, single or dual; see figure 8-8. Some also have disk brakes in the rear, while others have

Savvy Tip

Basically, if you've got a dead battery on your hands, you've got three options: jump the battery from another bike, jump the battery from a car, or push-start the bike. Walter Kern, motorcycle guru at About.com, talks you through all three of these procedures at http://motorcycles.about.com/cs/maintenance/a/jump.htm. Another option, if the bike is at your home or another location where it can be safely left, with access to electric power, is to buy a buy a Battery Tender (www.batterytender.com), which is attached to your battery via a small wiring harness and then plugged into an electrical outlet. These are nice gizmos to have if you live in a cold climate, if you don't ride that often, or if you are planning not to ride for an extended period. Read more about these below, in the section on winterizing/storing your bike.

---

rear drum brakes. Disk brakes have pads, drum brakes have shoes, and both have friction-type material that must be checked periodically for wear. Your owner's manual will tell you what kind of brakes your bike has and how and how often you should check them. Disk brakes almost always have a wear indicator you can keep an eye on; drum brakes can be more difficult to monitor, often requiring removal of the wheel, although some also have a wear indicator. The maintenance schedule in my V-Star's owner's manual specifies checking all brake components, including brake fluid level, hoses, and cables, at every 4,000-mile service interval. If the brakes don't feel right—if they're spongy or are making noises you've never heard before—you'll want to have them checked right away.

Antilock braking systems (ABS) obviously, are more complicated because of the electronics involved. I've never owned a bike that had one of these systems, but from what I understand, they have a self-checking function built into them and a light will come on somewhere on your instrument cluster if there is a problem of some sort.

The Winter of Our Discontent, the Spring of Our Hope

Here in Florida, we ride pretty much all year round (if the summer heat doesn't do us in). Maybe you also live in an area where this is possible. Or maybe you don't—and you're in the position of having to store your bike for the winter months.

It's not just a matter of shoving your machine into the rear of the garage or your backyard shed and ignoring it until the spring thaw. If you want to have it up and running with minimal fuss when the riding season rolls around again—and if you want to prolong its life—you'll need to do right by it before you store it away. Sometimes your owner's manual will tell you exactly what to do. In general, however, here's the drill:

Fig. 8-8: My bike has dual-disk front disk brakes.

- First and foremost, give it a good cleaning. You can't go wrong by following advice from the Wrench Wench later in this chapter. Make sure to dry it thoroughly.
- Change the oil and oil filter.
- Drain the carburetor; the easiest way is to turn the fuel **petcock** to Off and run the motorcycle until the engine dies. Leave the petcock in the Off position.
- Disconnect and remove the battery. Store it in a warm, well-ventilated place (out of the reach of children and pets). You may want to hook it up to a Battery Tender (www.batterytender.com) if you have one.
- Fill the fuel tank all the way up—this keeps condensation from forming—and add a bit of a fuel stabilizer.
- Mark Zimmerman, in his *Essential Guide to Motorcycle Maintenance*, advises spraying a little WD-40 into the exhaust pipe(s) and then covering the opening(s) with duct tape. "Likewise, seal the air-filter opening to prevent it from becoming a mouse condo," he advises (page 220).
- If it's cold where you'll be storing the bike, you may want to think about removing the seats and bringing them inside, as excessive cold can cause cracks and other damage to leather and vinyl.
- To protect the cylinders, piston rings, etc., from corrosion, you'll need to remove the spark plugs (easier to get to on some bikes than others; check your owner's manual), put a tablespoon or so of clean engine oil into the spark plug holes, screw the plugs back into the sockets, and then use the electric starter to spin the engine a few times and distribute the stuff.
- Fill tires to their proper pressure levels and then do what you can to get the weight of the motorcycle off its tires. If your bike has a centerstand, that's ideal. If not, you may be able to buy a work stand or jerry-rig something. If none of these options are available, roll the bike

Savvy Tip

Although your motorcycle owner's manual may be essential reading, maybe you've lost yours or never got one to begin with and can't lay your hands on a replacement. Or maybe you're eager for more information that what the typical owner's manual provides. Most experienced riders recommend obtaining a Clymer Repair Manual for the specific make, model, and year of your motorcycle. These are do-it-yourself repair guides designed for someone working on a bike in a home garage—as opposed to the OEM shop manuals used at your dealer's service department, which often call for OEM-specific or other expensive equipment. Even if you are not the do-it-yourself type, it's good to have a Clymer manual around as a reference. They retail for about $40 but can often be obtained for less on eBay or from online book vendors; www.clymer.com.

onto a large piece of cardboard and, at least every couple of weeks throughout the winter, roll the bike and/or turn the wheels a little. The object is to keep it from resting in the same location for a protracted period, which will cause degradation in one spot on each of the two tires.

Some folks advise covering the bike, while others discourage the use of covers, maintaining that they promote the accumulation of moisture, which causes corrosion. Some cover manufacturers claim that their covers "breathe." At any rate, you may want to ask in online forums or check with other motorcyclists in your locale.

Check out Adam Glass's comprehensive *Winter Storage for Motorcycles* guide, www.clarity.net/~adam/winter-storage.html, for detailed advice on resources and techniques.

The winter months can drag by when you are eager to be out riding again, but sooner or later, it will be time to get back on the road. Glass's guide, mentioned above, provides information on taking the bike out of storage. You may also want to look at "Breaking Out of Hibernation" in *Biker Ally*, a magazine for women motorcyclists (www.bikerallymag.com/Web/Articles/Web/Wrench/Breaking%20out%20of%20Hibernation.pdf).

KAONA, OR KEEPING IT CLEAN

This section taken by permission from *Hula and the Art of Motorcycle Maintenance*, www.wrench-wench.com/maint/maint1.htm, by Hawaii writer/artist Leilehua Yuen (aka, the Wrench Wench; see figure 8-9).

Fig. 8-9: Leilehua Yuen, the Wrench Wench.

Kaona is the deeper or "hidden" meaning in a hula. Sort of like a sacred pun. It is what is on the inside, not the external part that you see. It is what gives strength and spirit to a hula. The parts you don't see give strength and spirit to your bike.

It is important to do more than just polish the chrome when you clean your bike. You need to really get in there and clean the frame, between the fins, polish the fork tubes, the inside of the fenders—all the places you *cannot* see are at least as important to keep clean as the places you *can*. That includes the engine, too—change your oil regularly and keep your fuel fresh.

I get a real sense of satisfaction knowing that I fully understand my hula, and that from the inner meaning out, I know the dance. I get the same sense of satisfaction from knowing that I have cared for my bike from the inside of the transmission to the covers on the side.

And, from a practical, worldly viewpoint, thoroughly cleaning your bike will extend its life and maintain the value. Dirt holds moisture, and moisture enables rust. All those little pockets of dirt hiding under trim and between components are rust breeders which eventually will affect the strength, performance, and longevity of your motorcycle.

My Favorite Bike Washing Tools:

- rags—lots of old, soft, and clean ones
- newspapers
- Q-tips
- toothbrushes
- toilet brush
- 000 steel wool

- flexible brush (found them on sale at Wal-Mart once, bought all I could get away with)
- long skinny tweezers and picks for getting stones out of fins and screws out of strange places
- big paint bucket—I store my stuff in this and sit on it while cleaning the bike
- second bucket for holding soapy water

Other Stuff:

- Simple Green
- dish soap
- waterless cleaner/wax
- leather/vinyl conditioner (but not the kind that slick up our seats!)
- chrome polish
- aluminum polish
- brake cleaner

Using a System

Just as we learn a new hula in a systematic manner, we clean the bike systematically. It doesn't really matter which system you use, so long as you are consistent and get to everything. Me, I start at the top and front, and work down and back, inspecting each component as I go. If the bike is very dirty, I'll wash it first—going for the engine, underbelly, and then the wheels. Then I'll go back up to the top and dry it, going over each part with a waterless cleaner/wax.

Water or Waterless?

I use both, depending on the level of dirt and grease involved. If the bike is filthy, covered in road grime, or oily, I'll gently mist it down with water and spray Simple Green on the engine and wheels. Avoid the paint! Let that set for a while. You can keep busy by pulling off the bags and seats and cleaning them. Mist to rinse, and spray again. Now take that toilet brush and scrub the engine, getting into the fins, between the jugs, and everywhere you can reach—being, as Elmer Fudd would say, "vewwwy, vewwwy carefuw" of all small parts and electrical wiring, connectors, etc. Mist it down and see if it needs another go. Repeat until clean.

Now get down and look under the bike. Get all of the grime off the underbelly. While you are down there, check for loose parts, bolts, floppy stuff, oil drips which might indicate leaking seals, etc.

Rinse the brush thoroughly and go for the wheels. A soft toilet brush does wonders to get the grime from between spokes, or off detailing on a cast wheel.

Brakes

While you are down at the wheels, take a good look at the brakes. I'm talking about disc brakes right now. Those are the ones that have a flat circular metal thing next to the wheel, and a box at the back edge which encloses a small portion of it. Inside that box are the calipers and pads. Over time and mileage, the pads can get a build-up of road grease which needs to be cleaned off.

If the bike is grimy enough to wash, there's probably a fair amount of road grease on the brakes. I like to cover my wheels and nearby paint with old newspapers, and then thoroughly clean the brakes with—brake cleaner! It comes in an aerosol can with a little tube you poke in the top pushy-downy thing. Stick the tube down the calipers and give the pads a good squirting. If you see gunky stuff running out, keep squirting until the fluid runs clear. Keep your face well away from this stuff. Get it in your eyes, and it can blind you. It's not very healthy for the rest of you, either.

Then again, neither is brake failure.

You'll want to move the bike back and forth a bit to work the cleaner under the pads. When the brakes are clean, roll up the newspapers and put them in your icky toxic rubbish container for proper disposal.

Return to scrubbing the wheels. It's likely that some of the fluid got on the tires or other parts. Rinse it off thoroughly. A mild dish soap, well diluted, is good for washing off the painted surfaces. Now, back to the wheels . . .

After you have finished the wheels with the toilet brush and gotten into any small hard-to-reach places (like behind the brake calipers) with the toothbrush, rinse, and then spray more Simple Green on the tires. This is where that flexible scrub brush is great! But whatever you are using, scrub the tires thoroughly. Clean tires stick to the street better and last longer! Use this opportunity to check for nails, cuts, glass, or other nasties in your tires. Give a final rinse, stand up and stretch. Now we get to go back to the top of the bike!

The Rest of the Bike

Now is the time to break out the waterless cleaner.

I start with the mirrors, checking them for chips, looseness, etc., and polishing them. The mirror backs, risers, and fittings are inspected, cleaned, and polished. I start on the left, and work my way across to the right. Then I head down the middle, and clean the instrument housing—again checking for damage, rust, loose parts, etc. As a matter of fact, just assume that you will check for these things everywhere you clean!

Work your way over the fork bridge, down the headlamp, steering head, etc., checking all joins for dirt and rust, cleaning and polishing as you go. It's painstaking, but this inch-by inch cleaning and inspection will pay off in the long run. You will know your bike better than some mechanics!

Continue with this process, going from top to bottom, working your way back, component by component. (Someone once asked my Hunny if he didn't get tired of all that cleaning. He compared it to foreplay, and said . . . well, never mind what he said. I'm sure you can figure it out!)

An important—though often overlooked—place to keep spotless is the front fork, specifically the slidey-inney tubes. If you take a good look at your bike, you'll see rubber gaskets here. Any rust on the inney tube thingies will damage those gaskets, causing them to leak, and leaking fork seals are an expensive thing to fix. So keep those tubes clean and waxed!

If you give a good, thorough cleaning to your bike on a regular basis, then all you need between times is a soft cloth and a little waterless cleaner to catch smudges, stray dirt and bugs, and keep your bike looking its best!

Note: The Wrench Wench, a multitalented woman, also does graphic design. See figure 8-10.

Fig. 8-10: © Leilehua Yuen. Leilehua is Tutu (grandparent) to a wonderful preschooler and can't wait to have him help her wrench her ride! When she's not riding, wrenching, or teaching the hula, she designs charming clothing and gifts for lady riders and their families: www.CafePress.com/Wrench_Wench.

181

Walter Kern

Motorcycles Guide, About.com

Freehold, NJ

2000 Honda Gold Wing SE with Motor Trike conversion

http://motorcycles.about.com

I got started in motorcycling in 1989. I was 51 and never been on a bike before. A chance trip back to my hometown in Illinois found my wife and me surrounded by motorcycles at my brother-in-law's house. Both he and my wife's sister had been riding BMW motorcycles for years. Somehow, we came away with the desire to ride and a motorcycle bug that we couldn't get rid of.

We wanted to do it right. We found a Motorcycle Safety Foundation (MSF) riding course at a college in South Jersey. Yes, both my wife and I decided to take up motorcycling together. We passed the course, got a small, 400cc bike, and practiced. My wife got the first new bike, a Honda Shadow VLX600. We were active in all things motorcycle.

In 1999, I came upon the Mining Company, which was a different sort of Web site run by guides running individual sites under the Mining Company network. I noticed that they were looking for more guides. Better still, they were looking for a guide for cycles. I applied, spent a month in training, got them to change the name from "Cycles" to "Motorcycles," and was live in July 1999.

The Mining Company changed its name to About.com just as I became a guide. The Motorcycles site started with three subjects, one article, and 200 links. Then growth took off. After three months, I was allowed to add a forum to the site, also called Motorcycles. That gave me a window on the real world of motorcycling.

Six years of work on the Motorcycles site has resulted in six forums, a twice-weekly newsletter, and many thousands of pages of motorcycle content, features, picture galleries, and a front page that's a blog. We even have a forum-sponsored rally each year in Maggie Valley, North Carolina.

Now, the site is teeming with features such as women on motorcycles, recalls, specifications, road tests, user reviews, pictures of the week, how-tos, glossary, quizzes, book reviews, FAQs, e-mail courses, and numerous original articles on motorcycling.

My job these days is more about creating content than riding. Both my wife and I have gravitated to riding motorcycle trikes.

For the future, I expect to be providing even more motorcycle content to satisfy the cravings of that motorcycle bug within all of us.

9 EXPANDING YOUR HORIZONS: PLACES TO GO, PEOPLE TO RIDE WITH

◆ Motorcycle clubs

◆ Bike nights

◆ Bike rallies

◆ Taking to the open road

◆ If you can't ride it there . . .

MOTORCYCLE CLUBS

What some people relish about motorcycling is the chance to get out there solo—away from everybody and everything. Riding can be a form of meditation. But many folks are attracted to the social aspects of motorcycling; indeed, it's an excellent way to meet new and interesting people you probably wouldn't encounter in other areas of your life. The only thing that really matters when you get together is a shared love of riding. (See figure 9-1.)

Riding clubs can be brand-specific, regional—or both. Large organizations like the Harley Davidson Owners Group (www.hog.com), which has more than 900,000 members worldwide, typically have hundreds of local chapters, sometimes scattered all over the world.

Usually you can find a chapter near you by contacting local dealers or browsing the Web sites of national or international organizations. You'll find a list of the major ones in the sidebar "Major Brand/Model-Specific Motorcycle Owners Groups."

MAJOR BRAND/MODEL-SPECIFIC MOTORCYCLE OWNERS GROUPS

Airheads Beemer Club
BMW
www.airheads.org

American Voyager Association (AVA)
Kawasaki
www.amervoyassoc.org

BMW Motorcycle Owners of America (BMW MOA)
www.bmwmoa.org

BMW Riders Association (BMWRA)
www.bmwra.org

Concours Owners Group (COG)
Kawasaki
www.concours.org

Ducati Enthusiast Sport Motorcycle Association (DESMO)
www.desmoducati.org

Ducati Online
(Not just an online club)
www.ducati.net

Gold Wing Road Riders Association (GWRRA)
www.gwrra.org

Harley-Davidson Owners Group (HOG)
www.hog.com

Honda Riders Club of America (HRCA)
http://hrca.honda.com

Honda Sport Touring Association (HSTA)
"All brands welcome"
www.ridehsta.com

International Oilheads Club
BMW
www.oilheadsclub.org

International Star Riders Association (ISRA)
Yamaha
www.star-riders.org

Magna Riders Association (MRA)
Honda
www.magnariders.com

Marauder Intruder Group (MIG)
Suzuki
www.migcruisers.com

Moto Guzzi National Owners Club (MGNOC)
www.mgnoc.com

Riders of Kawasaki Club (ROK)
www.kawasaki.com/gtoc

ShadowRiders.org
Honda (other brands welcome)
www.shadowriders.org

Star Riding and Touring Association (STAR)
Yamaha
www.startouring.org

Suzuki Owners Club USA
www.soc-usa.org

Triumph International Owners Club (USA)
http://members.aol.com/tiocbima/index.htm

V-Max Owners Association (VMOA)
Yamaha
www.v-max.com

Valkyrie Owners Association International (VOAI)
Honda
www.valkyrie-owners.com

The Venturers
Yamaha
www.venturers.org

Vulcan Riders Association (VRA)
Kawasaki
www.vulcanriders.org

Vulcan Riders and Owners Club (VROC)
Kawasaki
www.vroc.org

Fig. 9-1: Motorcyclists have always liked getting together. This group showed up for the motorcycle races on July 4, 1941, in Vale, Ore. Photograph by Russell Lee. Library of Congress, Prints & Photographs Division, FSA/OWI Collection, [reproduction number, LC-USF3301-013094-M1].

While you may get together semi-regularly with a small group of friends for a ride, your best chance for an organized group ride is with a riding club. Despite its name, Southern Cruisers (www.south erncruiser.net) is a club that ranges far and wide, with chapters in almost every state and a few foreign countries. It is a family-oriented motorcycle club that welcomes riders of all makes and models, and various chapters often hold events to raise money for St. Jude Children's Research Hospital.

While the number of women riders is growing exponentially, we are still in the minority. Most women motorcyclists are thrilled to meet other women who "ride their own." And there are riding clubs just for women, such as Women in the Wind (www.womeninthewind.org), which has about a thousand members throughout the United States and Canada. Maybe there's a chapter near you. See figure 9-2.

You'll find a long list of motorcycle clubs for women—national, international, regional, and local—at BikerLady's Wind Sisters page: www.bikerlady.com/bikerladyweb/pages/windsisters.htm, which also includes other resources for women riders such as e-mail lists, women-friendly accessory and gear dealers, events calendars, and more.

The law enforcement community tends to be very close-knit, and there are a number of active motorcycle clubs for these folks, such as the Blue Knights International Law Enforcement

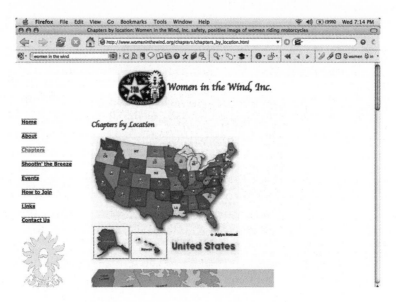

Fig. 9-2: Women in the Wind says, "We welcome all kinds of motorcycles, and our members are from all walks of life: everything from students to secretaries, real estate agents and teachers, factory workers, and police officers. Our members are married and single, mothers and grandmothers. We have them all!" www.womeninthewind.org.

Motorcycle Club (www.blueknights.org) and the Blood Brothers Motorcycle Club (www.bloodbrothersmc.org; see figure 9-3).

The Red Knights Motorcycle Club (www.redknightsmc.org) is for members of the fire services and their families, as is (obviously) the American Firefighters Motorcycle Club (www.aff-mc.com). Some other examples of affinity-type motorcycle clubs:

- Military/Veterans
    - Leathernecks Motorcycle Club (Marines, active duty or retired), www.leathernecksmc.com
    - Military Veterans Motorcycle Club, www.geocities.com/lotas_1

- Religious/Ethnic
    - Christian Motorcyclists Association, www.cmausa.org
    - Christian Sport Bike Association, www.christiansportbike.com
    - Jewish Motorcyclists Alliance, www.jewishbikers.com
    - Latin American Motorcycle Association, www.latinbikers.com
    - National Association of Black Bikers, www.nabbweb.org

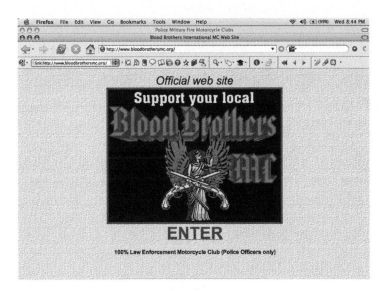

Fig. 9-3: If you're not a LEO, you'll have to find another club to join. The Blood Brothers Motorcycle Club is "100% Law Enforcement." www.bloodbrothersmc.org.

— National Association of Buffalo Soldiers Motorcycle Clubs (African American, primarily military/law enforcement), www.buffalosoldiersnational.com

• Potpourri

— Antique Motorcycle Club of America ("All makes are welcome, thirty five years old or older."), www.antiquemotorcycle.org

— Bald Guys Motorcycle Club ("Motorcycle club for the follically challenged"), http://baldguysmc.com

— Bikers Against Child Abuse ("Exists to provide aid, comfort, safety, and support for children that have been sexually, physically, and emotionally abused"), www.bacausa.com

— British Biker Cooperative ("Dedicated to the preservation of the British motorcycle"), http://britishbiker.net

— Brothers of the Third Wheel (trikes), www.btw-trikers.org

A good place to start looking for motorcycle clubs in your area is to check the American Motorcyclists Association's database. You can search by state, AMA district, or city. See figure 9-4.

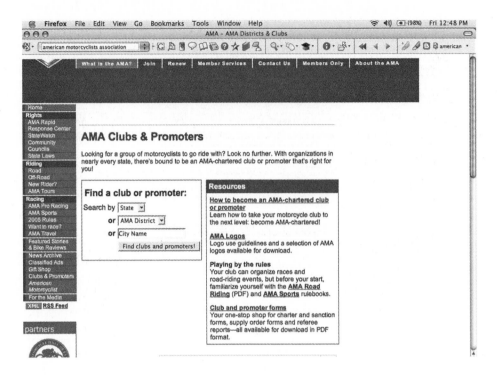

Fig. 9-4: The American Motorcyclist Association maintains a database of AMA-chartered clubs. Look here to find a group in your area: www.ama-cycle.org /clubs/index.asp.

– Disabled Riders of America ("To pursue and protect the interests of disabled motorcyclists"), www.disabledriders.com
– Iron Butt Association (long-distance riders), www.ironbutt.com
– RETREADS Motorcycle Club International (age 40-plus), www.retreads.org
– Vintage Japanese Motorcycle Club (owners of 15-year-old and older Japanese motorcycles), www.vjmc.org

BIKE NIGHTS

Depending on where you live and how active you want your social calendar to be, every night could be a bike night for you. With more and more people riding motorcycles, more and more restaurants are looking to attract the biker crowd—which attracts other customers who enjoy looking at motorcycles. Some of these events attract hundreds of bikers. Cities or towns often sponsor bike nights of their own, sometimes on a monthly basis, and these can draw large crowds of motorcyclists from all over the region. (See figure 9-5.)

Fig. 9-5: Plant City, Florida is known as the "Winter Strawberry Capital of the World." But on the first Saturday night of each month, the bikers take over. And the local chamber of commerce is thrilled to have them. According to this Web site, between 9,000 and 12,000 motorcyclists attend this event each month, with as many or more nonriding folks coming to look at the bikes and soak up the atmosphere. Bikers are good for business. How much money do you figure the local merchants are raking in? http://plantcitybikefest.com,

Most dealers know when and where the area bike nights are happening, as do the local m/c clubs, who often like to ride to these things as a group. You'll usually find free motorcycle-oriented newspapers at dealerships that tend to include advertisements and event calendars. Eating and drinking establishments that attract bikers often give these away as well. Or you can search the large online calendar offered by the Motorcycle Events Association at www.motorcycleevents.com/calendar.php. Be aware that some of these bike nights are so popular that you'll find "authority figures" in the parking lot directing traffic and telling you where to park. Don't feel obligated to park in any place you consider unsafe or that will present a problem for you when you want to leave—for example, on a steep slope or uneven surface.

BIKE RALLIES

I am an introvert by nature; it's probably safe to say that most writers are. So I haven't had a great deal of experience with massive bike rallies, though I've allowed myself to be goaded into attending a few smaller ones. A rally is simply a large (or large-ish) get-together of motorcyclists that usually lasts more than one day. It may take place over a weekend or it may encompass an entire week. Besides lots and lots of other riders and their machines, you'll usually find vendors of motorcycle gear and paraphernalia, bike shows (for custom-builts, restored bikes, etc.), and a variety of organized (or semiorganized) activities, sometimes including racing. Although a fee may be charged for participation in events, in truth, most motorcyclists tend to just show up and hang out.

Rallies, by the way, are not a recent phenomenon, as the panoramic photo in figure 9-6 shows. In March 2005, Daytona Bike Week celebrated its 64th anniversary. The Sturgis Rally in South Dakota has been going on since 1938.

The first time you attend a rally, you'll see more motorcycles than you've ever seen in one place before. You'll get to look at unfamiliar and unusual bikes. And you'll meet people from all over; the larger and more famous the rally, the more geographic diversity you'll encounter. For an optimal experience, you'll want to plan your trip in advance. Thanks to the Internet, this is easier than ever. Bike rallies usually have their own Web sites, including event schedules, maps and directions, information about hotels and motels, campgrounds, restaurants, activities, and more. Often, you can sign up to receive ongoing information about the rally by e-mail. Check the sidebar "Significant U.S. Motorcycle Events" for a list of the larger, better-known rallies, along with Web site links.

TAKING TO THE OPEN ROAD

Sooner or later, you're gonna wanna do it . . . either by yourself, with a passenger, or with another rider or two. Take a motorcycle trip, that is. The Great American Road Trip is the very essence of

Fig. 9-6: As long as there have been motorcyclists, apparently, there have been motorcycle rallies. This picture was taken in Venice, CA somewhere around 1910. Library of Congress, Prints and Photographs Division, LC-USZ62-132370.

SIGNIFICANT U.S. MOTORCYCLE EVENTS

AMA Vintage Motorcycle Days
(Lexington, Ohio; American Motorcyclist Association)
www.amadirectlink.com/vmd/2005/home.asp

Americade
(Lake George, N.Y.)
http://tourexpo.com/04/index2.html

Biketoberfest
(Daytona Beach, Fla.)
www.biketoberfest.org

BlackBikeFest
(Myrtle Beach, S.C.)
www.blackbikefest.net

BMW MOA International Rally
(moves around; BMW riders; link is to site for 2005 rally)
www.bmwmoa.org/rally/rally05/index.htm

Daytona Bike Week
(Daytona Beach, Fla.)
www.daytonachamber.com/bwhome.html

Four Corners Rally in the Rockies
(Ignacio, Colo.)
www.rallyintherockies.com

Golden Aspen Rally Association
(Ruidoso, N.M.; two per year)
www.motorcyclerally.com

Hollister Independence Rally
(Hollister, Calif.)
www.hollisterrally.com

Honda HomeComing
(Marysville, Ohio)
www.ohio.honda.com/news/homecoming/index.cfm

Honda Hoot
(Knoxville, Tenn.)
www.hondahoot.com

Laconia Motorcycle Week
(Laconia, N.H.)
http://laconiamcweek.com

Laughlin River Run
(Laughlin, Nev.)
www.laughlinriverrun.com

Little Sturgis Rally
(Sturgis, Ky.)
www.littlesturgisrally.net

Love Ride
(Glendale, Calif.; large fundraiser; supports MDA and other groups)
www.loveride.org

Mid-Atlantic Women's Motorcycle Rally
(Gettysburg, Pa.; women only)
www.mawmr.com

Myrtle Beach Bike Week
(Myrtle Beach, S.C.)
www.myrtlebeachbikeweek.com

Rolling Thunder
(Washington, D.C.)
www.rollingthunder1.com

Steel Pony Express
(New Orleans, La.)
www.steelponyexpress.com

Sturgis Motorcycle Rally
(Sturgis, S.D.)
www.sturgismotorcyclerally.com

Trail of Tears Commemorative Motorcycle Ride
(begins in Chattanooga, Tenn., and ends in Waterloo, Ala.)
www.al-tn-trailoftears.org

Wing Ding
(moves around; basically Gold Wing and Valkyrie riders)
www.wing-ding.org

freedom; but freedom moves to a whole 'nother level when you take off on two wheels instead of sitting inside a four-wheel, climate-controlled, air-bag-and-seat-belt-encumbered cage.

Of course, a motorcycle road trip is not for everybody. But you know you're going try it at least once. Keep in mind that even if you're up for it, your prospective passenger may not be. Cruising around the area on the weekend is one thing. Spending hours in the **pillion** seat—let's face it; as far as the passenger is concerned, the view straight ahead never changes—is *definitely* not for everyone. If your significant other or your kid just doesn't want to go, there is nothing to be gained by nagging or pleading until you get reluctant compliance.

To Camp or Not to Camp

The way I look at it, motorcycle travel comes in two flavors—camping and noncamping (or, if you prefer, "credit card camping"). Of course, you can always combine the two, sometimes sleeping outside and sometimes sleeping inside. I am not a camper . . . never have been. So I'm not one to give advice on this. But there are other sources for this information; for starters, I commend your attention to Bob Woofter's *Motorcycle Camping Made Easy*, which you'll see listed in the bibliography at the end of this book. And of course there is the Internet. Two recommended sites:

- Bill Johns' Excellent Motorcycle Camping Guide, www.wetleather.com/reference/camping.html
- Biggest Bike-Camping List Ever, http://users.pullman.com/viking/CampingList.htm

Pack in Haste, Repent at Leisure

Packing for a motorcycle trip is no casual endeavor. Although "just throw a few things in a bag and take off" sounds great, it's likely that you will come to regret it, especially if you aren't a kid anymore.

For one thing, there's the weight and balance issue. Your motorcycle can only carry so much weight. Your owner's manual may provide you with the "maximum load" information—total weight of rider, passenger, cargo, and accessories. If not, you can figure this out by subtracting the motorcycle's "wet weight"—including a full tank of fuel and all other fluids—from the gross vehicle weight rating (GVWR), which is the maximum allowable total weight of the motorcycle, riders, luggage, accessories, and anything else you choose to put on it. If you don't have an owner's manual, check for this information on manufacturers' Web sites or call a dealership.

The owner's manual for my V-Star 1100 states a maximum load of 441 pounds. Now, that is not a concern for me, a smallish woman who always rides solo. But if you are a large-ish person with a large-ish passenger, you can see where it might become a problem. If you have a Gold Wing or a large BMW

Savvy
Tip
What to take with you? Some things will depend on your own specific needs (and those of your passenger, if you'll be traveling 2-up). But whether you're planning to camp out or just cruise from motel to motel, you can generate a good packing list online, at the Micapeak Web site. Choose either the full Motorcycle Trip Checklist if you'll be camping out—www.micapeak.com/ info/mclist.html—or the abbreviated "credit card camping" version if you plan on a roof and four walls each night—www.micapeak.com/checklists/ccard.html.

touring bike, weight rarely becomes a concern, and you can easily tow a small trailer behind behemoth machines like this. If you have a sport bike, however . . . well, let's just say it's unlikely to be the ideal vehicle for an extended road trip. Not every motorcycle makes a good touring bike.

We discussed motorcycle luggage in chapter 6; basically, you have your choice of hard luggage or soft luggage, but the type of bike you've got may narrow your options considerably—for example, a motorcycle with high exhaust pipes affords limited room for saddlebags. Check with a dealer, browse enthusiasts' Web sites or ask in online forums. Whatever you are riding, somebody, somewhere has likely taken a trip on it and, if nothing else, can provide information on what *not* to do. Everyone will want lots and lots of bungee cords. And you may as well pick up a couple of bungee cargo nets while you're at it; these are cheap ($6 or $7 at most dealerships) and can be very handy for securing odd-shaped items (see figure 9-7).

Even if you are keeping within the recommended weight limit, you can't just go loading all sorts of stuff onto your motorcycle without taking certain things into consideration—mainly, those things that affect the balance and handling of the machine:

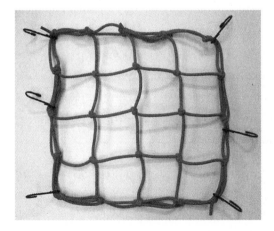

Fig. 9-7: The amazing bungee cargo net. Don't leave home without it.

195

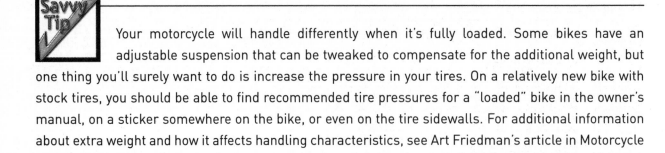

Your motorcycle will handle differently when it's fully loaded. Some bikes have an adjustable suspension that can be tweaked to compensate for the additional weight, but one thing you'll surely want to do is increase the pressure in your tires. On a relatively new bike with stock tires, you should be able to find recommended tire pressures for a "loaded" bike in the owner's manual, on a sticker somewhere on the bike, or even on the tire sidewalls. For additional information about extra weight and how it affects handling characteristics, see Art Friedman's article in Motorcycle Cruiser, "Getting Loaded: How Much Weight Can Your Motorcycle Handle?" (http://motorcyclecruiser.com/streetsurvival/Overload/).

- Keep your cargo weight as low as possible, closest to the motorcycle's center of gravity.
- Distribute weight as evenly as possible on both sides of the motorcycle.
- Make sure everything is tied down firmly; shifting weight can be dangerous. Check cargo restraints/mounts frequently.
- Don't attach anything heavy or bulky to the handlebars, front fork, or front fender.
- Be mindful of your exhaust pipes; keep luggage or other objects from touching them or you could have a fire on your hands.
- On the back of the bike, pack your bundles pyramid-style, with the widest, most solid objects on the bottom and smaller, squishier things on the top.

The American Motorcyclist Association offers *Loaded for the Road*, an excellent guide to carrying stuff on your bike. See figure 9-8.

Planning Your Trip . . . or Choosing a Tour

Planning a motorcycle trip is the same as planning a car trip—only different. You'll still need the standard stuff like maps (or a GPS system, for the gadget freak—www.gpsy.com/gpsinfo/), guidebooks, reservations (even if you're camping—campgrounds do fill up, especially in popular tourist locations during desirable times of the year). Rather than taking mainly to the superslabs in the interest of saving time, however, the motorcyclist tends to prefer "the road less traveled." Some experienced riders caution against "overplanning," since a trip can be more relaxing and enjoyable if you don't feel pressure to stick to a schedule . . . and you won't get upset if there's a delay or necessary change in plans due to the weather, unexpected road construction, etc.

Discounting the state of your bladder, your appetite, or your desire to pull over for reasons other than basic creature comforts—to gawk, shop, talk with other motorcyclists—how far you can travel without stopping depends on the range of your motorcycle. How large is your gas tank? How many

Fig. 9-8: Read this excellent "guide to carrying stuff on your motorcycle" at www.ama-cycle.org/magazine/2003/luggage/luggage.asp, which includes information about different types of motorcycle luggage and links to major vendor Web sites.

miles do you get to the gallon? Remember that your mileage will drop when your bike is fully loaded, if you're doing a lot of hill climbing or high speed riding, if you're fighting the wind, etc. One thing is for sure—you will definitely not be able to travel as far between fuel stops as you would in a car. Plan accordingly. Obviously, you don't want to get stuck in the middle of nowhere; likewise, you don't want to find yourself stranded in a small town on a Sunday where the only gas station is closed.

Excellent advice on motorcycle touring abounds. There's some good reading in the bibliography of this book. Motorcycle magazines typically feature trip reports (as do motorcyclists' weblogs and personal Web sites). See the sidebar "A Dozen Web Sites for the Motorcycle Traveler" for sources of helpful information.

Another motorcycle travel option is to take an organized trip. With the growing popularity of motorcycling, you'll have no trouble finding a tour operator catering to the two-wheeled crowd. You'll definitely need a credit card and a motorcycle license (or endorsement on your driver's license). What else you'll need depends on the tour. Are motorcycles supplied or must you provide your own? What about gear? What about rain gear? Other information you'll want to know:

- What level of expertise is recommended? If you've just passed the MSF course and you haven't even purchased your own bike yet, maybe you don't want to sign up for that trip through the Pyrenees. Not this year, anyhow.
- How much extra does it cost if you want to bring a passenger?

197

> **Savvy Tip**
>
> A former California Highway Patrol motorman passed along this bit of advice to me, which he said he received from his training officer. Always go to the bathroom before you start out on your ride, and pull over to use the bathroom as soon as you feel the urge. Why? If you're in an accident, a full bladder is much more likely to rupture than an empty bladder, greatly complicating any other problems you might have.

- Who covers which expenses—lodging, meals, tolls, tips, gas, insurance, entrance fees, etc.?
- If meals and accommodations are part of the package, what can you expect in terms of quality? Even if you don't mind spartan arrangements, it's best to know ahead of time if you'll be staying at five-star accommodations, inns and B&Bs, flophouses, or whatever. And particularly if you have dietary issues, you'll want to know something about the meal arrangements.
- Can you break off and go touring by yourself or must you stay with the group the entire time?
- Will there be a "chase vehicle" and/or trained mechanic along for the ride?

How to find a tour? The backs of the bike magazines are full of ads, often with Web site addresses. The Web itself can be helpful; Ronnie Cramer's Motorcycle Web Index includes a long list of links to tour operators, http://sepnet.com/cycle/tours.htm. Naturally, you'll want to check these places out before you lay your money down—ask online, check the Better Business Bureau database (www.bbb.org), see if you can find out how long the company has been in business. And you may want to consider trip cancellation insurance in case your plans are disrupted by inclement weather, illness, or other difficulties.

If You Can't Ride It There . . .

What if you live in Sturgis and want to attend Daytona Bike Week? Or live in Daytona, but yearn to make it out to the Sturgis Rally? Well, you could ride there, of course. But many of us do not have the physical stamina or experience (not to mention the desire) to endure hours and hours in the saddle of a motorcycle, regardless of weather or road conditions. And if you're only going to go a few hundred miles a day or less, there's a limit to how far you can get before your vacation time runs out.

Renting a Motorcycle

One increasingly popular option is to fly to your destination and rent a motorcycle once you get there. It's not inexpensive and, depending on where you're headed, it's often not easy to find anything but Harleys to rent—which is OK if you're a Harley rider, but maybe not if you'd like some-

---

A DOZEN WEB SITES FOR THE MOTORCYCLE TRAVELER

33 Secrets for Smart Touring (AMA)
("Useful suggestions that have made our tours more organized and more fun")
www.ama-cycle.org/roadride/riderresc/33secrets.asp

BIKE-STAY
("Motorcycle-friendy accommodations")
www.bike-stay.net

Horizons Unlimited
("The web site motorcycle travelers trust")
www.horizonsunlimited.com

International Help 'N Hands (AMA)
("Wherever you ride, there's a friend nearby.")
www.ama-cycle.org/roadride/helpnhands.asp

LDriders.com
("It's not the destination. It's the ride.")
www.ldriders.com

Moto-Directory: Touring and Travel
(resources and travel sites)
www.moto-directory.com/touring/travel.asp

Motorcycle Cruiser: Summer Travel Safety
("Here's how to beat the heat, fight fatigue, and make those long rides fun and safe.")
http://motorcyclecruiser.com/streetsurvival/summer

Motorcycle Cruiser: What to Do if Your Motorcycle Breaks Down
("Your bike can stop running when your least want it to do so")
http://motorcyclecruiser.com/streetsurvival/breakdown

Motorcycle Escape: Trip Q & A
("The most frequently asked tour-oriented questions")
http://motorcyclistonline.com/escape/tripqna/123_0444_qna

Motorcycle Misadventures
("Real time dispatches filed from the road," by Carla King. Eat your heart out.)
www.motorcyclemisadventures.com

Motorcycle Touring for Beginners
("A tutorial for people new to motorcycle touring")
www.visi.com/~dalebor

Motorcycle.com: The Touring World
("Motorcycle tours from around the world written by our globe-trotting staff")
www.motorcycle.com/mo/mcworld/world.motml

---

thing other than a heavy cruiser or have a strong preference for another marque. On the other hand, if you've ever thought you might want a Harley some day, this might be a good way to take one for an extended test ride.

To get an idea of what's involved here, check out Eaglerider, at (I kid you not) www.hogrent.com. They've been around since 1992, operate nationwide (more or less, including popular tourist destinations and a few foreign locations), and their Web site works pretty much like that of any rental car company. You can make reservations online. (They also rent ATVs, snowmobiles, dirt bikes, and "personal watercraft.") Although their two-wheeled fleet features Harley-Davidsons, it's also possible to rent bikes from Yamaha and Honda, including small machines like the Honda Rebel or Yamaha Virago that are beginner-friendly. Scooters are available, too. Click on "Rates and Models" to see the selection. They won't rent to anyone under the age of 21, and you'll need a valid motorcycle license—and a credit card; deposit upon pickup starts at $1,000 and goes up from there, depending on the machine you're taking. A helmet and basic liability insurance is included in the rental fee. You may bring your own helmet, of course, and/or purchase additional insurance if desired. Clicking around the site, I noticed that they impose a $45 per day "rally surcharge" if you're renting for Daytona, Sturgis, or a number of other large get-togethers. Econ 101 at work here—supply and demand, you know—so take this into consideration. (Note: American Motorcyclist Association members get a small discount from Eaglerider.)

Find links to other motorcycle rental firms (and tour operators) at

- DJ's Motorcycle Rentals, http://harleys.com/cgi-bin/listings/mdb/filter.pl?selregion=usa
- Moto-Directory: Motorcycle Rental Companies, www.moto-directory.com/touring/rental _usa.asp

Also, check the back pages of the bike magazines. Or you can try an online yellow pages directory for the destination of your choice. You may do best at a local establishment. Captain Tussing, the technical editor for this book, uses a small local-to-Tampa company when he needs to rent a bike. Their fees are reasonable, their fleet is diverse—you can even rent a BMW—and they will bring the bike right to your door on a trailer.

Towing or Hauling

If you live in a large metropolitan area but you don't enjoy riding in traffic at all, towing—or hauling—your bike out of town to a quieter, more picturesque location can be a good option for you. Ditto if you'd like to have your bike available to you on vacation but don't feel up to riding it for hundreds (or thousands) of miles.

If you already have a pickup truck or figure you might want to buy one, you can set it up for hauling a motorcycle . . . or maybe two; at minimum, you'll need a ramp and ratcheted tie-downs, which you'll normally fasten to eyebolts screwed into strategic locations in the truck bed. Getting a large motorcycle into (and out of) the back of a pickup truck is not for the faint of heart. (See figure 9-9.) There's almost always someone at your local dealership who can provide guidance and tell you what you need, since they do it all the time. And you can always throw money at the problem and shell out for a motorized lift. Plenty of ads for these in the backs of the bike rags.

The other alternative is a trailer for your bike—which works even if you don't have a pickup truck, as long as you can have a hitch installed on your four-wheeled vehicle. On the low end, there are plenty of used barebones trailers around, including some that are not motorcycle-specific but can easily be modified to haul your bike. A knowledgeable friend is invaluable here. See figure 9-10.

Fig. 9-9. It eventually took four of us to get my 1980 Suzuki GS1000G—aka the Beast—into the back of this pickup truck from Wayne Cycle in Waynesboro, Va. (Very nice folks, by the way, if you're in the vicinity.) This top-heavy bike weighed at least 800 pounds.

Fig. 9-10. This makeshift trailer was good enough to deliver a nice used Beemer to its new owner. Having three strong guys to manage the process was definitely a plus. We get by with a little help from our friends. That's Captain Tussing in the middle.

Fig. 9-11. Motorcycle trailers can be rather elegant. While on the road myself, I met the guy who owns this one. A fully enclosed trailer can protect your bike from the elements and is a secure place to store it overnight when you are traveling. Plus you can haul all sorts of stuff. This man had a fully equipped workshop in there, plus changes of gear for all kinds of weather.

You're still going to have to get your bike up some sort of ramp (and then down again when you arrive at your destination).

On the high end, you can find fully enclosed trailers that not only protect your bike from the elements but allow you to carry your gear and an entire workshop with you. I met the guy in figure 9-11 on the road in Virginia. From what I could gather, he's a semiretired contractor who spends a lot of time hauling his custom Harley Sportster around so he can ride it in a variety of locations and take it to bike shows. He was only too glad to offer assistance when I needed to replace the windshield on my bike—and he had exactly the right tools, too.

If you think trailering might be for you, start exploring the options at webBikeWorld's Motorcycle Trailers page, www.webbikeworld.com/motorcycle-trailer.

Magnifying Glass: Would you like to ride you own motorcycle in Europe? It's doable. H. Marc Lewis has Been There, Done That, and he tells you how, incorporating information from other folks who've been through the experience. See "Shipping a Motorcycle from the USA to Europe," www.micapeak.com/~marcl/pages/shipbike.html.

Shipping a Bike

What if you want to take a motorcycle trip but only have time to ride one way? Or you know you'll be tired at the end of your journey and you'd just as soon fly home? Well, there are any number of companies willing and eager to transport your machine for you. It's not inexpensive, but then again, you'd have to spend money on food, lodging, gas, etc., during your days on the road. And maybe you can snag a cheap one-way airfare.

As it says on webBikeWorld's Motorcycle Shipping-Transport page (www.webbi keworld.com/motorcycle-shipping-transport), "Motorcycles can be shipped crated or uncrated, and some shipping companies have specialized containers to hold motorcycles." When I shipped my old Suzuki from Waynesboro, Virginia, to Tampa, Florida, in September 2004, it cost about $600. More than half of that went towards building a custom crate for the bike. Why so high? Well, plywood was at a premium just then. It was being shipped in quantity to the Middle East for tent floors, plus Florida was in the process of being socked by four destructive hurricanes. (You've seen the Weather Channel footage of all those people lined up to buy plywood at Home Depot? Happens before every storm. Not sure what people are doing with all the plywood in between hurricanes. Eating it?)

As with so many things, you'll need to call around to get shipping quotes, although some companies will provide you with a quote online or via e-mail. As you might expect, if you're in or near a major metropolitan area, you'll have more options. For instance, if you can deliver the bike to the trucking terminal and then pick it up at the terminal on the other end, you'll save a significant amount over what it would cost to have it shipped door-to-door. You'll probably be required to drain the gas and maybe the oil out of the motorcycle, so when you go to fetch it, you'll need to bring dino juice with you, as well as a crowbar, since you may need to uncrate the thing yourself. (I did—which is why I also brought along my bigger-stronger-younger next-door neighbor.)

Again, the backs of the motorcycle magazines are full of ads from companies that will ship your bike. Check webBikeWorld (www.webbikeworld.com/motorcycle-shipping-transport/) for information on more shipping companies. If you're a member of the American Motorcyclist Association, you can get

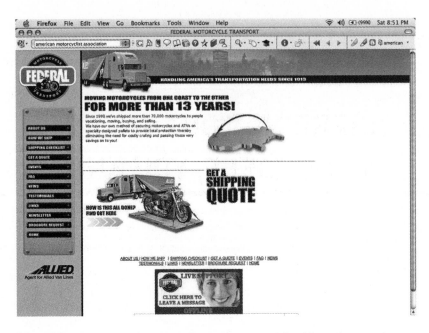

Fig. 9-12. Federal Motorcycle Transport says it's shipped more than 70,000 motorcycles since 1990. According to their Web site, they have a system of securing the bike to a pallet in such a way as to eliminate the need for an expensive crate; www.funtransport.com.

a discount from Federal Motorcycle Transport (figure 9-12), which ships bikes uncrated and has plenty of experience doing so. Speaking of the AMA, you'll find an article about bike shipping on its Web site: "To Ship or Not to Ship: 13 Questions to Help Find the Answer," www.ama-cycle .org/roadride/shipping.asp.

10 YOU'RE NOT OUT THERE BY YOURSELF, YOU KNOW

◆ How to ride in a group

◆ Riding two-up

◆ To wave or not to wave

◆ Don't touch other people's machines without permission, and other caveats

Some folks are really into the social aspects of motorcycling, and why not? As was discussed in chapter 9, when you buy a bike, you instantly become part of a large, diverse community. At any stage of life, it's interesting to meet new people. But the older we get and the more ruts we dig ourselves into, the fewer opportunities we have to socialize with folks who are not connected to the workplace, the neighborhood, our children's schools and activities, our houses of worship, professional associations . . .

Motorcyclists are interested in other motorcyclists. We can talk endlessly about our bikes and riding. We can debate the merits and liabilities of helmet laws, loud pipes, and synthetic oil versus dino juice. We can rail about the abuse we take from the cagers, and we can seek advice for mechanical problems. It's not surprising that so many motorcyclists like to get together for a weekend ride or maybe a longer road trip. (This is hardly a new pastime, as figure 10-1 clearly demonstrates.)

Even solitary bikers on the road tend to gather, according to Captain Glenn Tussing, MSF instructor and technical editor for this book. "Total strangers who happen to be sharing the same stretch of road for a few miles will actually adjust their speed if possible to fall into an ad hoc formation together. They will usually ride together for as long as possible, even having conversations at inter-

Fig. 10-1: "Motorcycle club out to enjoy the fall coloring along the Mohawk Trail, Massachusetts." Taken by John Collier in October 1941, this picture is part of the Farm Security Administration/Office of War Information collection at the Library of Congress. Library of Congress, Prints & Photographs Division, FSA/OWI Collection, [LC-USF34-081032-D]

sections or during pauses in traffic. When they finally reach the point at which they must part ways, they usually ride off while rendering their version of the 'motorcycle wave,' as dictated by the type of ride they are on."

ALL OF US TOGETHER: THE INS AND OUTS OF GROUP RIDING

As far as visibility on the highways is concerned, a group of motorcyclists is much harder to overlook than a solitary rider—so yes, there is a certain amount of safety in numbers. But some people do not enjoy group riding at all, and the larger the group, the more complicated things can get.

When it's only a few motorcyclists meeting up for a ride someplace, a brief chat beforehand will usually do it:

Savvy Tip

"Ride your own ride" is another one of those hoary motorcycle maxims that you'll hear over and over again. For good reason. You should never allow yourself to be pressured or goaded into riding faster than your comfort level, on roads that you find too challenging (hills, curves, traffic), under conditions (rain, high winds, late nights) that make you feel unsafe. If you start to experience that sort of pressure during a group ride, your best bet may be to drop out and head home. And find another group to ride with next time.

- How far can you go before you have to stop for gas?
- What is your comfort level as far as speed goes?
- Where and when should we stop for lunch?
- Do you have to be home at a certain time?

If more than a couple of motorcyclists are riding together and you don't establish certain things ahead of time, there could literally be trouble down the road. For one thing, no one is "in charge"—for example, to lead the group at a safe speed and to keep an eye on potential stragglers. Negative group dynamics can take over, like riders racing one another or pulling dangerous stunts to show off. Or worse, pressuring a slower, less experienced motorcyclist to ride beyond his or her capabilities.

But when it's a full-bore group ride, the planning and preparation can rival what must have taken place in advance of the Normandy invasion—especially one of those charity rides that can attract a thousand or more motorcyclists. But that is hardly typical.

Most group rides are purely recreational, usually organized by a club or a dealership. The optimum size is 10 or fewer bikes; if you've got more riders than this, it is usually recommended that the group be split into two or more smaller groups. Some fairly universal organizational rules apply to group riding:

- The **road captain** is basically in charge of organizing the ride and specifying rules/guidelines.
- The **lead bike** heads up the group and is responsible for transmitting information to the other riders via standard hand signals, as shown in figure 10-2. The lead rider sets the pace for the group in terms of speed, direction, preferred lane, and formation. Often, he or she is called upon to make quick decisions when confronted with the unexpected obstacle—road construction, surface condition, confusing signage, etc. The road captain may or may not ride in the lead position, but if a large group has been divided into smaller groups, each one will have its own lead bike.

Fig. 10-2: Motorcyclists have developed a standard set of hand signals to communicate with each other while riding together. At minimum, make sure everyone knows a few critical signals before starting out: for example, "Let's stop," "Need gas," etc. Keeping it simple, perhaps the best way of warning other riders about road hazards is a quick flash of your brake light. Download the Motorcycle Safety Foundation's Group Riding Quick Tips brochure: www.msf-usa.org/downloads/Group_Ride .pdf.

- The **drag bike**, or the **sweep bike**, brings up the rear. Typically, this is the most experienced rider in the group, as he or she will be the one to stop and help other riders who get into trouble or experience mechanical problems. This is also the person responsible for nailing down a lane for the group as it merges into faster traffic. He or she will move over first and block traffic approaching from the rear until the rest of the group has moved over. Yet another name for this rider is the **tail gunner**. (Note that it may not be possible for the entire group to change lanes at the same time, depending on traffic conditions. And each rider should pass slower vehicles individually, when it's safe. Don't try this as a group.) The lead rider and the drag rider should have some means of communicating with each other—cell phones, a radio system, etc.

- Group riders typically arrange themselves in **staggered formation**, with the lead bike on the left-hand side of the lane ("left track"), the second rider in the right track, the third rider in the left track, and so on. Proper spacing is one second behind the next bike and two seconds behind the bike riding in the same track. Each bike should have enough space to move from side to side in a lane when necessary to avoid obstacles, etc. When cornering, it's a good idea to spread out a little so no one ends up running off the road.

- Depending on the circumstances—entering or exiting the freeway, moving through toll plazas, in tight turns, if the road surface is bad—riders may ride single file—lined up behind each other in same lane position. Riding two abreast (**parade formation**) is not usually recommended for this type of situation as it doesn't leave enough room for each bike to maneuver—for example, if the cage in the next lane starts drifting over into your lane or if road hazards multiply. When stopped at a traffic light, though, bikes will often move two abreast, so the group takes up less space.

- Newer riders and those who prefer to ride slow should be nearer the lead bike, who can adjust the pace as required. Faster riders should be toward the back.

- Given differences in riding ability, traffic conditions, and so forth, it is likely that the group will split apart on more than one occasion. Discuss ahead of time how these situations will be handled. Having each rider wait for every other rider after a turn is an easy way to keep a smaller group together. Larger groups, before starting out, should decide on scheduled stops and determine that the group will wait at each stop until all the riders have caught up.

- When stopping, the entire group should try and get off the road as quickly as possible. Make sure the parking lot can accommodate everyone in the group; pass-through parking would be ideal.

- Each rider is responsible for arriving on time, at the designated location, with a full gas tank and a motorcycle in good mechanical condition. A riders' meeting should be held prior to starting out to brief everyone on the route, rest stops, hand signals, etc.

- Be aware of all the additional distractions that come into play when you are riding with a group, such as the unfamiliar riding styles of other motorcyclists, the challenges of staying with the group, and riding on unfamiliar roads, especially in scenic areas where the urge to sightsee is strong.
- Each rider is ultimately responsible for his or her own personal safety. *Ride your own ride.*

Check your bike over systematically before you set out on your ride. As previously discussed, the Motorcycle Safety Foundation recommends a T-CLOCS inspection:

- T—Tires and wheels (air pressure, tread, cracks/dents/loose spokes, bearings, brakes)
- C—Controls (levers, switches, cables, hoses, throttle)
- L—Lights and electrics (working condition)
- O—Oil and other fluids (coolant, hydraulic fluid, fuel)
- C—Chassis (suspension, drive components—chain or helt or drive shaft)
- S—Sidestand

RIDING 2-UP

It takes more love to share the saddle than to share the bed.

—The Daily Funnies

That old motorcycling maxim may or may not be true for you. However, most motorcyclists ride solo most of the time. Some will ride solo all of the time. I swapped out the stock seat and pillion pad on my V-Star for an upgraded solo seat because I don't anticipate ever riding with a passenger. I am a small woman, and almost anyone I would take on my bike would be bigger than me, which seems a little too unsafe for my personal comfort level.

I cringe whenever I see a pair of young kids on a sport bike, neither of whom is wearing proper equipment. I look at these scantily-clad young girls clinging to their boyfriends, who are weaving in and out of heavy traffic at a high rate of speed, and all I can think of are the parents sitting home somewhere, blissfully ignorant . . . until the phone rings one day and there's a state trooper on the line with bad news. OK. I thought I was immortal at that age, too. But I know better now—especially since I am a parent myself. This is not my idea of 2-up riding, and it's probably not what you had in mind, either.

Make no mistake about it; when you take a passenger on your motorcycle, you are also taking on a

---

The epigraph is from the Daily Funnies: Biker Wisdom, http://dailyfunnies.org/page/214.

Fig. 10-3: Sometimes it is downright nice to have company on the road. Photo courtesy of Honda Motorcycles.

lot of responsibility. But if you do it right, it's a great way to introduce others to the sport of motorcycling—and to have companionship while pursuing a pastime you love. Women, in particular, often get involved in motorcycling after riding behind a significant other. See figure 10-3.

When you decide to carry another person on your bike, it is your responsibility to:

- Make sure he or she is wearing proper gear—at minimum, a helmet, eye protection, long-sleeved shirt and long pants, gloves, and boots that come up over the ankle. If you're going to be riding with your spouse, significant other, child, etc., on a regular basis, you'll want to invest in the same quality of gear that you've purchased for yourself.
- Make sure he or she knows which parts of the motorcycle could cause injury and should be avoided—the hot exhaust pipe, chain, wheel spokes, moving suspension parts, etc.
- Make sure he or she understands that motorcycles turn by leaning, so panic will not ensue the first time you go around a corner. The passenger should always look over the shoulder of the operator in the direction of the turn, which not only puts him or her in the correct position, but doesn't hinder the operator's vision.
- Make sure the passenger knows to keep both feet on the footpegs when the bike is stopped—for example, at a traffic signal. Make sure he or she knows how and where to hold on—your hips, your waist, or handles/arm rests if the bike is so equipped.

- Make sure your passenger understands at least something about how motorcycles work. At minimum, explain the controls, how you start the bike, how you stop the bike, how you accelerate and how you slow down. It may help to compare/contrast the motorcycle with an automobile, with which your passenger likely has a fair amount of personal experience.
- Understand that your passenger—especially if he or she is a novice—should be the one to determine the speed and distance of the ride. Don't overdo either at first, and keep everything as smooth as possible. Go out of your way to avoid abrupt turns, sudden acceleration, hard braking, and excessive lean angles. It's also helpful to brief your passenger ahead of time on the route you plan to take.

Instruct your passenger not to get onto the bike until you've started it up, gotten it securely balanced, and indicated it's OK to proceed. At this point, the passenger generally places his or her left hand on the operator's left shoulder for balance, steps on the left passenger footpeg with his or her left foot, and swings his or her right leg over the bike. This can be a less-than-graceful procedure the first couple of times—particularly if your bike is tall and your passenger is short—but it will get easier with practice. (Captain Tussing, who is as anal about the appearance of my bike as he is about his, suggests warning the mounting/dismounting passenger to avoid scraping his/her right heel across the paint on the tail section of the bike or the top of the hard bags . . . which is a good idea, but don't be surprised if it happens anyhow.)

When it's time to dismount, it's pretty much the same thing in reverse; the passenger waits until the operator has come to a complete stop, shut down the engine, gotten the bike balanced, and indicated that it's OK to get off. As a passenger, you'll want to remember:

- Not to wear any loose or floppy articles of clothing that could get caught in the bike's moving parts or flap excessively in the wind, which is very annoying.
- Not to make any sudden movements or shifts in weight while under way, as this could throw the motorcycle off balance.

Motorcycles are noisy. The wind is noisy. Absent the luxury of an electronic communications system, you will likely not be able to carry on any sort of conversation. Ask all questions up front—or save them for a rest stop—and let the operator know what your comfort level is in terms of speed and length/distance of ride. Establish ahead of time a few basic signals, such as how to indicate you would like to stop or turn right/left.

Do not climb onto a motorcycle behind any operator who makes you feel uncomfortable—for example, someone who has a penchant for recklessness, is inexperienced, or who has been drinking. Likewise if the weather or road conditions make you uneasy.

When you take someone with you on the back of your bike, even if that person is an experienced motorcycle passenger, you need to be aware that your machine will operate quite differently because of the additional weight. If your passenger weighs as much as you, you are doubling the load on the motorcycle's suspension system. Depending on the manufacturer, you may be able to adjust your bike's suspension to better accommodate the extra weight. Check your owner's manual. You may also need to increase tire pressures. Also keep in mind the differences in:

- **A**cceleration: It will take a bit longer to start out and get up to speed. Do it smoothly. If the bike leaps forward too quickly because you've been aggressive with the throttle, your passenger will be jerked around—and possibly decide, then and there, that he or she wants to get off.

- **B**raking: With the added weight of a passenger, it will take a bit longer to get stopped, so start rolling off the throttle and braking sooner. If you stop too suddenly, your passenger will slam into you from the rear, pushing you forward—which may well cause you to lose control of the bike. Remember that your passenger does not have the same unobstructed view of the road ahead that you do and may be blissfully unaware that you're about to apply the brakes because some critter has emerged from the grass at the shoulder of the road and dashed out in front of the bike. If you're going to ride with a passenger often, it's probably a good idea to find a vacant parking lot somewhere and practice panic stops with a second person aboard.

- **C**ornering: Remember that a motorcycle turns by leaning. Even if you've explained this in advance, it's often an unsettling feeling for the novice passenger, who may go into panic mode the first time you attempt to turn. The instinctive reaction under such circumstances is to throw his or her weight to the opposite side of the bike—not the most expeditious maneuver for you, as you struggle to get the motorcycle leaned over far enough to complete the turn without running off the road or drifting across the center line into the oncoming lane. And if your bike already has limited ground clearance—for example, most cruisers— the extra weight of the passenger means you're going to drag a footpeg or a heel a lot sooner than you would if you were riding solo. Inflating your tire pressure in accordance with what your owner's manual suggests for 2-up riding will help. So will managing your turns better; take the corners more sedately, with a larger radius.

- **D**own (and up): When you are going up a hill with a passenger seated atop the rear wheel, the extra weight back there kinda makes your bike want to do a wheelie—even if you, as the operator, most definitely do not. Depending on how steep the incline and how heavy the passenger, you may want to stand up and lean forward on the footpegs to shift more weight to the front. When you are headed downhill and your passenger shifts forward, right up against you, your problem is increased load on the front wheel, which will make stopping more difficult. Particularly on roads with steep downhill turns, start braking well in advance.

The Motorcycle Safety Foundation offers a helpful brochure, *Quick Tips: Guidelines For Carrying a Passenger on Your Motorcycle.* Download it at www.msf-usa.org/downloads/ Passenger_Tip_Sheet.pdf.

To Wave or Not to Wave

The brand you ride, or the price tag or nationality associated with it, or the "exclusivity" of your ownership, should not preclude you from waving to the rider going the opposite direction on their Rebel 250, Boss Hoss, GSX-R, Harley, or new MV Augusta. As a relatively small group of society, we can't really afford the special interest mentality, and the exclusionary attitude that goes along with it.

—*Willy Ivans*

"Harley riders don't wave."

"Sport bike riders don't wave."

"BMW riders don't wave."

"Gold Wing riders don't wave."

My, but we do go on . . . and what is this all about, anyhow, this waving-at-other-motorcyclists thing?

This is a topic that regularly pops up in the online motorcycling world. Whatever happened to the "good old days," when "we were all in this together," and every motorcyclist greeted every other passing motorcyclist with a wave, regardless of make, model or style (with the exception of the **1%-ers**, of course)? Why does this matter so much?

It is, of course, largely symbolic. Although there is this lingering image of the motorcyclist as lone wolf and nonconformist, most of us understand (and kind of like) the idea that when we buy a motorcycle and hit the highway on two wheels, we become members of this unique "band of brothers" (and sisters). Somehow, we are all supposed to experience a feeling of connectedness to every other motorcyclist—regardless of make or model of machine, occupational or financial status, etc. At the very least, we recognize that it's "us"—the bikers—against "them"—the cagers. Which is why motor-

The epigraph is from Willy Ivans, "What Happened to the Family?" *Motorcycle Digest,* November 16, 2002.

cyclists are prone to wave at each other . . . and many of us feel it is a Good Thing for the cagers to see this, as perhaps it makes them more aware of us out there on the roads.

Given all of this, you can see why the simple act of waggling your hand or wiggling your fingers takes on a significance far in excess of a simple greeting.

Some people feel there is less waving now because motorcycling has become more fragmented—more types of bikes, more types of bikers. Others come up with their own, often bizarre explanations—newbies who are afraid to remove their hands from the handlebars, non-helmet-wearing Harley riders who won't wave to anyone in a full-face helmet whose face they cannot see, sport bike riders who want to stay hunched over and aerodynamic, Gold Wing riders who are too busy fiddling with their GPS systems and other electronics. And then there is snobbery and prejudice: "those kids all dressed up in their clown suits on their little plastic bikes," "that yuppie **poseur** in his black leather jacket and doo-rag on his $25,000 Harley."

You'll be glad to know that the vast majority of mainstream motorcyclists regard this kind of stuff as nonsense. For better or for worse, motorcycling *is* a community of sorts. Most of us are brand-agnostic and will wave at anybody—even people on scooters, which sometimes startles them. Of course, when it's unsafe to take your hand off the handlebars—in stop-and-go traffic, tricky curves, etc.,—a nod of the head will do just fine.

DON'T TOUCH OTHER PEOPLE'S MACHINES (AND OTHER FINE POINTS OF MOTO-ETIQUETTE)

If the rules of motorcycle etiquette are actually codified somewhere, I haven't stumbled across them yet. But there are certain things that people just . . . know. Like not touching someone else's bike without permission.

Even if there are thousands of bikes lined up along the street during some rally, you must keep your hands to yourself. "Touch with your eyes, don't look with your fingers." (See figure 10-4.)

True story: I had wandered across the street from my office to use the ATM at the credit union. When I returned, there was a Harley-Davidson Road King in the parking lot in front of our building—with its turn signal flashing. I stopped. I looked. All it would have taken was for me to press and cancel the signal . . . but I did not. Instead, I went into the building and wandered around inside until I saw a guy with a motorcycle helmet and jacket sitting at one of the machines in our computer lab. I went up to him. I tapped him on the shoulder. I said, "You know, your turn signal is still flash-

Fig. 10-4: Look but don't touch—especially when it's a beautifully restored classic.

ing out there in the parking lot." I jerked my thumb in the appropriate direction. "Thank you," he said. And got up, went outside, and dealt with the turn signal himself.

And I knew I'd done the right thing.

Yes, people do it, but it is generally considered poor etiquette to dis someone else's bike because of its brand or style. Along with this comes the stereotyping of owners, for example, the young and reckless **squid** on the sportbike, the **Rich Urban Biker** and his midlife crisis Harley, the old fart on the Gold Wing ("Winnebiko"), the snobbish and anal-retentive BMW owner, the Harley wanna-be on the Japanese cruiser . . .

Some of this is all in good fun, of course; you'll see a lot of good-natured kidding in the online motorcycle forums. And there's nothing really wrong with pride of ownership. When it turns mean-spirited, however, is when it starts to become . . . well, immature and tacky.

This also applies to how people accessorize their bikes. As our bikes become an extension of our personalities, aesthetics can take on outsized significance. Personally, I am a minimalist; you will not see much chrome and no leather fringe on my bike. A fellow at my work bought a similar cruiser a little larger than mine, and added everything but the kitchen sink to it, including decals for the gas tank. I rag on him about "whoring up his bike," and I'm sure he regards mine as a plain Jane, but he

Savvy Tip

If you happen to see a motorcyclist rolling along with the rear passenger pegs down in the absence of a passenger, know that this is one way of commemorating a fallen rider. In a procession for a fallen rider, all of the bikes are likely to have the rear passenger pegs down. It's analogous to saluting a fallen commanding officer by reversing a pair of empty boots in the stirrups on a horse. As a general rule, however, it's not a good idea to ride around with the pegs down if no one is using them, since there is a danger they may get caught on something, although Captain Tussing tells me they can serve as an alternate place to put your own feet on a long-distance ride—depending on your stature and your bike, I guess—"for that half-tank stretch."

stops by my office regularly to talk motorcycling and regularly invites me to join his brand-agnostic group of friends on their midweek evening ride.

When it comes right down to it, most motorcyclists realize that a love for two-wheeled motorized transportation unites us more than brands or models could ever divide us. For one thing, we all know that we are largely invisible to the cagers out there. And we all like to look at each other's bikes. More than once, my sons have rolled their eyes in a restaurant when their mother, hearing a motorcycle pass by, stops talking in mid-sentence, whips her head around, and cranes her neck to look out the window.

So you're riding along and spot another motorcyclist stopped on the side of the road with his or her helmet on the ground next to the bike, usually facing oncoming traffic. This almost always indicates that there's been some sort of mechanical breakdown, and traditional biker etiquette holds that you should always stop to help. Obviously, there are some caveats here.

From a personal safety standpoint that requires no elaboration, a woman should probably never stop. Guys can probably make a spur-of-the-moment decision based on gut reaction and physical prowess, that is, if you're a six-foot, four-inch Navy SEAL, you're unlikely to be at a disadvantage should the operator of the disabled motorcycle turn out to be a bad apple. If you've got mechanical skills and tools and you feel comfortable with the situation, your help will most likely be gratefully appreciated by any stranded motorcyclist. Even if you're mechanically inept, you might want to stop and offer the use of your cell phone.

Although I hate watching people talk on cell phones while driving and I despise hearing personal conversations in public places, I would no sooner ride without my cell phone than I would without my helmet. Personally, if I saw a stranded motorcyclist alongside the road, I'd proceed to the nearest freeway exit, gas station, or other convenient stopping place and I'd make a call to the highway patrol or local constabulary and let them deal with the unfortunate biker.

Frankly, given the realities of the world we live in, this is a reasonable course of action for any motorcyclist, male or female. But do make that call.

APPENDIX A:
MOTORCYCLISTS IN YOUR BLIND SPOT

As the driver of a car or other four-wheeled vehicle, have you ever been in the position where you are preparing to make a lane change and then have to make a quick adjustment back into your lane because you hear a horn sound? You may have looked in your sideview and rearview mirrors but saw nothing. Now back in your lane a motorcyclist rides up in the lane beside you. You give the ol' "I'm sorry I didn't see you" wave and then drive on, remorseful for at least a little while.

If this has happened to you, you're not alone; a recent National Highway Traffic Safety Administration study found that over two-thirds of motorcycle-involved accidents were caused by other vehicles encroaching upon the motorcyclist's right-of-way. The majority of motorists involved in an accident with a motorcycle usually state they never saw the motorcycle, or saw it too late to correct any action.

Here are some tips to help you avoid this situation:

- Make a mental note each time you drive to look for motorcyclists on the roadways.
- Don't just use your sideview/rearview mirrors but turn your head to ensure no one is in your blind spot.
- Properly adjust your sideview mirrors to see the lanes on each side of you, not the sides of your vehicle.

This appendix is written by Captain Glenn L. Tussing Jr., USAF. Tussing, the technical editor for this book, is motorcycle safety coordinator at MacDill Air Force Base in Tampa, Fla.

- Use your blinkers when making a lane change; this will make motorcyclists aware of your intention and give them time to react if you don't see them.
- Don't be in a hurry or make last-minute lane-change decisions; give yourself time to get over.
- Treat a motorcycle as a full-sized vehicle; provide it the same room and rights to the road as any other vehicle.
- Stay off your cell phone when you are driving. Cell phone use makes you inattentive to your surroundings.
- Don't drink and drive, as alcohol impairs your judgment and reaction time.

These tips should help you avoid a potential accident with a motorcyclist—or any other vehicle that could be in your blind spot. As we all know, motorcyclists are not as protected as automobile drivers are when it comes to accidents. Let's all help reduce the risk to our motorcycle riders.

And if you are a motorcyclist, be sure you are operating your vehicle safely and within the rules of the road, and be proactive by taking one of the many motorcycle safety courses available. This applies to everyone from "I have never touched a motorcycle but want to try riding" to "I have been riding for 45 years and would like to see what is new out there for me to learn."

APPENDIX B:
CHECKLIST FOR USED-BIKE BUYERS

The checklist on the next pages is reproduced here courtesy of MotorcycleBeginners.com. If you would like to print extra copies, go to http://motorcyclebeginners.com/downloads/used-bike-questionnaire-2.pdf. Take a copy with you when you are checking out a used motorcycle you're thinking of buying.

MotorcycleBeginners.Com

Date			
Principal			
Address			
Phone		Fax	
Make		Model	
Year		Size	
Cost			

First (Over-the-Phone) Questions:
1. What is the general condition of the bike?
2. What is the history of the bike, and how was it used? Raced?
3. Has the bike been tipped or crashed?
4. Do you have the documentation? Title, tags, repair/service history?
5. What is the mileage on the bike?
6. What repairs and maintenance have been performed? (If mileage over 30K, clutch changed? How often oil changed?)
7. What enhancements/modifications have been made?
8. What repair does the bike need now? Anything wrong with it?
9. What "extras" come with the bike?
10. Why is the bike being sold?

Quick check at the seller's:
- Does title match bike (tags, odometer, VIN?) Lien on title?
- Does wear & tear match age/mileage/use?
- Generally clean and straight?
- Maintenance history? Include receipts for parts/oil/work done?

FROM THE TOP:	
Brake fluid level in reservoir? Cracks on mounting? Cable adjustment screw OK?	
Clutch lever OK? Cracks in mounting? Cable adjustment screw OK?	
Look nasty, with cracks and scratches?	
Signs of impact damage?	
Welds look OK?	
Cracks? Look at triple tree, frame	
Gas cap works?	
Dents in gas tank from accident/drop?	
Rust in gas tank?	
Gas dark? How much in tank?	
Seat cover intact? Cover material OK?	
Seat locking release OK? Works with ignition key?	
Seat stable, latches OK?	
Original seat?	
Battery level OK?	
Battery posts clean?	
Battery and cradle OK, clean, no cracks?	

FRONT	
Pump suspension. Return to position after 2 ½ strokes?	
Chromed fork legs show no sign of oil?	
Fork seals ever changed (after 15-20,000 miles)?	
Look symmetric?	

REAR	
Pump suspension. Return to position after 2 ½ strokes?	
Look symmetric?	

BOTH SIDES	
Wheels round, smooth, not dented?	
Spokes OK?	
Tires have tread? (Lincoln penny rule: top of Abe' shead shouldn' tshow when top of penny is inserted into thread)	
Sidewalls OK?	
Tires with rough edges, balled-up rubber buildup suggests racing.	
Tires OK on edges, but completely smooth in center suggests burn-out; look closely at other care of bike.	
Tire pressure OK?	
Also check tire date guide, appended at end of questionnaire.	
Brake wear indicator visible? Brake cable has some slack?	
Scoring in brake disks?	
Shocks: bushing OK? Leaking?	
Springs: Breaks or cracks?	
Signs of impact damage?	
Welds look OK?	
Cracks in engine mounts, front fairing bracket (if any), frame...	
Motor mount bolts OK?	
Fasteners look stripped or gouged?	
Footpegs match?	
Wiring harness looks redone?	

BOTH SIDES	
Rust? Where? (Check exhaust system, subframe...)	
Dents from accident or drop?	
Belt drive: Condition of belt and sprockets?	
Shaft drive: Leaks?	
Chain drive: Chain aligned?	
• Kinked links when spin back wheel?	
• Rusty?	
• Can you pull back a full link?	
• Sprocket teeth bent/broken/worn?	
Cooling:	
• Air-cooled: Fins OK? Options in way of cooling?	
• Oil-cooled: leaks? Radiator OK?	
• Water-cooled: Leaks? Radiator OK? Coolant pure? Coolant level OK?	
Oil clean? Level OK?	
Engine hot/warm/cold? Why?	
Head gasket: Signs of burned gas (defective head gasket)? Crystallization (water leak)?	
Aftermarket engine cover suggests racing.	
Bolts drilled for retaining wires suggests racing or other heavy use.	
Parallel scratches on engine or bodywork suggest crash if high up (lower scratches may be low turns - ask!)	

BOTH SIDES	
Bodywork seams fit OK & appear even? Tabs, &c., may have broken in crash	

LEFT SIDE	
Shift lever OK? Sign of oil leak?	

RIGHT SIDE	
Both brakes trigger brake light?	

SIT ON BIKE:	
Brake power levels after two pumps?	
Bottom out when you sit on it?	
Horn works?	
Lights work? (High/low beam? All idiot lights come on when engine starting? Lights go out appropriately?)	
Signals work?	
Brake lever feels OK? Lever comes all the way to handlebar? (It shouldn' t...)	
Rear brake smooth?	
Clutch smooth? Feels like neutral when you roll bike (possibly a little more resistance).	
Levers match? Why not? (Crash?)	
Choke? (Where is it?)	
Kill switch?	
Gas reserve petcock? Does it move?	

START BIKE:	
Starts OK? Twice?	
Idle near 1000 rpm?	

START BIKE:	
Sound OK? Piston slap on startup?	
Engage clutch. Smooth? Find friction zone OK?	
Blip throttle: black smoke (rich fuel mix) or blue smoke (oil in fuel mix)?	
Kickstand cutoff works?	
Engine kill-switch works?	
Engine running: does headlight brighten when engine revved? (It' s supposed to...)	

OVERALL:
Do I like this bike enough to pay for it?

TIRE DATE GUIDE

You can check the date of manufacture of the tires on the bike. Tires made after 1/1/2000 will have a date code beginning with the letters DOT and ending with a code for the date of tire manufacture in this format: DOT???????WWYY, where the WW indicates the number of the week of the year (with the first week of the year being 01 and the last week of the year, presumably, being 52), and the YY indicates the last two digits of the year of manufacture (the ??????? indicates other coding between the letters DOT and the date code). A tire manufactured in mid-February of 2002 will have a number like DOTAX126GH70602.

Tires manufactured prior to 1/1/2000 will not have all the additional data (the number will not start with DOT??????), but will have a three-digit code stamped into the sidewall in the format WWY, where WW indicates the number of the week of the year, and the Y indicates the last digit of the year of manufacture; a tire manufactured in mid-February 1999 will have a number like 069 or 079.

COPYRIGHT AND DISCLAIMER

GLOSSARY

As an activity with a rich history and folklore, motorcycling has developed a rather colorful, specialized vocabulary over the years. Here's a quick study guide to motorcycle terminology, jargon, and slang.

1%-er (or one-percenter)—According to legend, the **AMA** blamed the problems at Hollister, California, in 1947 (see chapter 1) on the so-called "outlaw" motorcycle clubs, claiming that 99 percent of motorcyclists were upstanding, law-abiding citizens, yada yada. Those belonging to non–AMA sanctioned clubs—"outlaw" does not necessarily mean "criminal"—continue to refer to themselves as "one-percenters."

2-up—Riding with a passenger. See **pillion**, **ridin' bitch**.

ABS—Antilock braking system. Computerized braking system that senses when your wheels are about to lock up and automatically interrupts pressure to the brakes so as to prevent a skid. Tends to be offered as an accessory on some higher-end bikes, but many motorcyclists are wary of it because they feel it takes control away from the operator.

AMA—American Motorcyclist Association (www.ama-cycle.org). Special-interest and lobbying organization for the motorcycling community. Claims 260,000-plus dues-paying members.

aftermarket—Motorcycle parts and accessories made by companies other than the original motorcycle manufacturer. See **OEM**.

ape hangers—High handlebars that position the rider's hands higher than his or her shoulders. Mostly for show. Often there are state laws restricting how high the handlebars can be on a bike that is ridden on public streets.

apex—The tightest point of a curve.

asphalt surfing (or pavement surfing or eating asphalt)—Slang term for what happens when the rider is thrown from the motorcycle and slides along the road surface. If you aren't wearing adequate protective gear, this results in **road rash**.

Beemer—BMW motorcycle; as opposed to Bimmer, which is a BMW automobile.

blip the throttle—Quick twist of the wrist that provides a short burst of the accelerator. Sometimes done at stoplights, with the clutch in, to attract attention, especially by those with an affinity for "loud pipes."

bone yard—Motorcycle salvage operation where used parts can be scavenged.

cager—Automobile driver. Motorcyclists universally refer to cars, SUVs, light trucks, vans, etc., as **cages**.

centerstand (or center stand)—Stand that is spring-mounted under the motorcycle to hold it vertical when it is parked.

choke—Knob or other device that restricts air intake so that a fuel-rich mixture can get a cold engine started. Not needed on motorcycles that have **fuel injection systems** rather than carburetors.

chopper—Originally used to describe stripped-down, post-World War II motorcycles that had most of their body parts removed, ostensibly to make them go faster. Now refers to highly customized motorcycles with an extreme front **rake**, **ape hanger** handlebars, and no rear suspension. These tend to be more for show than regular use, as they are difficult to handle and may not even be street legal.

colors—Motorcycle club patches, often worn on denim or leather vests. Not exclusive to "outlaw" clubs; many AMA-sanctioned club members wear an AMA patch along with a club-specific patch. But since colors are commonly associated with outlaw groups like the Hell's Angels, any pack of bikers decked out in their patches, thundering down the highway, may strike fear into the hearts of the non-motorcycling public.

conspicuity—Being conspicuous, standing out. White helmets, brightly-colored gear, and reflective materials all increase motorcyclist conspicuity, making us more likely to be seen by the **cagers**.

contact patch (or footprint)—That part of the tire tread that actually touches the road when you are riding.

Cordura—"CORDURA® is the registered trademark for INVISTA certified performance fabrics containing proprietary INVISTA fibers and, in some cases, other companion fibers" (www.invista.com/prd_cordura.shtml). It's a tough, abrasion-resistant material commonly used for camping equipment, soft luggage, and motorcycle protective gear. (See chapter 6.)

countersteer—At all but the slowest speeds, you turn a motorcycle by countersteering—push on the left handlebar to go right and push on the right handlebar to go left. For some reason, most people find this intuitive … as long as they don't stop to think about it too much.

crash bars (or engine guards, highway bars)—Usually metal loop (one piece) or two half-loops that you bolt to the frame of your bike behind the front wheel in the area of the engine. In the event of a serious crash, they are not going to provide much protection. But if the bike tips over while stopped or at low speed, they could prevent expensive engine or bodywork repair and possibly save you from a broken leg. You can buy attachable footpegs for most of them, so a taller rider can stretch out his or her legs while on the highway.

crotch rocket—Sport bike; sometimes referred to as a **rice rocket**, since the vast majority are Japanese.

dirty side—Bottom of the motorcycle (e.g., the "shiny side" is the top)."Keep the dirty side down" and "Keep the shiny side up" mean the same thing—ride safe, or "Stay vertical."

drag bars—Flat, straight handlebars that look very cool and sporty, but may require you to lean forward slightly while riding. Those with shorter arms may have more difficulty handling a bike equipped with drag bars.

drag bike (lieutenant, sweep bike, tail gunner)—This is the person who brings up the rear during a group ride. Ideally, this would be the most experienced motorcyclist in the group, since he or she will be the one to stop and help any riders who have problems.

enduro—When used to describe a motorcycle, it's a dual-sport machine that is suitable for both street and off-road use. When used to describe a race, it's a competition that tests endurance rather than speed.

fairing—A body panel mounted on the front of a bike that protects it—and its rider—from the elements and flying debris. Some of these are quite elaborate, wrap-around constructs, with integrated windshields and other features. Some motorcycles—particularly touring models—come with a fairing, but they are widely available as **aftermarket** add-ons for other bikes.

final drive—Delivers power from the transmission to the rear wheel. Comes in three flavors—chain, belt, and shaft. (See chapter 4.)

forks—The two telescoping metal tubes which hold the front wheel to the rest of the bike, a key element of the front suspension system.

forward controls—You can move your foot pegs, rear brake pedal, and shifter further out in front of you if you are more comfortable in this riding position. Usually better for extended highway travel than city riding.

friction zone—That area of the clutch between fully released and fully engaged. The friction zone starts when you let the clutch out slowly, power starts to be transmitted to the rear wheels, and the bike begins moving forward. It ends when the clutch is all the way out and the rear wheel is fully powered. Using the friction zone is vital to controlling your motorcycle at slow speeds. It tends to be a bit different from bike to bike—longer, shorter, touchier, etc.

fuel injection—Electronic system that adjusts the fuel/air mixture to the engine. No manual **choke** required.

fully dressed (or full dresser, or full bagger)—A touring bike set up with hard luggage, a fairing, and other amenities for long-distance travel.

garbage wagon—Slang term for a large, fully-dressed touring bike. Synonyms: Geezer Glide, Winnebiko.

gearhead—Someone with a strong interest in mechanical things. You don't really have to be a gearhead to be a motorcyclist, but a little bit of mechanical knowledge never hurts.

hard bags—Side bags made from hard polymer materials. They require permanent mounting hardware; the brackets stay on, even if you remove the bags. However, they are usually lockable and waterproof, making them ideal for touring and commuting.

high side—Type of crash that typically occurs when the rider brakes suddenly, locks up the rear wheels, then suddenly releases the brakes so that the rear wheel jerks upward, pitching the rider off over the handlebars or the side of the bike facing away from the ground.

HOG—Harley Owners Group; "Hog" is a nickname for Harley-Davidson motorcycles

Hurt Report—Detailed 1979 University of Southern California study of over 3,600 motorcycle accidents. The findings of this study served as the underpinnings of the Motorcycle Safety Foundation's courses and launched the helmet wars that continue to this day (see chapter 6). Named for the lead investigator, Harry Hurt—which is kind of an ironic name, if you think about it. Believe it or not, no such detailed study has been done since then, despite the growing popularity of motorcycling and the resultant rise in injuries and fatalities, although Congress allocated funding for this in its 2005 session.

hydroplane—When you're riding on a wet road and your tires cease to make contact with the ground, so that you're actually traveling on top of the water, meaning that you have zero traction. Not a good thing.

ink—Slang for tattoo.

iron butt—Long-distance rider. The annual Iron Butt Rally is, arguably, one of the most grueling ordeals in organized motorcycling—11,000-plus miles in 11 days. If this is your thing, the Iron Butt Association is for you (www.ironbutt.com).

lane splitting—Riding between lanes of traffic. Normally done at low speeds, during traffic congestion. Not legal in most states and not for the novice or faint-of-heart rider. Watch for cagers suddenly changing lanes or opening their doors.

laying it down—In an emergency situation, deliberately dropping the motorcycle in a way that will cause the least amount of damage—to you and the machine. Make no mistake about it: "laying it down" is crashing. Not a recommended accident avoidance strategy.

lead bike—First rider in a group ride. Sets the pace for the group, watches for obstacles, etc. Should be an experienced rider.

LEO—Law enforcement officer.

low-side—Type of crash that results from allowing the motorcycle to lean so far over in a turn that it loses traction and drops to the ground.

lugging the engine—Riding the motorcycle in a gear that is too high for the speed you are traveling.

MSF—Motorcycle Safety Foundation. "The Motorcycle Safety Foundation (MSF) is a national, not-for-profit organization promoting the safety of motorcyclists with programs in rider training, operator licensing and public information. The MSF is sponsored by the U.S. manufacturers and distributors of BMW, Ducati, Harley-Davidson, Honda, Kawasaki, KTM, Piaggio/Vespa, Suzuki, Victory and Yamaha motorcycles" (www.msf-usa.org).

naked bike—A motorcycle with no fairing and an exposed chassis.

OEM—Original equipment manufacturer. Typically, parts and accessories made/offered by the same company that manufactured your motorcycle.

outlaw—Technically speaking, describes motorcycle clubs that are unwilling to go along with the rules and regulations necessary to gain the blessings of the **AMA**. See **1%-er**.

parade formation—Group of motorcycles riding two-by-two, side-by-side in a single lane. Generally not recommended for a group ride; **staggered formation**, which gives each rider a better space cushion, is preferred.

petcock—Fuel valve. (See chapter 2.)

pillion—Rear or passenger seat, or riding on the rear or passenger seat, thus, "riding pillion." See: **ridin' bitch**.

pipes—Exhaust system.

poker run—Organized event—often with a charitable purpose—in which motorcyclists pay a fee to participate and follow a prescribed course, picking up a playing card at each location. Whoever ends up at the last checkpoint with the best hand is the winner, and there is usually a party. Remember not to drink and ride.

poseur—Generally speaking, someone who buys an expensive motorcycle, gear, and accessories, but does very little actual riding. Likes to hang out at bike nights and show off. See *Diary of a Poseur* (www.harleyrendezvous.com/98poseur.htm).

power cruiser—Cruiser-style bikes with large engines—e.g., Honda VTX 1800, Yamaha V-Max, Triumph Rocket, Kawasaki Vulcan 2000.

rake—The angle of the front forks from the vertical. On a bike that is "raked out"—e.g., a chopper—the angle can be extreme.

rat bike—Usually, an older motorcycle that looks ill-maintained. "[A] Rat Bike is a motorcycle which is ridden instead of cleaned, maintained at the lowest possible cost with whichever parts are at hand, and which is usually painted matte black. There's no room on a Rat Bike for things like chrome or, horror of horrors, bolt-on plastic pretending to be chrome" (Rat Bike Zone: www.ratbike.org).

rice burner—Japanese motorcycle.

ridin' bitch—Riding on the rear or passenger seat. Given that it's usually a woman riding as a passenger, well … use your imagination. See **pillion**.

road captain—Organizer of a group ride who plans the route, stops, etc. May or may not serve as **lead bike**.

road crown—High point of a road, in the middle, to allow for water to drain off to either side. You're unlikely to find standing water close to the centerline of a road.

road gators—Those big chunks of rubber shed by tractor-trailer retread tires. Definitely a hazard for motorcyclists.

road rash—Abrasion injury that results from asphalt surfing if the motorcyclist is not wearing adequate protective gear. In extreme cases, the effect is like that of a third degree burn, requiring skin grafts.

Rolling Thunder—Veteran-oriented group that publicizes the POW/MIA issue, mainly by a huge annual Ride for Freedom that attracts several hundred thousand motorcyclists to Washington, D.C., over the Memorial Day weekend. (www.rollingthunder1.com/)

scoot—Slang term for a motorcycle. See **sled**.

shaft jacking—On shaft-driven bikes, acceleration causes the frame of the bike to move in the opposite direction from the shaft rotation, creating a somewhat bumpy motion.

sidecar—A small cart with a single wheel that attaches to the side of a motorcycle and provides extra carrying capacity or room for an additional passenger.

sidestand (side stand)—On a bicycle, this is called a kickstand. Push it down with your foot from the left side of your bike and it supports your motorcycle in a slightly left-leaning position while parked.

sissy bar—Backrest behind the passenger seat. Enhanced comfort and security for your passenger; it's also a useful gizmo to which you can bungee luggage, etc.

slab (super slab)—Freeway; limited access high-speed road.

sled—Slang term for motorcycle. See **scoot**.

snick (or snicking)—Nudging a transmission into gear; the sound a well-tuned transmission makes when it moves smoothly from one gear to another.

squid—Stupid, Quick, Underdressed, Imminently Dead. Those sport bike riders you see, zipping in and out of traffic at high speeds, often wearing nothing more than t-shirts, shorts, and flip-flops. (See Squid Purity Test—www.bytebrothers.org/SquidTest.htm.)

staggered formation—Preferred formation for group riding; bike one, in the lead, is in the left track of the lane, bike two is behind bike one in the right track, bike three is behind bike two in the left track, etc. Allows each bike a space cushion on either side.

stock—How your motorcycle comes set up, directly from the factory, before you open your wallet a little wider and modify it with accessories.

stoppie—Show-off maneuver in which the motorcycle is stopped with its rear wheel in the air, balancing on its front wheel. Don't try this at home, especially on a large touring bike.

T-bone—The most common kind of motorcycle accident involving another vehicle, where the oncoming **cager** either doesn't see or misjudges the speed of the motorcycle and turns left across its path.

thumper— Large displacement, single cylinder, four-stroke engine that makes a distinctive "thumping" sound.

track day—A racetrack-sponsored event where ordinary motorcyclists like you and I can learn racing techniques that will make us better street riders.

trike conversion (trike)—Three-wheeled motorcycle created by taking (usually) a large touring bike, removing its rear wheel and replacing it with two automobile tires and making the necessary mechanical accommodations. Walter Kern, About.com's motorcycle guru, rides a trike and offers extensive information about them on his site: http://motorcycles.about.com/od/trikes/.

twist the wrist—Accelerate. Whee!

twisties—Roads with a challenging series of curves.

UJM—Universal Japanese Motorcycle. Four-cylinder, standard-type motorcycle imported in quantity from Japanese manufacturers back in the 1970s.

wheelie—When a rider raises the front wheel of a motorcycle and rides along on the rear wheel only. Don't try this at home. See **stoppie**.

wrench—Slang term for a mechanic or, when used as a verb—e.g., "wrenching on my bike"— means performing mechanical work on your machine.

BIBLIOGRAPHY AND RESOURCES

BOOKS

Ayres, Ron. 2002. *Going the extra mile: insider tips for long-distance motorcycling and endurance rallies*. North Conway, N.H.: Whitehorse Press.

Bennett, James S. 1999. *The complete motorcycle book: a consumer's guide*. New York: Facts on File.

Carrington, William G. 1999. *Cowboys with chrome horses: a historical explanation of America's most popular and unique phenomenon*. Durham, N.C.: Jarrett Press.

Carstens, Rosemary. 2003. *Dream rider: roadmap to an adventurous life*. Longmont, Colo.: Black Lightning Press.

Code, Keith. 1997. *A twist of the wrist: the motorcycle road racers handbook*. Glendale, Calif.: Code Break.

———. 1993. *A twist of the wrist: volume 2, The basics of high-performance motorcycle riding*. Glendale, Calif.: Code Break.

Coombs, Matthew. 2002. *Motorcycle basics techbook*. Newbury Park, Calif.: Haynes.

Davidson, Jean. 2003. *Jean Davidson's Harley-Davidson family album: 100 years of the world's greatest motorcycle in rare photos*. Stillwater, Minn.: Voyageur Press.

Davidson, Willie G. 2002. *100 Years of Harley-Davidson*. Boston: Bulfinch Press.

Drew, A .J. 2002. *The everything motorcycle book: the one book you must have to buy, ride, and maintain your motorcycle*. Avon, Mass.: Adams.

Egan, Peter. 2002. *Leanings: the best of Peter Egan from* Cycle World *magazine*. St. Paul, Minn. : MBI.

Ferrar, Ann. 1996. *Hear me roar: women, motorcycles, and the rapture of the road*. New York: Crown.

Hahn, Pat. 2004. *Ride hard, ride smart: ultimate street strategies for advanced motorcyclists*. St. Paul, Minn.: MBI.

Harrison, Greg. 2005. *American Motorcyclist Association ride guide to America*. Center Conway, N.H.: Whitehorse Press.

Holmstrom, Darwin, and Charles Everett. 2004. *The complete idiot's guide to motorcycles*, 3d ed. Indianapolis: Alpha Books.

Hough, David L. 2003. *More proficient motorcycling: mastering the ride*. Irvine, Calif.: BowTie Press.

———. 2000. *Proficient motorcycling: the ultimate guide to riding well*. Irvine, Calif.: Bow Tie Press.

———. 2001. *Street strategies: a survival guide for motorcyclists*. Irvine, Calif.: BowTie Press.

Hufnagle, Bill. 2004. *Biker Billy cooks with fire*. North Conway, N.H.: Whitehorse Press.

———. 2000. *Biker Billy's freeway-a-fire cookbook*. New York: W. Morrow.

———. 2003. *Biker Billy's hog wild on a Harley cookbook*. Boston: Harvard Common Press.

Ienatsch, Nick. 2003. *Sport riding techniques: how to develop real world skills for speed, safety, and confidence on the street and track*. Phoenix, Ariz.: D. Bull.

Jacobs, David H. 2002. *Motorcycle detailing made easy*. North Conway, N.H.: Whitehorse Press.

Joans, Barbara. 2001. *Bike lust: Harleys, women, and American society*. Madison: University of Wisconsin Press.

La Plante, Richard. 2002. *Detours: life, death, and divorce on the road to Sturgis*. New York: Forge.

Larsen, Karen. 2004. *Breaking the limit: one woman's motorcycle journey through North America*. New York: Hyperion.

Larson, Kent. 2005. *Motorcycle track day handbook*. Osceola, Wis.: Motorbooks International.

Maher, Kevin, and Ben Greisler. 1998. *Chilton motorcycle handbook manual*. West Chester, Pa.: Chilton.

McKechnie, Gary. 2002. *Great American motorcycle tours*. Emeryville, Calif.: Avalon Travel.

Miller, Stuart, and Geoffrey Moss. 2002. *The biker code: wisdom for the ride*. New York: Simon & Schuster.

Motorcycle Safety Foundation. 2005. *The Motorcycle Safety Foundation's guide to motorcycling excellence: skills, knowledge, and strategies for riding right*. North Conway, N.H.: Whitehorse Press.

Mullins, Sasha. 2003. *Bikerlady: living and riding free!* New York: Kensington.

Noren, Allen. 2000. *Storm: a motorcycle journey of love, endurance, and transformation*. San Francisco: Travelers' Tales.

Parks, Lee. 2003. *Total control: high-performance street riding techniques*. St. Paul, Minn.: Motorbooks International.

Peart, Neil. 2002. *Ghost rider: travels on the healing road*. Toronto: ECW Press.

Pierson, Melissa Holbrook. 1997. *The perfect vehicle: what it is about motorcycles*. New York: W. W. Norton.

Richman, Jana. 2005. *Riding in the shadow of saints: a woman's story of motorcycling the Mormon trail*. New York: Crown.

Seeley, Alan. 2003. *The motorcycle book*. St. Paul, Minn.: MBI.

Siebert, Diane, and Leonard Jenkins. 2002. *Motorcycle song*. New York: HarperCollins.

Solomon R. Guggenheim Museum. 2001. *The art of the motorcycle*. New York: Guggenheim Museum.

Stermer, Bill. 1999. *Motorcycle touring and travel: a handbook of travel by motorcycle*. North Conway, N.H.: Whitehorse Press.

Wilson, Hugo. 1999. *Motorcycle owner's manual*. New York: DK.

Woofter, Bob. 2002. *Motorcycle camping made easy*. North Conway, N.H.: Whitehorse Press.

Zanetti, Geno. 2002. *She's a bad motorcycle: writers on riding*. New York: Thunder's Mouth Press.

Zimmerman, Mark. 2004. *The essential guide to motorcycle maintenance*. North Conway, N.H.: Whitehorse Press.

MAGAZINES

Librarian's note: You've probably been on the Internet long enough to realize that Web links come and go—or move. If you hit a dead one, you may want to try searching for it by title, using Google or your own preferred search tool. Remember to put quotation marks around the title so it will be searched for as a complete phrase.

American Iron, www.americanironmagazine.com

Born To Ride, www.borntoride.com

Cycle World, www.cycleworld.com

Full Throttle, http://fullthrottleusa.com

Hot Bike, www.hotbikeweb.com

IronWorks, www.ironworksmag.com

Motorcycle Consumer News, www.mcnews.com/mcn/

Motorcycle Cruiser Magazine, www.motorcyclecruiser.com

Motorcycle Escape, www.motorcyclistonline.com/escape/

Motorcycle Times, www.motorcycletimes.com

Motorcycle.Com (online subscription magazine), www.motorcycle.com

Motorcyclist, www.motorcyclistonline.com

Paisano Publications (*Easyriders, V-Twin,* etc.), http://v-twin.com/

Rider, www.riderreport.com

Roadracing World and Motorcycle Technology, www.roadracingworld.com

RoadRUNNER, www.rrmotorcycling.com/

The Robb Report: Motorcycling, www.motorcyclingmag.com

Sport Rider, www.sportrider.com

Thunder Press, www.thunderpressinc.com

Wing World, www.wingworldmag.com

VIDEOS/DVDs

Recommended: the Ride Like a Pro series from motorman Jerry Paladino:

Ride Like a Pro

Ride Like a Pro III

Ride Like a Pro for the Ladies

Paladino's newest offering, *Learn to Ride the Easy Way*, is geared toward the beginning rider. Order these directly from Paladino's Web site: www.ridelikeapro.com/NewOrderOptions.htm.

WEB SITES

A totally subjective listing based on content, frequency of updates, etc.

About.com: Motorcycles, http://motorcycles.about.com/

The Art of the Motorcycle (Guggenheim Museum), www.guggenheim.org/exhibitions/past_exhibitions/motorcycle/motorcycle.html

Discover Today's Motorcycling (Motorcycle Industry Council), www.motorcycles.org

BikePics.com, www.bikepics.com

Bikez.com, www.bikez.com

The Hurt Report (Summary, *Motorcycle Accident Cause Factors and Identification of Countermeasures*), www.clarity.net/%7Eadam/hurt-report.html

Infomonger Motorcycle Page, www.slack.net/%7Ethundt/mc.htm

MicaPeak dot com, www.micapeak.com: "A free Web site for motorcyclists. Providing World Wide Web and electronic mailing list services to the motorcycling public of planet Earth (and particularly the Pacific Rim of North America)." Known also for its searchable motorcycle registries, www.micapeak.com/reg/bikes.

Moto-Directory.com, www.moto-directory.com

Motorcycle City, www.motorcyclecity.com

Motorcycle Daily, www.motorcycledaily.com

Motorcycle Hall of Fame Museum, www.motorcyclemuseum.org/halloffame/halloffame.asp

Motorcycle Info and Accessories, http://motorcycleinfo.calsci.com

Motorcycle Misadventures ("realtime dispatches filed from the road" by Carla King), www.motorc
yclemisadventures.com

Motorcycle USA, www.motorcycle-usa.com

MotorcycleBeginners.Com, www.motorcyclebeginners.com

MotorcycleGearReview.com, www.motorcyclegearreview.com

MotorcyclePictures.com, www.motorcyclepictures.com

National Agenda for Motorcycle Safety (National Highway Traffic Safety Administration),
www.nhtsa.dot.gov/people/injury/pedbimot/motorcycle/00-NHT-212-motorcycle/toc.html

North American Sportbike Road Registry (directory of "twisties"), http://sportbikeroads.com/

Rat Bike Zone, www.ratbike.org

Ronnie Cramer's Motorcycle Web Index, http://sepnet.com/cycle

Speed Trap Exchange, www.speedtrap.org

SportbikeS.com, www.sportbikes.com

Sport-Touring.Net, www.sport-touring.net

Total Motorcycle, www.totalmotorcycle.com

webBikeWorld, www.webbikeworld.com

WhyBike.com: motorcycle weblogs, www.whybike.com/other_blog.htm

Wrench Wench Home Page, www.wrench-wench.com

ORGANIZATIONS

*Note: Brand-specific and local/regional organizations are not included here. There are a number of
Web pages with extensive listings. Use a search engine, or try these links:*
   www.motorcycleclubsindex.com
   www.dropbears.com/bikelinks/clubs.htm
   www.google.com/Top/Recreation/Motorcycles/Associations_and_Clubs?tc=1
   http://dir.yahoo.com/Recreation/Automotive/Motorcycles/Clubs_and_Organizations

Also see chapter 9 for more motorcycle clubs.

ABATE (chapter listing), www.google.com/Top/Recreation/Motorcycles/Associations_and _Clubs/American_Bikers_Aimed_Toward_Education/

American Cruisers Alliance, http://americancruisers.us

American Firefighters Motorcycle Club, www.aff-mc.com.

American Motorcyclist Association, www.ama-cycle.org

Antique Motorcycle Club of America, www.antiquemotorcycle.org

Bald Guys Motorcycle Club ("This is a virtual club with some members who probably actually ride."), www.baldguysmc.com

Blood Brothers Motorcycle Club (law enforcement), www.bloodbrothersmc.org

Blue Knights International Law Enforcement Motorcycle Club, Inc. (law enforcement), www.bl ueknights.org

British Biker Cooperative, http://britishbiker.net

Brothers of the Third Wheel, (trikes), www.btw-trikers.org

Canadian Motorcycle Association, www.canmocycle.ca

Christian Motorcyclists Association, www.cmausa.org

Disabled Riders of America, www.disabledriders.com

Institute of Advanced Motorcyclists (UK), www.iam.org.uk

Iron Butt Association, www.ironbutt.com

Jewish Motorcyclists Alliance, www.jewishbikers.com

Latin American Motorcycle Association, www.latinbikers.com

Motorcycle and Moped Industry Council (Canada), www.mmic.ca

Motor Maids, Inc., www.motormaids.org (the oldest motorcycling organization for women in North America)

Motorcycle Industry Council, www.mic.org

Motorcycle Riders Foundation, www.mrf.org

Motorcycle Safety Foundation, www.msf-usa.org

Motorcycle Touring Association, www.mtariders.com

National Association for Bikers With a Disability (UK), www.nabd.org.uk

National Association of Black Bikers ("NABB Welcomes Bikers of ALL Nationalities!"), www.nabbweb.org

National Association of Buffalo Soldiers Motorcycle Clubs (African American), www.buffalosoldiersnational.com

National Association of State Motorcycle Safety Administrators, www.smsa.org

National Coalition of Motorcyclists, www.aimncom.com/ncom

North American Three-Wheeler Association, www.geocities.com/indycycler

Red Knights MotorCycle Club (fire services), www.redknightsmc.org

Retreads Motorcycle Club International (age 40-plus), www.retreads.org

Ride to Work, Inc., www.ridetowork.org

Rolling Thunder, Inc., www.rollingthunder1.com/

Sidecar Industry Council, www.sidecar-industry.com

Southern Cruisers Riding Club, www.southerncruisers.net

Trike Riders International, www.trikes.org

United Sidecar Association, www.sidecar.com

U.S. Military Vets Motorcycle Club, http://usmvmc.org

Vintage Japanese Motorcycle Club, http://vjmc.org

Vintage Motor Cycle Club Limited, www.vmcc.net

Women in the Wind, www.womeninthewind.org

Women on Wheels, www.womenonwheels.org

Women's International Motorcycle Association, www.wimaworld.com

INDEX

ABOUT THE AUTHOR

Shirl Kennedy lives in St. Petersburg, Fla., and is the base librarian at MacDill Air Force Base in Tampa. She also writes about technology and the Internet and is deputy editor of two information industry weblogs, ResourceShelf.com and www.DocuTicker.com. A former newspaper reporter, she has a master's degree in library and information science from the University of South Florida. She has two amazing sons and a 2005 Yamaha V-Star 1100 Midnight Custom motorcycle. Her personal Web site is at www.uncagedlibrarian.com.

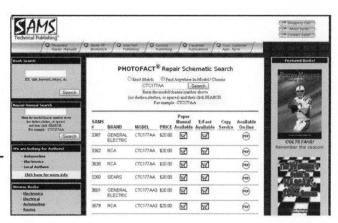